T0304137

The Minor Marshallians and Alfred Marshall

Alfred Marshall, Professor of Economics at Cambridge University (1885–1908), produced a distinguished crop of students, many of them leaders in the economics profession in subsequent generations. Pigou, Keynes and Dennis Robertson are undoubtedly the most famous of these Marshall 'pupils' but there were many more, even if more minor forces in the development of early twentieth century economics. This book intends to examine the major work of ten of these 'minor' Marshallians – Sydney John Chapman (1871–1951), John Harold Clapham (1873–1946), Charles Ryle Fay (1884–1961), Alfred William Flux (1867–1942), Frederick Lavington (1881–1927), Walter Thomas Layton (1884–1966), David Huchinson MacGregor (1877–1953), Joseph Shield Nicholson (1850–1927), Charles Percy Sanger (1871–1930) and Gerald Francis Shove (1888–1947), to name them in alphabetical order.

The broad aim of this book is to evaluate the more important contributions of these 'minor' Marshallians by selective examination of their major economic work. That evaluation has at least two dimensions. First, it focuses on the significance of the author's individual contributions to the development of twentieth century economic thought. Second, it attempts to assess the Marshallian credentials of these contributions in order to indicate how Marshallian in their economics these 'pupils' of Marshall's economics teaching actually stayed.

This book presents a detailed study of ten, 'minor' Marshallians who spread the 'organon' of Marshall's economics to later generations of economists via the impact Marshall had on their own work. That impact, the book shows, came directly via Marshall's teaching or indirectly via their study of Marshall's published work.

Peter Groenewegen is Honorary Associate and Emeritus Professor of Economics at the University of Sydney, Australia.

Routledge studies in the history of economics

1 **Economics as Literature**
Willie Henderson

2 **Socialism and Marginalism in Economics 1870–1930**
Edited by Ian Steedman

3 **Hayek's Political Economy**
The socio-economics of order
Steve Fleetwood

4 **On the Origins of Classical Economics**
Distribution and value from William Petty to Adam Smith
Tony Aspromourgos

5 **The Economics of Joan Robinson**
Edited by Maria Cristina Marcuzzo, Luigi Pasinetti and Alesandro Roncaglia

6 **The Evolutionist Economics of Léon Walras**
Albert Jolink

7 **Keynes and the 'Classics'**
A study in language, epistemology and mistaken identities
Michel Verdon

8 **The History of Game Theory, Volume 1**
From the beginnings to 1945
Robert W. Dimand and Mary Ann Dimand

9 **The Economics of W.S. Jevons**
Sandra Peart

10 **Gandhi's Economic Thought**
Ajit K. Dasgupta

11 **Equilibrium and Economic Theory**
Edited by Giovanni Caravale

12 **Austrian Economics in Debate**
Edited by Willem Keizer, Bert Tieben and Rudy van Zijp

13 **Ancient Economic Thought**
Edited by B.B. Price

14 **The Political Economy of Social Credit and Guild Socialism**
Frances Hutchinson and Brian Burkitt

15 **Economic Careers**
Economics and economists in Britain 1930–1970
Keith Tribe

16 **Understanding 'Classical' Economics**
Studies in the long-period theory
Heinz Kurz and Neri Salvadori

17 **History of Environmental Economic Thought**
E. Kula

18 **Economic Thought in Communist and Post-Communist Europe**
Edited by Hans-Jürgen Wagener

19 **Studies in the History of French Political Economy**
From Bodin to Walras
Edited by Gilbert Faccarello

20 **The Economics of John Rae**
Edited by O.F. Hamouda, C. Lee and D. Mair

21 **Keynes and the Neoclassical Synthesis**
Einsteinian versus Newtonian macroeconomics
Teodoro Dario Togati

22 **Historical Perspectives on Macroeconomics**
Sixty years after the 'General Theory'
Edited by Philippe Fontaine and Albert Jolink

23 **The Founding of Institutional Economics**
The leisure class and sovereignty
Edited by Warren J. Samuels

24 **Evolution of Austrian Economics**
From Menger to Lachmann
Sandye Gloria

25 **Marx's Concept of Money: The God of Commodities**
Anitra Nelson

26 **The Economics of James Steuart**
Edited by Ramón Tortajada

27 **The Development of Economics in Europe since 1945**
Edited by A.W. Bob Coats

28 **The Canon in the History of Economics**
Critical essays
Edited by Michalis Psalidopoulos

29 **Money and Growth**
Selected s of Allyn Abbott Young
Edited by Perry G. Mehrling and Roger J. Sandilands

30 **The Social Economics of Jean-Baptiste Say**
Markets and virtue
Evelyn L. Forget

31 **The Foundations of Laissez-Faire**
The economics of Pierre de Boisguilbert
Gilbert Faccarello

32 **John Ruskin's Political Economy**
Willie Henderson

33 **Contributions to the History of Economic Thought**
Essays in honour of R.D.C. Black
Edited by Antoin E. Murphy and Renee Prendergast

34 **Towards an Unknown Marx**
A commentary on the manuscripts of 1861–63
Enrique Dussel

35 Economics and Interdisciplinary Exchange
Edited by Guido Erreygers

36 Economics as the Art of Thought
Essays in memory of G.L.S. Shackle
Edited by Stephen F. Frowen and Peter Earl

37 The Decline of Ricardian Economics
Politics and economics in post-Ricardian theory
Susan Pashkoff

38 Piero Sraffa
His life, thought and cultural heritage
Alessandro Roncaglia

39 Equilibrium and Disequilibrium in Economic Theory
The Marshall–Walras divide
Michel de Vroey

40 The German Historical School
The historical and ethical approach to economics
Edited by Yuichi Shionoya

41 Reflections on the Classical Canon in Economics
Essays in honour of Samuel Hollander
Edited by Sandra Peart and Evelyn Forget

42 Piero Sraffa's Political Economy
A centenary estimate
Edited by Terenzio Cozzi and Roberto Marchionatti

43 The Contribution of Joseph Schumpeter to Economics
Economic development and institutional change
Richard Arena and Cecile Dangel

44 On the Development of Long-run Neo-Classical Theory
Tom Kompas

45 F.A. Hayek as a Political Economist
Economic analysis and values
Edited by Jack Birner, Pierre Garrouste and Thierry Aimar

46 Pareto, Economics and Society
The mechanical analogy
Michael McLure

47 The Cambridge Controversies in Capital Theory
A study in the logic of theory development
Jack Birner

48 Economics Broadly Considered
Essays in honour of Warren J. Samuels
Edited by Steven G. Medema, Jeff Biddle and John B. Davis

49 Physicians and Political Economy
Six studies of the work of doctor-economists
Edited by Peter Groenewegen

50 The Spread of Political Economy and the Professionalisation of Economists
Economic societies in Europe, America and Japan in the nineteenth century
Massimo Augello and Marco Guidi

51 **Historians of Economics and Economic Thought**
The construction of disciplinary memory
Steven G. Medema and Warren J. Samuels

52 **Competing Economic Theories**
Essays in memory of Giovanni Caravale
Sergio Nisticò and Domenico Tosato

53 **Economic Thought and Policy in Less Developed Europe**
The nineteenth century
Edited by Michalis Psalidopoulos and Maria-Eugenia Almedia Mata

54 **Family Fictions and Family Facts**
Harriet Martineau, Adolphe Quetelet and the population question in England 1798–1859
Brian Cooper

55 **Eighteenth-Century Economics**
Peter Groenewegen

56 **The Rise of Political Economy in the Scottish Enlightenment**
Edited by Tatsuya Sakamoto and Hideo Tanaka

57 **Classics and Moderns in Economics, Volume I**
Essays on nineteenth and twentieth century economic thought
Peter Groenewegen

58 **Classics and Moderns in Economics, Volume II**
Essays on nineteenth and twentieth century economic thought
Peter Groenewegen

59 **Marshall's Evolutionary Economics**
Tiziano Raffaelli

60 **Money, Time and Rationality in Max Weber**
Austrian connections
Stephen D. Parsons

61 **Classical Macroeconomics**
Some modern variations and distortions
James C. W. Ahiakpor

62 **The Historical School of Economics in England and Japan**
Tamotsu Nishizawa

63 **Classical Economics and Modern Theory**
Studies in long-period analysis
Heinz D. Kurz and Neri Salvadori

64 **A Bibliography of Female Economic Thought to 1940**
Kirsten K. Madden, Janet A. Sietz and Michele Pujol

65 **Economics, Economists and Expectations**
From microfoundations to macroeconomics
Warren Young, Robert Leeson and William Darity Jnr

66 **The Political Economy of Public Finance in Britain, 1767–1873**
Takuo Dome

67 **Essays in the History of Economics**
Warren J. Samuels, Willie Henderson, Kirk D. Johnson and Marianne Johnson

68 **History and Political Economy**
Essays in honour of P.D. Groenewegen
Edited by Tony Aspromourgos and John Lodewijks

69 **The Tradition of Free Trade**
Lars Magnusson

70 **Evolution of the Market Process**
Austrian and Swedish economics
Edited by Michel Bellet, Sandye Gloria-Palermo and Abdallah Zouache

71 **Consumption as an Investment**
The fear of goods from Hesiod to Adam Smith
Cosimo Perrotta

72 **Jean-Baptiste Say and the Classical Canon in Economics**
The British connection in French classicism
Samuel Hollander

73 **Knut Wicksell on Poverty**
No place is too exalted
Knut Wicksell

74 **Economists in Cambridge**
A study through their correspondence 1907–1946
Edited by M.C. Marcuzzo and A. Rosselli

75 **The Experiment in the History of Economics**
Edited by Philippe Fontaine and Robert Leonard

76 **At the Origins of Mathematical Economics**
The Economics of A.N. Isnard (1748–1803)
Richard van den Berg

77 **Money and Exchange**
Folktales and reality
Sasan Fayazmanesh

78 **Economic Development and Social Change**
Historical roots and modern perspectives
George Stathakis and Gianni Vaggi

79 **Ethical Codes and Income Distribution**
A study of John Bates Clark and Thorstein Veblen
Guglielmo Forges Davanzati

80 **Evaluating Adam Smith**
Creating the wealth of nations
Willie Henderson

81 **Civil Happiness**
Economics and human flourishing in historical perspective
Luigino Bruni

82 **New Voices on Adam Smith**
Edited by Leonidas Montes and Eric Schliesser

83 **Making Chicago Price Theory**
Milton Friedman–George Stigler correspondence, 1945–1957
Edited by J. Daniel Hammond and Claire H. Hammond

84 **William Stanley Jevons and the Cutting Edge of Economics**
Bert Mosselmans

85 **A History of Econometrics in France**
From nature to models
Philippe Le Gall

86 **Money and Markets**
A doctrinal approach
Edited by Alberto Giacomin and Maria Cristina Marcuzzo

87 **Considerations on the Fundamental Principles of Pure Political Economy**
Vilfredo Pareto (Edited by Roberto Marchionatti and Fiorenzo Mornati)

88 **The Years of High Econometrics**
A short history of the generation that reinvented economics
Francisco Louçã

89 **David Hume's Political Economy**
Edited by Carl Wennerlind and Margaret Schabas

90 **Interpreting Classical Economics**
Studies in long-period analysis
Heinz D. Kurz and Neri Salvadori

91 **Keynes's Vision**
Why the great depression did not return
John Philip Jones

92 **Monetary Theory in Retrospect**
The selected essays of Filippo Cesarano
Filippo Cesarano

93 **Keynes's Theoretical Development**
From the tract to the general theory
Toshiaki Hirai

94 **Leading Contemporary Economists**
Economics at the cutting edge
Edited by Steven Pressman

95 **The Science of Wealth**
Adam Smith and the framing of political economy
Tony Aspromourgos

96 **Capital, Time and Transitional Dynamics**
Edited by Harald Hagemann and Roberto Scazzieri

97 **New Essays on Pareto's Economic Theory**
Edited by Luigino Bruni and Aldo Montesano

98 **Frank Knight & the Chicago School in American Economics**
Ross B. Emmett

99 **A History of Economic Theory**
Essays in honour of Takashi Negishi
Edited by Aiko Ikeo and Heinz D. Kurz

100 **Open Economics**
Economics in relation to other disciplines
Edited by Richard Arena, Sheila Dow and Matthias Klaes

101 **Rosa Luxemburg and the Critique of Political Economy**
Edited by Riccardo Bellofiore

102 **Problems and Methods of Econometrics**
The Poincaré lectures of Ragnar Frisch 1933
Edited by Olav Bjerkholt and Ariane Dupont-Keiffer

103 **Criticisms of Classical Political Economy**
Menger, Austrian economics and the German historical school
Gilles Campagnolo

104 **A History of Entrepreneurship**
Robert F. Hébert and Albert N. Link

105 **Keynes on Monetary Policy, Finance and Uncertainty**
Liquidity preference theory and the global financial crisis
Jorg Bibow

106 **Kalecki's Principle of Increasing Risk and Keynesian Economics**
Tracy Mott

107 **Economic Theory and Economic Thought**
Essays in honour of Ian Steedman
John Vint, J. Stanley Metcalfe, Heinz D. Kurz, Neri Salvadori and Paul Samuelson

108 **Political Economy, Public Policy and Monetary Economics**
Ludwig von Mises and the Austrian tradition
Richard M. Ebeling

109 **Keynes and the British Humanist Tradition**
The moral purpose of the market
David R. Andrews

110 **Political Economy and Industrialism**
Banks in Saint-Simonian economic thought
Gilles Jacoud

111 **Studies in Social Economics**
Leon Walras, Translated by Jan van Daal and Donald Walker

112 **The Making of the Classical Theory of Economic Growth**
Anthony Brewer

113 **The Origins of David Hume's Economics**
Willie Henderson

114 **Production, Distribution and Trade**
Edited by Adriano Birolo, Duncan Foley, Heinz D. Kurz, Bertram Schefold and Ian Steedman

115 **The Essential Writings of Thorstein Veblen**
Edited by Charles Camic and Geoffrey Hodgson

116 **Adam Smith and the Economy of the Passions**
Jan Horst Keppler

117 **The Analysis of Linear Economic Systems**
Father Maurice Potron's pioneering works
Translated by Christian Bidard and Guido Erreygers

118 **A Dynamic Approach to Economic Theory: Frisch**
Edited by Olav Bjerkholt and Duo Qin

119 **Henry A. Abbati: Keynes' Forgotten Precursor**
Serena Di Gaspare

120 **Generations of Economists**
David Collard

121 **Hayek, Mill and the Liberal Tradition**
Edited by Andrew Farrant

122 **Marshall, Marshallians and Industrial Economics**
Edited by Tiziano Raffaelli

123 **Austrian and German Economic Thought**
Kiichiro Yagi

124 **The Evolution of Economic Theory**
Edited by Volker Caspari

125 **Thomas Tooke and the Monetary Thought of Classical Economics**
Matthew Smith

126 **Political Economy and Liberalism in France**
The contributions of Frédéric Bastiat
Robert Leroux

127 **Stalin's Economist**
The economic contributions of Jenö Varga
André Mommen

128 **E.E. Slutsky as Economist and Mathematician**
Crossing the limits of knowledge
Vincent Barnett

129 **Keynes, Sraffa, and the Criticism of Neoclassical Theory**
Essays in honour of Heinz Kurz
Neri Salvadori and Christian Gehrke

130 **Crises and Cycles in Economic Dictionaries and Encyclopaedias**
Edited by Daniele Bensomi

131 **General Equilibrium Analysis**
A century after Walras
Edited by Pascal Bridel

132 **Sraffa and Modern Economics, Volume I**
Edited by Roberto Ciccone, Christian Gehrke and Gary Mongiovi

133 **Sraffa and Modern Economics, Volume II**
Edited by Roberto Ciccone, Christian Gehrke and Gary Mongiovi

134 **The Minor Marshallians and Alfred Marshall**
An evaluation
Peter Groenewegen

The Minor Marshallians and Alfred Marshall

An evaluation

Peter Groenewegen

LONDON AND NEW YORK

First published 2012
by Routledge
2 Park Square, Milton Park, Abingdon, Oxon OX14 4RN

Simultaneously published in the USA and Canada
by Routledge
711 Third Avenue, New York, NY 10017 (8th Floor)

Routledge is an imprint of the Taylor & Francis Group, an informa business

British Library Cataloguing in Publication Data
A catalogue record for this book is available from the British Library

Library of Congress Cataloging in Publication Data
Groenewegen, Peter, 1972–
The minor Marshallians and Alfred Marshall:
an evaluation/Peter Groenewegen.
p. cm.
Includes bibliographical references and index.
1. Marshall, Alfred, 1842–1924. 2. Economists–Great Britain. 3. Economics–Great Britain–History. I. Title.
HB103.A3.G76 2011
330.092'241–dc23

2011022535

ISBN: 978-0-415-57020-6 (hbk)
ISBN: 978-0-203-15471-7 (ebk)

Typeset in Times
By Wearset Ltd, Boldon, Tyne and Wear

Contents

Preface and acknowledgements

This study of 'minor Marshallians' spreading the 'organon' of economics as initially developed by their 'master', Alfred Marshall, arose out of the contents of one of the concluding chapters of my biography of Alfred Marshall, dealing with his legacy to future generations of economists. Such a legacy is reflected in the title of this study of ten minor Marshallians: *Spreading the Organon: Marshall's Impact on Ten Minor Marshallians.* However, the specific selection of the subjects for the ten key chapters also owed much to my desire to learn more about these ten persons, the majority of whom were for me names of authors who had written key interpretations of Marshall's work (for example, those of MacGregor and Shove discussed in Chapters 7 and 11 respectively). Alternatively, they were persons who had extended the research programme which Marshall himself had managed to complete by examining topics such as money, banking, saving and investment, the capital market, the trade cycle, industry economics, labour economics, distribution, taxation economics and public finance, which Marshall either had not fully tackled himself, or which needed updating from the ravages caused by the passage of time on the specific state in which Marshall had left his discussion of them.

The structure of the book adopted enabled gradual preparation of the individual case studies of 'minor Marshallians'. A few of these were earlier presented as parts at conferences, or were published in a preliminary form in various history of economic thought journals. Thus Chapter 3 on Flux was first published in *History of Economics Review* No. 48 (Summer 2008, pp. 63–77) and a paper on Walter Layton's *The Relations of Capital and Labour* (1914) as published in *Economic History Review* No. 46 (Summer 2007, pp. 19–31) was expanded into Chapter 9. Chapter 8 on Lavington was first presented at a conference in a form which exclusively concentrated on his 1922 book, *The English Capital Market*, while Chapter 11 on Shove was initially submitted to the Amsterdam ESHET Conference (2010), which ill health prevented me from presenting there. Chapter 10 on Fay was likewise presented at an earlier conference, and later substantially altered and revised.

In addition, I gratefully acknowledge permission to reproduce extracts from work for which they hold the copyright from Palgrave Macmillan with respect to 332 words from an article by Austin Robinson which appeared in Don Patinkin and J. Clark Leith, eds., *Keynes, Cambridge and the General Theory* which appeared in 1977, p. 28; from Cambridge University Press for an extract of text from page 250 within A.F.W. Plumtre, 'Maynard Keynes as Teacher' in Milo Keynes, ed., *Essays on John Maynard Keynes*, 1975; from Michael Holroyd for extracts from *Lytton Strachey. A Biography*, Penguin Books, reprinted with revisions, 1979, pp. 169, 1028; and from David Winch, on behalf of the Royal Economic Society, for enabling me to reproduce significant extracts from A.C. Pigou, ed., *Memorials of Alfred Marshall*, 1925.

Apart from comments received during discussion of the mentioned chapters presented at conferences, chapters benefited from comments of others. Annalisa Rosselli assisted by supplying copies of material on Shove's lectures; the referees appointed by Routledge provided valuable comments on both the structure of the book and the contents of the specific draft chapters they looked at. These reviews saved me from errors of omission and commission, and thereby improved the contents of this book. Any remaining errors of interpretation and completeness are my responsibility.

University of Sydney
November 2010

1 Introduction

Ten 'minor Marshallians' and spreading the economic organon

This book is a by-product of my biography of Marshall (Groenewegen 1995a) with special reference to its Chapter 20, the Marshall Legacy through the establishment of the Cambridge School of Economics and the spread of Marshall's economics elsewhere through the efforts of his former 'pupils'. Marshall himself was very conscious of the fact that many of his best students frequently became academics themselves, and in this way spread his economics in the widest sense to various parts of the United Kingdom and even occasionally universities in the Empire, with special reference to Canada. This he had made a major aim when taking up his professorship at Cambridge in 1885 (Marshall 1885, 1925, esp. pp. 172–174).

The ten 'minor Marshallians' discussed in this book – that is, J.S. Nicholson, A.W. Flux, C.P. Sanger, S.J. Chapman, J.H. Clapham, D.H. MacGregor, F. Lavington, W.T. Layton, C.R. Fay and G.F. Shove, in chronological order by year of birth – were all students of Marshall, either directly during the years when he himself was the major teacher of economics at Cambridge, or indirectly, in the case of Lavington and Shove, when they were taught by Marshall's own pupils at Cambridge (that is, by Pigou and Maynard Keynes) in the years immediately following Marshall's retirement as professor in 1908. Of the ten, therefore, eight had studied economics directly under Marshall at Cambridge, often after completing a degree at another university or for a different Cambridge Tripos (either the Classical, the Historical, or the Mathematical). The six older Marshallians studied economics under Marshall either in the Moral Sciences Tripos or, less frequently, in the Historical Tripos (Clapham). All of them completed their economic studies at Cambridge before the start of the First World War, and may be broadly described as the first generation of Marshall's 'pupils'.

Academic teaching, generally speaking immediately following their graduation, was carried out by nearly all of the ten. The exception is Lavington. He worked at the Board of Trade for six years after completing his economic studies at Cambridge, and then became a teacher at Cambridge from 1918 until his early death in 1927. Five (Nicholson, Clapham, MacGregor, Fay and Shove) were academics for the whole of their working lives, with two (MacGregor and Fay) having their academic work interrupted by active military service during the First World War. Two (Flux and Chapman) followed their positions as academics by public service, in both cases at the Board of Trade, one left economics teaching to become a barrister-at-law (Sanger) and one became a financial journalist and newspaper editor and proprietor (Layton) including therein ownership, and editing, of the weekly *Economist.* Of the academics, two taught at universities in Canada for some time (Flux at McGill University in Montréal from 1900 to 1908; Fay at Toronto from 1921 to 1931). Of those staying in the United Kingdom, two taught at Leeds (Clapham and MacGregor), three taught at Manchester (Flux, Sanger and MacGregor), one at Edinburgh (Nicholson), one at Oxford (MacGregor) and three at University College, London (Nicholson, Sanger and Layton). They thereby helped to spread various aspects of Marshall's economic organon far and wide.

The economics specialisations of these ten Marshallians were rather diverse. Both Flux and Sanger worked on mathematical economics and economic theory, the second also on the economics of taxation; both Clapham and Fay were essentially economic historians: Clapham published general economic history texts as well as detailed studies of the development of specific industries in Britain; Fay wrote work on economic history as well as a treatise on the cooperative movement in Great Britain and abroad. Nicholson wrote on economic history, on monetary economics, on Marxian economics, and on general economics; Chapman produced work on taxation economics and a small text; MacGregor concentrated on industry economics with special emphasis on industrial combinations such as trusts and cartels; Lavington worked on finance, the English capital market and the trade cycle; Layton wrote on labour economics and on the price level; and Shove contributed, as he himself put it, to the theory of value, broadly contemplated. It may also be noted that Nicholson published a three volume *Principles of Political Economy* in two editions; Flux produced a single volume *Principles of Economics* in two editions; while all ten published journal articles, largely, but not exclusively, for the *Economic Journal.*

From this brief resumé of the careers of these ten economics academics it can easily be suggested that they all share sufficient relevant characteristics in their studies and later work to make them good, if not loyal Marshallians. All had gained their major economics education from either Marshall himself in the case of eight of the ten, or from his leading 'pupils', Pigou and Keynes, in the case of the other two. All, like Marshall himself, taught economics either at Cambridge or at other universities or, in a few cases, both. All of them, moreover, wrote on topics which fitted broadly into the Marshallian economic research programme, or economic organon as Marshall called it in his inaugural lecture (Marshall 1885, 1925, pp. 165–166). This sought to combine economic principles, or the theory of value, with more specialised, and often applied, studies in industry economics, monetary and international trade economics, labour economics, taxation economics and public finance, economic policy, welfare economics, and the economics of cycles and progress. In varying degrees, all ten fully acknowledged their credentials as Marshall's students in the widest sense of the term. As such, they drew on both his published work and the contents of his lectures for inspiration in their research and saw themselves as basically continuing his work either in new directions not explored by Marshall himself or by advancing it in fields on which Marshall himself had published. From this perspective, in short, they are all good candidates for inclusion in a study into the nature of 'minor Marshallians' with special reference to the impact Marshall made on their work.

Why minor Marshallians?

This issue is perhaps best addressed by indicating reasons why it seems appropriate to omit the major Marshallians from this type of study. There can be little disagreement with the proposition that these major Marshallians are confined to three individuals: Pigou, Maynard Keynes and Dennis Robertson. Pigou and Keynes were the major Cambridge economics teachers in the immediate period following Marshall's retirement. At this stage, both did so as loyal Marshall pupils, building on the work of the master. Dennis Robertson was not a direct student of Marshall, who had retired as professor just before Robertson's entry into economic studies at Cambridge. Robertson, however, became an exceedingly loyal, if not devout student of Marshall's work which he regarded as the foundation of all future work in economics. By the 1920s, Pigou, Keynes and Robertson were the major economists writing economics at Cambridge in the Marshall tradition: Pigou and Keynes gaining this accolade by the second decade of the twentieth century, Robertson certainly achieving the reputation as a staunch Marshallian by the mid-1920s.

Given their enormous reputations as twentieth century economists, particularly in the case of Keynes, a very substantial amount has been published on their work and influence. For Keynes, the commentary literature frequently includes material on Marshall's considerable influence on Keynes's work. My essay (Groenewegen 1995b) dwelled on the Marshall/Keynes connection, concentrating on Keynes as Marshall's economics student at Cambridge, and to his subsequent contact with Marshall's thought. Robertson's work as influenced by Marshall has not been specifically dealt with in the literature, but is at least partly, and selectively, covered in some of the published Robertson studies (Presley 1978, 1992; Fletcher 2000). No detailed biographical study of Pigou exists, hence making his indebtedness to Marshall not a topic of systematic inquiry. However, Collard's (1981) study of Pigou does cover much of the relevant material, while Graaf's (1987) entry on Pigou in *The New Palgrave Dictionary of Economics* suggests the magnitude of the task of preparing a detailed study of Pigou's economics, given its abridged bibliography of nearly thirty entries for books written by Pigou, and his reference to a King's College list of work by Pigou in excess of 100 items. Particularly in the case of Pigou's early work during Marshall's lifetime, the impact of teacher on student would have been quite enormous, and Pigou, after all, had been given Marshall's imprimatur by the strong support he gave him to secure his succession to the Cambridge chair.

Enough has been said about the major Marshallians in economics to explain why their relationship with, and indebtedness to, Marshall and his work could not be included in this book and why the subject matter of this book has been confined to studying ten minor Marshallians. Adding systematic studies of Marshall's impact on Pigou, Robertson and Keynes would have made this study too large and unwieldy and, given the existing literature on these economists, also somewhat unnecessary.

Approach taken in this study of the ten minor Marshallians

In the ten chapters which follow, the sample of ten 'minor' Marshallians is systematically explored in chronological order by date of birth, starting with Nicholson and ending with Shove. The sample to me seems to be a reasonable one, even if it cannot claim to be complete. Some of the omitted 'minor' Marshallians include Foxwell, one of Marshall's earliest 'pupils' and until 1908, a close friend; John Neville Keynes, a particularly important Marshallian in the 1870s and 1880s; William Cunningham, the economic historian who had criticised Marshall's historical introductory chapters in the early editions of the *Principles* as most unsatisfactory; Henry Cunynghame, an early student, highly gifted in mathematical economics, and author of a 1904 text, *A Geometrical Political Economy*; and finally, his Oxford student, L.L. Price, who published work on 'Industrial Peace', 'Money in its Relation to Prices' and a short, but very popular, introduction to the history of economics from Adam Smith to Toynbee. Omissions from the subsequent generation include Claude Guillebaud and Hubert Henderson, and others in their class which graduated in the years before the First World War, who have already been mentioned (Robertson, but not Shove). However, their omission may be justified by the fact they failed to reach the same magnitude in their subsequent economic contributions to economics as teachers and writers, as was the case with the ten selected for this study. An exception perhaps is Henry Cunynghame but he, as far as Marshall was concerned, was never 'fully caught for economics'.

Each of the following ten chapters follows a specific pattern. After an introduction of a few pages, the first section of each of these chapters covers the biographical details of the economist in question with emphasis on the nature of their association with Alfred Marshall, the subsequent two or three sections assess the Marshallian character of their work as represented by a number of important samples. The final section presents some conclusions. Two aspects of the construction of these chapters deserve further comment. First, there is the process of selecting for each of the ten economists an appropriate sample of their published work by which to assess their Marshallian credentials. Second, the manner in which their Marshallian credentials are ascertained in these chapters needs to be disclosed. Although there are variations in the application of these tests for individual authors, by and large there are similar principles operating in these choices and assessment criteria for the ten minor Marshallians who are the subject of these chapters.

Take first the selection of appropriate published work for each of the ten minor Marshallians. This was easier in some cases than in others. In the case of Shove, for example, whose published output was quantitatively rather small, the selection boiled down to some of his articles, some of his book reviews, and his centenary assessment of Marshall's *Principles* published in the 1942 *Economic Journal.* For both Layton and Lavington, the choice was easily confined to their two published books as suitable vehicles for assessing the Marshallian content of their work. On the other hand, for Nicholson, whose published output in book form was quite substantial, the choice was more difficult. As Chapter 2 indicates, it includes Nicholson's first book (and Cobden Prize Winning Essay) on machinery and labour in its second edition, his book on money together with essays on monetary subjects in its third edition, and last but not least, the three volumes of the first edition of his *Principles of Political Economy* for detailed study. It thereby omits much other work by Nicholson in book form. Similarly, for Clapham, the choices of appropriate texts made, including therein his English Economic History and his famous *Economic Journal* article 'Of Empty Economic Boxes', had to exclude most of the other of his important contributions to economic history. For Flux, for Sanger, for Chapman and for MacGregor the choices were easier, concentrating as they do on major books and important articles from what were not quantitatively large published outputs. As already implied, choices had to be made in this context, if only to confine the size of this study to a reasonable length. Whether the choices were the correct ones, can be left to the reader though I indicate again that the choices made in my view are suitable in the light of each individual economists' published output.

Assessing the Marshallian credentials of the works selected rested on a broad, twofold test. First, the general Marshallian thrust of the work in question was examined for its use of Marshall's tools of analysis and the explicit acknowledgement of the fact by the author in question. An example may illustrate this further. It draws on the especially easy case of two of MacGregor's books and of his 1942 centenary assessment of Marshall and his book published in *Economica.* These all explicitly mention three of Marshall's analytical tools as exceedingly beneficial for the study of industry economics in particular, that is, the consumers' surplus analysis, the concept of the representative firm, and third, the device of the particular expenses curve. Moreover, MacGregor's books, as shown in more detail in Chapter 7, resemble Marshall's books by avoiding the use of mathematical symbols as much as possible, and by placing the diagrams in the footnotes rather than in the text. The second test for assessing the Marshallian content of a work generally adopted in the ten chapters that follow was the frequency of citation of Marshall's published work, and the nature of that citation, theoretical or factual, positive or negative. Negative citation was taken to indicate a critical attitude to the continuing value of Marshall's work, the former approval and continuing value of a point or set of points contributed by Marshall. More detail of the actual application of these types of tools by which to assess the Marshallian contents of a work would anticipate too much of the argument pursued in the following chapters, and would also tend to involve unwarranted generalisations. Whether they are satisfactory or not depends very much on the way they are used in what follows. This also allows assessment of the Marshallian content which, in their writings, they passed on to future generations of economists.

Little more needs to be added by way of introduction. The ten chapters which follow on each of the ten minor Marshallians selected, are largely self-explanatory. The findings which can be derived from this study are summarised in the conclusions offered in Chapter 12.

2 Joseph Shield Nicholson (1850–1927)

An early student of Marshall at Cambridge – later quite critical of Marshall and his economics

Joseph Shield Nicholson studied political economy at Cambridge with Marshall while taking the Moral Sciences Tripos. In the final examinations in 1876 he was equal second in the first class honours list, an excellent result. Nicholson was therefore one of Marshall's early students, and was described by Marshall in an undated fragment (probably from around his retirement in 1908) as one of the many persons sent from Cambridge who had become a 'leading teacher' of economics at London University and, though not mentioned by Marshall on this occasion, at Edinburgh (cited in Groenewegen 1995a, pp. 753–734). Nicholson's Cambridge studies, it may be added, followed his philosophical studies (logic and metaphysics) at King's College, London, and a year's further study at Edinburgh. They were in turn followed by legal studies at Heidelberg. However, Nicholson basically studied his political economy at Cambridge, where Marshall and Sidgwick were his main teachers (Rutherford 2004, p. 854).

In 1877, Nicholson won the Cambridge Cobden Club's Essay Competition with the contribution, *The Effects of Machinery on Wages*, the first edition of which was published in 1878, the second in 1892 (Nicholson 1892). John Neville Keynes, who had also entered the competition as one of Marshall's early students, came second. In 1878 Nicholson completed an MA at the University of London, winning the Gerstenberg Prize for Political Economy. Following his successful completion of the Moral Sciences Tripos, Nicholson earned his living at Cambridge by private tutoring for the next four years. In 1880, he successfully applied for the Chair of Law and Political Economy at Edinburgh University.

Marshall appears to have had reasonable collegial relations with Nicholson, inviting him to his home for dinner on several occasions at least. Moreover, over the decades following Nicholson's appointment at Edinburgh, they cooperated on general economists' issues in a very collegial manner. These included signing the 1903 Free Trade Manifesto, organised by Edgeworth, Bastable and Nicholson (Marshall to Brentano, 18 August 1903, in Whitaker 1996, III p. 53); supporting the establishment of a British Economic Association (later Royal Economic Society) and its *Economic Journal* (in which both also published a number of articles); and the introduction of the new Cambridge Economics and Political Sciences Tripos as a way of encouraging greater specialisation in the study of economics. For a number of years, Nicholson also served his former university as an official examiner in the Moral Sciences Tripos.

Marshall and Nicholson also exchanged books. For example, Nicholson sent Marshall a copy of his prize-winning Cobden Club Essay in 1878, while Marshall sent Nicholson a copy of his *Elements of the Economics of Industry* in 1892 (Groenewegen 1995a, p. 427n.). However, they frequently criticised each other as well. Marshall, for example, thought little of Nicholson's monetary contributions including the material he had submitted in evidence to the Gold and Silver Commission (see Marshall 1888, 1996, pp. 65–80). Marshall was somewhat dubious of Nicholson's article on 'human capital' for the 1891 *Economic Journal* (Marshall to F.Y. Edgeworth, 4 April 1891, in Whitaker 1996, II p. 28). Furthermore, Marshall criticised Nicholson's misunderstanding of the notion of consumer surplus on several occasions (Marshall to E.R.A. Seligman, 13 May 1900, in Whitaker 1996, II p. 279), as well as Nicholson's misinterpretation of his concept of quasi-rent (Marshall to N.G. Pierson, 30 April 1898, in Whitaker 1996, II p. 230). In 1904, Marshall strongly disagreed with Nicholson as an examiner for the Cobden Club Prize Essay competition in that year, as he had placed Làl's essay above MacGregor's entry. According to Marshall, MacGregor's study of the coal industry was far superior, and Nicholson had ranked Làl's highly only for the quality of its English expression (Marshall to Tanner, 9 December 1904, in Whitaker 1996, III p. 98).

More generally, Marshall wrote John Neville Keynes (6 February 1902, in Whitaker 1996, II p. 353) apropos Nicholson, that Marshall had never thought that [J.S. Nicholson] had studied theory too much, 'my increasing complaint is that he has not studied it enough'. On another occasion, Marshall (letter to H.S. Foxwell, 2 August 1903, in Whitaker 1996, III pp. 42–43) described Nicholson's work as 'intellectually slovenly' on virtually every page of his books, and that he was completely incapable of describing Nicholson 'as a man of high calibre' in economics.

Nicholson was equally critical of Marshall on occasions. In his review of Marshal's *Principles* for the *Scotsman* (in Groenewegen 1998, I pp. 166–168), he criticised much of the historical material in the book. Stronger criticism was reserved for private correspondence with friends such as John Neville Keynes, who recorded Nicholson's comment in his diary:

> On re-reading the review, I think, I let him off too easily on some things. His history is vague, old-fashioned, and excessively weak; his examples are mainly of the old a priori kind or at best curious rather than important; the repetition is so great that his plan must be faulty; but if he is to cover the whole ground of what I understand by P.E., he will at the same rate take six volumes. At the same time his pure theory is extremely good and deserves the highest praise, especially because he was really the first to introduce the ideas to England. The book, however, will never do as a textbook in its present shape, and I can only recommend it for honours students.
>
> (J.N. Keynes, Diary, 24 July 1890, cited in Groenewegen 1995a, p. 416)

The final falling out between Marshall and Nicholson occurred in 1908 over Pigou's appointment as Marshall's successor to the Cambridge economics chair, instead of Foxwell. At the 'celebratory dinner' for Pigou's success at Balliol Croft the evening following the selection committee meeting, Nicholson later reported that 'Marshall did not speak to him the whole evening' because he had voted for Foxwell. In addition, Foxwell himself reported in a letter to Clara Collet, that on the following day Nicholson 'paced up and down my garden for two hours abusing Marshall' (cited in Groenewegen 1995a, pp. 623–624). Correspondence between Marshall and Nicholson seems to have ceased after this, though in 1922 Nicholson did sign the congratulatory economists' letter to Marshall on the occasion of his eightieth birthday. Their relationship was, therefore, often on the stormy side, and they happily criticised each other over their academic lifetime.

Nicholson's use of Marshall's ideas in some of his work, is discussed in what follows. This is done by seriatim assessment of Marshall's possible influence on Nicholson's Cobden Club Prize Essay on wages and machinery (Section II), then on his monetary writings (Section III) and finally on the three volumes of Nicholson's *Principles of Political Economy* (Section IV), and, where possible, by testing Marshall's reactions to his work.

I

Nicholson was born at Wrawby, Lincolnshire, on 9 November 1850. He was the son of an independent minister, and was educated at congregational schools. He matriculated and graduated at King's College, London University, with an honours BA in logic and metaphysics. He then studied for a year at Edinburgh University (1872–1873), before entering Trinity College, Cambridge, as a student in the moral sciences. In 1876, he shared second place in the first class honours list. The previous year, in the context of the 1875 Tripos examinations, Marshall wrote Foxwell that Nicholson was examined at Trinity and had been bracketed second with Jacobs in the Part I examination for the moral sciences Tripos (Marshall to Foxwell, 9 April 1875, in Whitaker 1996, I pp. 35–36 and n. 9).

In 1877 Nicholson won the Cambridge Cobden Club Essay Prize for his essay, 'The Effects of Machinery on Wages'; he also passed the London MA winning the Gerstenberg Prize. He then studied law at Heidelberg, and became fluent in both German and French. The three novels he wrote at this time were not very successful, that is, *Thoth, A Romance* (1888), *A Dreamer of Dreams* (1889) and *Toxar, A Romance* (1890). In 1913, he prepared a commentary on *Orlando Furioso: Tales from Ariosto,* which went through several editions.

Nicholson was appointed Professor of Political Economy and Mercantile Law at Edinburgh in 1880 (aged thirty), a position he held until he retired. He expanded his department with additional lecturers and established an honours degree in 1890. In 1885, Nicholson married the daughter of his predecessor, W.B. Hodgson. From the marriage came three children: a boy who died during the First World War, and two daughters.

Nicholson was a very prolific author. His first book was an edition of Smith's *Wealth of Nations*. As Scott (1927, p. 496) indicated in Nicholson's obituary, this signalled his great love and admiration of Adam Smith, the major influence on his work and of whom he was 'a linear successor' in the full sense of this term (Scott 1927, p. 497). Nicholson's aims in preparing this edition were to defend Smith from his contemporary critics who all too frequently failed to understand him, and to stress his continuing relevance. Nicholson therefore not surprisingly used Smith's *Wealth of Nations* and J.S. Mill's *Principles* as his major texts, supplemented by more contemporary reading. These books are the major sources for Nicholson's three-volume *Principles of Political Economy*, though its prefaces also thank Marshall and Sidgwick as his teachers of political economy at Cambridge, and J.N. Keynes (in all three volumes) for correcting the proofs. Marshall was fairly frequently cited in the first volume, considerably less in the second and the third, a citation practice partly explicable by the contents of the specific volumes. In the context of Nicholson's teaching, it may be added that Scott (1927, p. 496) depicted Nicholson as an old-fashioned Scottish academic: a thorough teacher, who was completely devoted to his students during the winter months, but who worked exclusively on his research during the warmer months of April to September.

Given this research strategy, it is not surprising that Nicholson published much additional material in book form. Apart from his Cobden Club Essay on wages and machinery, these include a *Treatise of Money and Essays on Monetary Problems* in 1888 (third edition 1895, fifth and final edition, 1901); *Strikes and Social Problems* (1896); *The Tariff Question with Special Reference to Wages and Employment* (1903); *A History of the English Corn Laws* (1904); *A Project of Empire: A Critical Study of the Economics of Imperialism, with Special Reference to the Ideas of Adam Smith* (1909); *War Finance* (1918); *Inflation* (1919); and, his final book, *The Revival of Marxism* (1920). As indicated in the introduction, three of these books are assessed in more detail, that is, the prize-winning Cobden Club Essay on wages and machinery, the *Treatise* and essays on monetary topics, and the three volumes of his *Principles of Political Economy*.

For the first volume of the *Palgrave Dictionary of Political Economy*, which appeared in 1894, Nicholson contributed seventeen entries. These commenced with the entry on 'Abolition [of slavery]' and concluded with that on 'Credit'. Nicholson wrote only one entry, that on his by then deceased father-in-law, W.B. Hodgson, for the second volume (1896, II pp. 317–318). He contributed no entries to the third and final volume of this important reference work. During the late 1880s, Nicholson also produced five articles for the ninth edition of the *Encyclopaedia Britannica*, on 'Taxation', 'Usury', 'Value', 'Wages' and 'Wealth'.

In 1893, Nicholson was President of Section F (Political Economy) of the British Association for the Advancement of Science, giving his Presidential Address on 'The Reaction in Favour of the Classical Economy' at its meeting in Nottingham in September 1893 (Nicholson 1893, 1962 pp. 112–125), an address largely devoted to praising the continuing relevance of Adam Smith, and to criticism of some aspects of mathematical economics.

Nicholson contributed extensively to the burgeoning academic journal literature. In total, nineteen academic articles appeared between 1887 and 1920: three in the *Journal of the Royal Statistical Society* (in 1887 and 1893); two in the *Journal of Political Economy* (both in 1893); and the other fourteen in the *Economic Journal.* The topics covered by these articles varied widely. Three were devoted to measurement problems of the various monetary standards and two, published during the First World War, to problems of inflation including its measurement. Two articles concerned capital: one discussed the issue of 'human capital', considered by some to have been Nicholson's major contribution to economics; the other capital in its relation to labour. Nicholson contributed two articles on classical political economy, and one on Adam Smith's position on the public debt. Nicholson also published a piece on the economics of imperialism, and three on the work of individual economists: Friedrich List, Walter Bagehot and John Law. Of the remaining four articles, one was an address given by Nicholson to the inaugural meeting of the Scottish Society of Economists which had taken place on 9 November 1897; one was on Scottish banking; of the final two, one was critical of Marshall, and one examined the use, and abuse, of authority in economics.

The paper critical of Marshall, published in 1894, questioned his analysis of consumers' surplus as a device for measuring value (utility) with money. Nicholson argued first that competitive market prices were applicable to all market participants in equal measure, whereas the degree of utility for individuals compatible with these market prices were, generally speaking, quite different. Total utility of a commodity, Nicholson (1894, p. 345) also maintained, was not measurable. Nicholson also claimed that 'necessities' could not be given a finite marginal utility, mentioning here in particular the commodity, coal, which in the first edition of the *Principles of Economics* Marshall initially had used as an example in this context (Marshall 1890b, III Chapter IV; 1891, III Chapter VI). It was this use of coal that Nicholson particularly objected to in the estimates of consumers' rent (later consumers' surplus) Marshall presented. As far as Nicholson (1894, pp. 346–347) was concerned, applying a utility measurement to coal was impossible, given its place as a vital necessity in a household budget. By the 1895 third edition, Marshall had changed the nature of his example: coal was abandoned, the commodity 'tea' (then much less of a necessity) was its replacement. As already indicated, Marshall had complained to Seligman in 1900 about Nicholson's misinterpretation of consumer surplus, an issue Marshall had tried to explain even more fully in the fourth edition of his *Principles* (Marshall 1898, pp. 202n., 207n., 257n.). Nicholson, however, maintained his criticism of consumer surplus in the two editions of both the first and second volumes of his *Principles of Political Economy.*

The second paper, published in 1903, investigated the 'use and abuse of authority in economics', an investigation which twice mentioned Marshall. The first reference to Marshall related to his depiction of Adam Smith as 'the first [person] to make a careful and systematic inquiry into the way in which value measured the desires of purchasers to possess wealth on the one side and on the other the efforts and sacrifices of production', thereby making him a leading authority in economics (Nicholson 1903a, p. 560). Second, Marshall was mentioned for his 'guarded statement' warning of the limitations of mathematical economics, a matter on which he had been preceded by Cournot, another leading mathematical economist conscious of the dangers of mathematical argument for explaining parts of the science of economics (Nicholson 1903a, p. 565).

It may be noted here, and will be reiterated in Section III below, that some of the monetary essays published in his book on money (1888, 1895a) covered topics dealt with in these journal articles, more specifically those dealing with monetary standards, with John Law, with inflation and with problems and advantages of bi-metallism. In the context of bi-metallism it may also be mentioned that Friedman (1990, p. 96) described Nicholson 'as one of the ablest British economists in favour of bi-metallism', the type of praise assigned more generally by Schumpeter (1954, pp. 1076, 1081) to his monetary economics. Nor should it be forgotten that especially during the 1880s, that is, prior to the commencement of specialist economics journal literature, Nicholson published many essays in non-academic journals, and read papers to learned societies, of which his 1893 Presidential Address to Section F of the British Association for the Advancement of Science has already been mentioned.

Nicholson resigned his Edinburgh chair in 1925 due to illness. He had held it for forty-five years. He died less than two years later, on 12 March 1927.

II

Nicholson's first book on economics, published two years after his completion of studies for the Moral Sciences Tripos, was his prize-winning Cambridge Cobden Prize Essay on *The Effects of Machinery on Wages.* Nicholson (1892, p. ix) recorded that the first edition owed much to writers of the historical school, in particular to Thorold Rogers and Cliffe Leslie and, from Germany, to work by Held, Knies, Roscher, Nasse and Brentano. The first edition did not draw on Marshall's work. Moreover, Marshall was then assisting John Neville Keynes in preparing his entry for the Cobden Prize. Keynes had preceded Nicholson in the Moral Sciences Tripos by one year (being Senior Moralist in 1875). Marshall's assistance to Keynes meant that Keynes treated the topic in a more abstract Ricardian and Marshallian manner. This was a distinct disadvantage when Cliffe Leslie was the external examiner for the prize, and 'obviously destined to dominate' the two internal examiners: Henry Fawcett, then Professor of Economics at Cambridge, and Samuel Phear, a theologian (Deane 2001, pp. 36–37). Nicholson's historical approach to the topic, based very much on that of Cliffe Leslie, was not surprisingly favoured by the external examiner as against that of Keynes, whose theoretical approach conflicted with Cliffe Leslie's historical method of economic investigation.

The structure of Nicholson's prize-wininng essay in the first edition was an introduction, followed by five substantive chapters, and concluding with a summary of results. These chapters each concentrated on one of the five different aspects of the relationship between machinery and labour identified by Nicholson, that is, substitution of machinery for labour (Chapter I), machinery as auxiliary to labour (Chapter II), machinery as affecting the division of labour (Chapter III), machinery as affecting the concentration of labour and capital (Chapter IV) and machinery as affecting the mobility of capital and labour (Chapter V). Contents and structure were not basically altered for the second edition in 1892. That edition, as Nicholson explained in the preface, was only updated by the availability of 'new facts', and by references to more recent authorities. In addition, the second edition provided translations of quotations from foreign writers, while technical terms used in the *Essay* were more fully explained. Among the new authorities for Nicholson's second edition was Marshall, in particular the second edition of his *Principles* (1891), a work which was quoted by Nicholson on no less than half a dozen occasions.

The first reference to Marshall, perhaps also in the first edition, is in a note on the 'wages-fund theory', a theory which had been strongly criticised 'from the deductive side.... by Professors Sidgwick and Marshall' (Nicholson 1892, p. 5n. 1). A quotation from Cournot (Nicholson 1892, p. 15) leads to the second note on Marshall, who had 'followed Cournot's example both as regards "money" and "continuity"' (Nicholson 1892, p. 16n. 1). Four pages later, the first volume of Marshall's *Principles* is strongly recommended on the topic of the effectiveness of individual wage bargaining as against collective wage-bargaining by trade unions (Nicholson 1892, p. 20n. 1). On p. 33n. 1, Nicholson (incorrectly) suggested that Marshall had obtained his motto for the *Principles*, *natura non facit saltum*, from Cournot's *Revue sommaire des doctrines oeconomiques* (for example, Cournot 1877, 1982, p. 99) though it may be noted that the 1927 *Marshall Library Catalogue* does not indicate that Marshall owned a copy of this book. Nicholson (1892, p. 36n. 2) quoted Marshall on the fact that the Swiss watch industry was 'yielding ground' to the American system (Marshall 1891, p. 316). Subsequently, Nicholson (1892, p. 86) cited Marshall's *Principles* (Marshall 1891, p. 335) for reporting the employment characteristics of labour by industry, while a few pages later (Nicholson 1892, p. 89), Marshall (1891, p. 315) is quoted on repairs of machinery as undertaken by their owners. Nicholson (1892, p. 92) finally cited Marshall (1891, pp. 268–270) on the improvements of technical education which had taken place in England during the years after 1878, the publication year of Nicholson's first edition. We can agree with Nicholson's view that these references to Marshall's work are on the factual side, with the exception of the first reference to the 'deductivist' critique of the wages-fund doctrine. Moreover, Marshall's *Principles of Economics*, in its latest available edition, the second edition of 1891, was obviously a new authority in economics of the highest rank.

Nicholson's first book on economics, written when he was a recent graduate in the moral sciences, in its second edition demonstrated a reasonable indebtedness to Marshall's *Principles of Economics* largely as a source of new facts of relevance to Nicholson's topic. Moreover, Nicholson appears also to have gained his knowledge of the analytical errors in the wages-fund doctrine from the 'deductionist' critique thereof by Sidgwick and Marshall, implying that Marshall shared his influence on Nicholson with Sidgwick as his fellow economic teacher. In short, for the Cobden Prize Essay *The Effects of Machinery on Wages,* Marshall was one of many sources. As measured by the number of citations in the second edition, he had become a quite important one even if not as influential as Adam Smith and John Stuart Mill. Moreover, Marshall's political economy teaching, from which Nicholson undoubtedly benefited greatly, would also have contributed to Marshall's impact on the writing of Nicholson's first economic monograph.

III

In 1888, Nicholson published *Money and Monetary Problems*, a book divided into two parts. *A Treatise of Money*, likewise subdivided into two parts from the third edition of 1895, made up the first component of the volume. Essays, largely devoted to monetary topics, but not exclusively so in every edition, made up the second part of the volume. The book appears to have been a popular one, going into five editions, of which the last, dated 1901, remains housed in the Marshall Library according to its 1927 Catalogue, presumably a gift from this 'former student' to his by then still revered teacher. Part I of the *Treatise of Money* discussed the general theory of money in eight chapters; Part II's seven chapters particularly examined 'the influence of the production of the precious metals on industry and trade'.

After an introductory chapter which warned of the difficulty of the topic, Part I of the *Treatise* in the third edition dealt in Chapter II with the functions of money ('medium of exchange', 'measure of value', 'means of deferred payments'); the requisites of good coinage (Chapter III); Gresham's Law (Chapter IV); the quantity of money and the level of general prices (Chapter V); the effects of credit on prices (Chapter VI); influence of the price level in one country on that of other countries (Chapter VII); and effects on the price level from using both gold and silver as standard money, that is, bi-metallism (Chapter VIII).

Part II contained seven chapters in the third edition. Chapter I indicated the nature of current monetary problems in India, the United States and the United Kingdom. Chapter II described the differences between money and other commodities. Chapter III looked at the exchange values of gold and silver. Chapter IV reviewed the causes of changes in these values. Chapter V explained the quantity theory of money. Chapter VI discussed the interaction of gold and silver prices; while the final chapter (Chapter VII) reviewed the effects of the annual production of gold and silver as additions to the monetary stock. Walter Bagehot's *Lombard Street* was perhaps the major monetary source cited in Nicholson's *Treatise*, while Adam Smith was the most frequently cited author.

Marshall is quoted only once, from his submission to the Royal Commission on the Depression of Trade (Marshall 1886, 1926) in the context of his support for 'a tabular standard of value' (Nicholson 1895a, p. 30).

Nicholson's essays included with the third edition of his *Treatise of Money* virtually all deal with either aspects of the quantity theory of money or the defence of bi-metallism, both directly and indirectly. Their dates of previous publication range from 1886 to 1893, with most of the papers dating from the final years of the 1880s. The first essay is a lengthy study of John Law, the Scottish banker and financier. When discussing the collapse of the Mississippi scheme, Nicholson applied the quantity theory as a way of explaining the interaction of money growth and rises in the price level. Nicholson (1888, 1895a), however, strongly maintained that causality can run in various ways in the quantity theory as a relationship between money and prices. One example is the following. Price rises can frequently induce increases in money supply to enable the volume of exchange transactions to be maintained at the higher price level. In the context of Nicholson's on Law it is interesting to note that Antoin Murphy (1997, p. 6) described Nicholson's account of Law's scheme as 'more balanced' than that of Marx, and superior to that of Alfred Marshall. Nicholson's second essay presents the introduction of one pound (£1) notes as a good way of saving on gold use, since it would remove the gold sovereign from the wear and tear of active circulation. This essay is followed by a historical account of the long run impact of past gold and silver discoveries. Nicholson here sharply distinguished the increases in the world stock of silver from the bullion inflows associated with the discoveries and colonisation of the new world of the Americas, while the consequences of a large gold inflow are discussed in terms of the discoveries of the South African, Californian and Australian gold fields from the middle of the nineteenth century.

The remaining essays were substantially devoted to bi-metallism, and form the basis for Friedman's (1990) assessment of Nicholson's quality as a writer on that subject. The first essay, an address given in Manchester in March 1887, sought to demonstrate that bi-metallism was both advantageous and practicable as a major reform of the contemporary monetary system. The second paper addressed the 'morality of bi-metallism'. The third paper argued in support of the 'the stability of the fixed ratio between gold and silver under international bi-metallism', while the fourth paper reviewed the associated issue of measuring variations in the value of a monetary standard. The next paper in the volume explained the causes of general price movements, an excursion into the quantity theory in its broader sense. A critical overview of Giffen's attack on bi-metallism, together with comments on some other monetary reform proposals followed. Then came what Nicholson called 'a elaboration of the missing link' between gold and silver. The essays closed with a discussion of Indian currency experiments, a study of a silver standard country in essentially a gold standard world. Some of these essays, particularly Nicholson's critical explanation of the quantity theory as a theory of the price level, were indirectly critical of Marshall, who himself had criticised Nicholson's monetary views in a special memorandum he had submitted to the Gold and Silver Commission in June 1888. This episode (discussed in detail in Groenewegen 1996, pp. 65–77) can now be briefly mentioned.

The sequence of events is as follows. Marshall had drafted his comment criticising Nicholson's paper by 23 June 1888, discussing it with J.N. Keynes that weekend. Keynes later recorded in his diary that Marshall, sadly, had entered 'into controversy with Nicholson'. Marshall's critical remarks largely related to Nicholson's far too narrow perception of his view on the quantity theory. Marshall (1888, 1996, p. 74) addressed this aspect of the matter very clearly in his note on Nicholson, emphasising no less than seven variables as essential for the proper enunciation of the quantity theory. This position, Marshall argued, 'was in substantial agreement with the views of such writers as Professor Nasse'. These seven factors were as follows: 'the volume of the currency', 'population', the amount of goods produced per head of population and their wealth generally', 'the amount of business to which any given amount of wealth gives rise', 'the proportion of these payments that are made for currency', 'the average rapidity of circulation of the currency', under which head provision could be made for the quantity of hoarding by individuals and by business, and 'the state of commercial and political confidence, enterprise and credit'. These remarks conformed quite well with the view of the quantity theory Nicholson had put forward in his essay on that subject based on a talk to the Royal Society of Edinburgh, 30 January 1888, with the title, 'Causes of Movements in General Prices'. Part of that essay (Nicholson 1888, 1895b, pp. 370–374) reads like a criticism of Marshall given his position as explained in the note on Nicholson. It is also very likely that given the date of Nicholson's paper, 30 January 1888, its substance would have found its way into his submission to the Gold and Silver Commission. As I pointed out in 1996 (Groenewegen 1996, p. 67n. 8), a substantial segment of the contents of the second part of his *Treatise of Money*, although written in early 1895, could have appeared as part of his views on monetary theory in Nicholson's submission, no longer extant, to the Gold and Silver Commission.

Marshall's other criticisms of Nicholson's submission covered the following matters. First was Marshall's failure to see how he differed from Nicholson in accepting the 'many causes which the older economists believed to be capable of exerting an influence on the gold price of silver' (Marshall 1888, 1996, p. 70). Nor did Marshall accept Nicholson's argument that a 'fall in the gold price of silver' will ensure 'that all commodities exported to silver-using countries will at once fall in price' (Marshall 1888, 1996, p. 71). Marshall associated such an analysis with an increased output of silver from greater production in silver-producing countries, raising the silver price of goods in India and the gold price of silver in England. These shifts would continue until a new equilibrium was reached in which the gold price of silver was once more in harmony with the gold prices to silver prices ratio (Marshall 1888, 1996, p. 72). Likewise, Marshall objected to Nicholson's view that a depression of prices due to accidental causes would continue long after these causes had disappeared, an argument he claimed to have convincingly refuted in his evidence to the Commission (Marshall 1888, 1996, p. 74). Other differences of opinion between the two related to the assumed speed of adjustments of wage levels, and those of internationally traded commodity prices (Marshall 1888, 1996, pp. 76–77). Given my earlier discussion (Groenewegen 1996), the matter need not be further pursued here.

IV

As already indicated, the three volumes of Nicholson's *Principles of Political Economy* appeared sequentially in 1893, 1897 and 1901. A second edition appeared over the years 1902 to 1909. The contents and structure of Nicholson's treatise followed that of John Stuart Mill's *Principles* in which books on production and distribution preceded those on exchange and on the impact of progress on distribution, and, the final book, the role of government. In the same manner, Volume I of Nicholson's *Principles* looked at production in Book I and distribution in Book II; its Volume II presented Book III on exchange; while Volume III examined the importance of economic progress in Book IV and the economic functions of government in Book V. From the index, Adam Smith, closely followed by John Stuart Mill, were the major authorities used in writing the book. Marshall's *Principles* was fairly frequently mentioned in Volume I, often in a critical manner, less so in Volume II and Volume III. In the preface to the three volumes of Nicholson's *Principles*, Marshall shared acknowledgements with Sidgwick as Nicholson's valued teacher of political economy at Cambridge. Examining the impact of Marshall's work on Nicholson's *Principles*, both positive and negative, is the rationale for this section of the chapter. Section IV does not, therefore, pretend to cover the contents of Nicholson's *magnum opus* systematically.

Volume I of Nicholson's *Principles* cited Marshall on no less than twenty occasions, referring three times to the first edition (1879) of *Economics of Industry*; at least once to the first (1890) edition of Marshall's *Principles*, eleven times to the second (1891) edition of the *Principles*, and once to the *Elements of the Economics of Industry* (1892), of which Marshall had sent a complimentary copy to Nicholson when it was first published. The other five references to Marshall fail to mention a specific text.

Nicholson's longest references to Marshall occurred when Nicholson criticised him on points of his theory. This is the case of Nicholson's (1893, pp. 63–65) treatment of consumers' rent (later consumers' surplus) and of the nature and legitimacy of a concept of quasi-rent (Nicholson 1893, pp. 411–414). There are also cases of implicit disagreement with Marshall in Nicholson's text. A good example is Nicholson's structure for much of the book in terms of the three agents of production (land or nature, capital and labour), hence omitting 'organisation', Marshall's fourth agent of production, the importance of which Marshall stressed especially in the *Principles* (Nicholson 1893, I Chapter II, p. 33).

In what follows, the references to Marshall are taken seriatim as they occur in Nicholson's text. The first (Nicholson 1893, p. 50n. 3) indicates agreement with

Marshall on the lack of need to classify 'goods according to the orders in which they rank with respect to consumption', in the way Menger had done. The next reference to Marshall is a three pages 'note' to Book I Chapter III on consumption, in which Nicholson critically reviewed the notion of consumers' rent as an unwarranted concept if it was meant for practical application. Such application was indeed suggested by Marshall when he used it in his tax-bounty welfare argument.

Subsequently, Nicholson (1893, Book IV Chapter V, pp. 85–86) argued he could not agree with Marshall that 'the struggle for existence causes, in the long run, those races of men to survive in which the individual is most willing to sacrifice himself for the benefit of his environment; and what are, consequently, the best adapted collectively to make use of his environment' (from Marshall 1891, p. 302). This point, according to Nicholson, was made more validly in the previous century by Sir James Steuart, though where Steuart made this comment Nicholson failed to indicate. In the chapter on capital, Nicholson's lengthy discussion of Turgot's theory may have been implicitly inspired by Marshall's defence of that theory against Böhm-Bawerk's misleading criticism (Nicholson 1893, p. 88; cf. Groenewegen 1995a, pp. 473–475), but Marshall is not named in this context. Nicholson (1893, p. 94) cited *Economics of Industry* on the problem of classifying a doctor's carriage purely as capital, a statement Nicholson (1893, p. 94n. 1) suggested should be compared with Marshall's somewhat different account in his *Principles*. Nicholson's (1893, p. 95) next point referred to Marshall's *Principles* (1891, II Chapter IV, p. 125) and its treatment of human capital. At the end of the chapter on capital, Nicholson (1893, p. 103n. 2) approvingly mentioned Marshall's *Principles* (1891, VI Chapter II, note, pp. 572–576) for its criticism of Mill's four propositions on capital.

Nicholson (1893, p. 108) also approvingly mentioned Marshall's *Principles* (1891, p. 315) on the 'importance of interchangeability of parts of machinery' to facilitate and cheapen repairs to them. Six pages later (Nicholson 1893, p. 114n. 1), Marshall's *Principles* (Book IV Chapter X, 'Concerning of Specialised Industries in Particular Localities'), is praised as a very useful discussion of the importance of location for ensuring a satisfactory division of labour. Nicholson's (1893, I Chapter VIII) treatment of production on a large scale and a small scale praised Marshall's 'excellent treatment of this topic' and used the definitions Marshall (1891, p. 325) had given of these two terms. In the context of the laws of diminishing returns and increasing returns, Nicholson (1893, I Chapter X, p. 210) quoted Marshall's (1891, p. 210) remark on the importance of the 'marginal dose' applied to the fixed factor: 'all that is necessary is that it should be the last dose which can be profitably applied to the land.' This is also the last reference to Marshall in Book I of Nicholson's *Principles*.

At the start of Nicholson's (1893, p. 229) Book II, Marshall's *Principles* and those of Sidgwick are praised as 'the two most important works in Political Economy since Mill'. In this context, Nicholson noted that Sidgwick's Book II is called 'Distribution and Exchange' while Marshall called his Book VI, 'Value, or Distribution and Exchange', a difference on the significance of which

Nicholson failed to elaborate. It is, however, not until Chapter X of Book II on wages, that Nicholson (1893, p. 325n. 1) mentioned Marshall's 1891 edition of the *Principles* on the subject of land rent. The rationale for this reference is not easy to grasp, since wages are not mentioned by Marshall in the material referred to, except briefly in the context of some remarks Marshall had made in this chapter on quasi-rent. Nicholson (1893, p. 331 and n. 1) pointed to Marshall's remark in the *Principles* (1890b, p. 14) that custom can sometimes act as a form of slow competition; while two pages later, Nicholson noted the discussion of 'normal' in relation to wages as discussed in the 1879 edition of the *Economics of Industry* (Book II chapters I and XIII) comparing it with the later remarks in Marshall's *Principles* (1891, p. 84) on 'normal' in relation to 'economic laws'. In connection with the impact of trade unions on wage levels, Nicholson (1893, pp. 383–384) cited Marshall's *The Elements of the Economics of Industry* (1892, VI, Chapter XIII).

Nicholson's chapter on profits (Book II Chapter VIII) contained several references to Marshall's work. Nicholson (1893, pp. 390–391) indicated that Marshall substituted the term 'waiting' for that of 'abstinence' (introduced by Nassau Senior) in the context of interest rate determination. Later on, Marshall and Walker were credited (Nicholson 1893, p. 399) with having developed Smith's notion of the 'wages of superintendence' in their analyses of entrepreneurial incomes. In Book II Chapter XIV, devoted to economic rent, Nicholson queried the legitimacy of Marshall's use of the term, 'quasi-rent', particularly since 'he has made a very extensive application of his theory'. However, Nicholson regarded use of the quasi-rent concept as wrong, largely because it conflicted with Ricardo's notion that rent, as a return, related to productive powers which were 'indestructible'. Furthermore, the classical theory of rent, especially that of Ricardo, the leading authority on the subject in Nicholson's view, showed rent as arising from the 'niggardliness of nature' and not from its 'benevolence'. Such 'benevolence' arose from the high productivity implied in the returns to investment in machines and human skills to which Marshall applied his notion of quasi-rent. Nicholson (1893, pp. 413–414) conceded, however, that his quarrel over Marshall's use of quasi-rent was simply 'a question of classification and analogy' but that even these types of issue could have significant consequences for the understanding of a problem.

Nicholson's second volume (1897) contained far fewer references to Marshall even though the third book of which it was composed was completely devoted to 'exchange'. For Nicholson, this topic included both money and international trade, topics not covered in Marshall's Book VI which combined value, distribution and exchange in its title. Other topics which Nicholson covered in his Book III came in Marshall's book on consumption and demand, production and supply, and the theory of equilibrium of demand and supply.

The less than half a dozen citations and other implicit references to Marshall's work fall virtually all within the first third of Nicholson's second volume, largely devoted to issues of domestic exchange and value. The first cited Marshall's 'nomenclature' of demand elasticity as a useful device, referring readers to Book III

Chapter IV of the second edition of the *Principles* (Nicholson 1897, p. 29n. 1). Nine pages later, Nicholson (1897, p. 38) referred his readers to Marshall's analysis of 'temporary equilibrium of supply and demand' in Book V, Chapter II of the second (1891) edition of the *Principles*. Nicholson (1897, Book III Chapter V) on cost of production in relation to value made a reference to the 'normal' not coinciding with the 'average' rate, not attributed to Marshall, even though he made this point in this context. The third direct reference to Marshall, Nicholson (1897, p. 62n. 1) made when discussing monopoly and profit maximisation, in a general note which apart from Marshall, mentioned valuable contributions by Cournot and Edgeworth on the topic. A fourth reference to Marshall occurred in Nicholson's (1897, pp. 80–82) treatment of quasi-rent, essentially a short period concept since in the long run Marshall admits that 'the normal price of the product depends on the cost of the factors'. Nicholson concluded from his discussion that '*quasi-rent* is an unforseen and unstable exceptional profit or loss' (Nicholson 1897, p. 82), inconsistent with the meaning Marshall gave to this concept.

The many chapters on monetary topics (Chapter XI–XXII) contain no references to Marshall directly or indirectly, even in the context of Nicholson's (1897, p. 166n. 1) reference to the Report of the Royal Commission on Indian currency, or to the other Royal Commissions on monetary and related issues to which Marshall had contributed evidence in the 1880s and early 1890s.

Two possible indirect references to Marshall occur in the context of Nicholson's lengthy chapters on the pure theory of foreign trade. The first relates to Marshall's choice of cloth and linen as examples of traded goods in the two commodities–international barter situation in his *Pure Theory of International Trade* (Marshall 1879, 1930). However, cloth and linen were likewise used in this way in J.S. Mill's international trade theory. The second is Nicholson's (1897, p. 323) critical remark on the use of 'consumers' rent' as a means of estimating the gain for consumers from international trade.

Volume III of Nicholson's *Principles of Political Economy* covered 'economic progress' in its Book IV and 'functions of government' in Book V. There are several direct references to Marshall in this volume, as well as some indirect ones. The first citation comes in a note in which Nicholson (1901, p. 116n. 2) favourably mentioned Marshall's 1879 *Economics of Industry* (p. 85n. 1) correction of 'a curious error in Mill', in which the algebra came from Nicholson, not Marshall. In the chapter 'On Progress and Profits' (Book IV Chapter VI), Nicholson (1901, pp. 121, 123) used the concept of consumers' rent 'to adopt the fashionable phrase', for explaining the gains of borrowers in paying the market rate of interest. Marshall, however, was not mentioned in these remarks by Nicholson. Later in the chapter, Nicholson (1901, pp. 141, 142 and n. 2) mentioned quasi-rent as an 'exposition of the resemblance between the rent of land and other forms of income' on which Marshall's *Principles* (Book VI Chapter VIII) is cited as the major reference. Nicholson's by now frequently mentioned differences of opinion with Marshall on quasi-rent are described by him as only 'a matter of language'. Finally, in the chapter on 'Wages and Progress', Nicholson (1901, p. 151) cited census data reported by Marshall in his *Principles* (1898, fourth edition, p. 355n. 1).

There are only two direct references to Marshall in Nicholson's Book V. First, Nicholson (1901, pp. 305–306) approvingly quoted Marshall's *Principles* (1898, p. 524n. 2) on the view that the theory of the shifting of taxation is 'an application of the theory of value in the broadest sense'. Ten pages later, Nicholson (1901, p. 315n. 1) referred his readers to Marshall's *Principles* (1898, Book V Chapter XIII) as a presumably useful analysis of 'taxes on monopolies'. Earlier, in Chapter III of Book V, Nicholson (1901, pp. 221, 235–236) referred approvingly to quasi-rent in the context of a reference to *Industrial Democracy* by the Webbs; and in the second page reference, to the concept of 'net value' in a very Marshallian way. In both cases, Marshall is not explicitly mentioned by Nicholson.

Overall, Marshall's *Principles* and his other writings (*Economics of Industry* 1879; *Elements of the Economics of Industry*, 1892) are used by Nicholson in his three-volume text as one set of sources among many others. Marshall is never the major authority except, and then often critically, on particular points (consumers' rent, quasi-rent). For Nicholson, Adam Smith and J.S. Mill remained the leading authorities on political economy, and only in the first volume, is Marshall, together with Sidgwick, described as a major authority from the 'new generation' of economists. For the second and third volumes, Marshall's work was a much less frequently used reference, only valuable on a few specific points for his readers, so Nicholson thought. For example, Marshall is overshadowed for Nicholson on international trade and public finance by Bastable, Seligman, and Edgeworth; on progress Marshall is barely mentioned, and the few Marshall citations Nicholson made are on small technical points. Whether Nicholson thought Marshall too difficult for the readers of his text, which he had, after all, designed for pass students and not for the honours students targeted by Marshall's *Principles* in Nicholson's view, is one explanation. The restricted nature of many areas covered by Marshall in his published work, provides another. Marshall's own assessment of Nicholson's lack of theoretical ability may also be a factor here, since it may have made Nicholson increasingly suspicious of theory, as he got older. This type of argument is, however, best left to the concluding section, where it can be pursued on a broader front.

V

A student of Marshall, who appeared less and less enamoured with the work of the 'master' as he grew older, such was the Professor of Political Economy and Law at Edinburgh, J.S. Nicholson. On the surviving evidence, Nicholson at first seems to have been a loyal follower of Marshall's political economy, always in tandem, however, with that of Sidgwick, whose *Principles of Political Economy* had appeared a good seven years before Marshall's *Principles*. However, despite Nicholson's gratitude to his two Cambridge teachers of political economy and the admiration Nicholson had for their books, Nicholson always showed a far greater historical bent in his approach to the subject, a result of his earlier education outside Cambridge. He also continued to show a tremendous admiration for the great classical authorities who continued to guide him, John Stuart Mill and, especially, Adam Smith. Neither of them had had their day in Nicholson's view, and both, despite their errors, still had much wisdom to impart. This is fully evident from Nicholson's citation practice in the three-volume *Principles of Political Economy*, and both Smith and Mill stayed the leading authorities for Nicholson over the whole of his professional life. His three volumes of *Principles*, it should not be forgotten, were completed over the 1890s, the same decade in which Marshall completed the first four editions of the first volume of his *Principles of Economics.*

Some aspects of Nicholson's treatment of Marshall as a source can here be reiterated. The first is the use Nicholson made of Marshall's books as a source of facts. This is the case for both the second edition of Nicholson's first book on *Machinery and Wages*, as well as his *Principles of Political Economy.* His reference to the *Elements of the Economics of Industry* on trade unions provides another good example of this. Second, there are the instances when Nicholson recognised Marshall as a great theoretician. This made his work valuable as an excellent reference for the more advanced theory on topics such as the refutation of the wages-fund doctrine, the theory of location of industry, the theory of temporary equilibrium of demand and supply, the notion of elasticity, the theory of monopoly and of profit maximisation, and the analysis of tax shifting. Third, there are issues on which Nicholson believed Marshall to have been wrong. In monetary discussion, this included what Nicholson (wrongly) described as Marshall's narrow presentation of the quantity theory; in economic theory and its application it included both the notions of consumers' rent and of quasi-rent, once again for basically wrong reasons on Nicholson's part. More broadly, there was Nicholson's criticism in his review of the first edition of the *Principles* of Marshall's approach to the structure of his *Principles*: poor history, poor structure and too much repetition.

Part of this type of relationship between Nicholson and Marshall can be explained by the fact that Nicholson was one of the old Moral Sciences Tripos students, taught in economics by Sidgwick as well as Marshall, and a friend and close associate of other early moral sciences students, J.N. Keynes and Foxwell. Keynes checked the proofs of the three volumes of Nicholson's *Principles*, an arduous task; Foxwell was Nicholson's preferred successor to Marshall on his retirement, a preference which greatly annoyed Marshall. It was also a strong indication of Nicholson's taste in the practice of economics. No wonder Marshall and Nicholson drifted apart, becoming respective anathemas as writers to each other. In the end Marshall thought very little of Nicholson's *Principles* and other parts of his later work, describing them as 'intellectually slovenly' on virtually every page, and at best 'low calibre' economics. Nicholson was a student whom Marshall occasionally counted (as in the 1908 fragment mentioned in the opening paragraph of this chapter) among his good products, but at other times as someone whose economic contributions he would prefer to forget. Nicholson likewise, over his lifetime, seems to have lost a great deal of respect for Marshall both as a person and, to a lesser extent, as an economist.

3 Alfred William Flux (1867–1942)

A mathematician successfully 'caught' for economics by Marshall

Flux was described by Marshall as his 'most important' find for economics in the years up to 1890 when searching for good economics students during the initial years of his professorship at Cambridge (Whitaker 1965, p. 33). He was a Senior Wrangler at Cambridge in 1887, and became a Fellow of St John's (Marshall's own College) in 1889, having switched to economics in the mean time. He left Cambridge in 1893 to go as a lecturer in economics to Owen College, Manchester, becoming its W.S. Jevons Professor in 1898. In 1901, Flux moved to the William Dow Chair of Political Economy at McGill University, in Montréal, Canada. He returned to England in 1908 to become Statistical Adviser to the Board of Trade, and subsequently built his statistical career by developing many official statistics and occasionally publishing articles for the *Journal of the Royal Statistical Society* on topics such as the measurement of price changes, indices of industrial productive activity and the national income.

Over his years as professor of political economy at Manchester and Montréal, Flux wrote many articles and book reviews for the *Economic Journal*, including his justly famous review of Wicksteed's *Essay on the Co-ordination of the Laws of Distribution* in 1894 (discussed in Section II of this chapter). While professor at McGill in 1904, he published his textbook, *Economic Principles*, with a second edition in 1923. Its prefatory note acknowledged the 'great inspiration' Flux had derived 'from contact with Professor Marshall as a Cambridge student, indicating that he himself was particularly 'conscious of a very special obligation to the teacher [i.e. Alfred Marshall] to whom he owed his chief guidance in economic study' (Flux 1904, 1923, p. v). Given its author designated status as a Marshallian text, the contents of Flux's *Principles* are discussed in some detail in Section III of this chapter.

The Marshallian credentials of Flux's economic contributions published during his early years as academic economist are the main focus of this chapter. To investigate these credentials, the argument is as follows. Section I provides biographical background, concentrating on Flux's years at Cambridge from the mid-1880s to 1893. In Section II, the Marshallian credentials of some of his early writings for the *Economic Journal* are investigated, with special reference to his review of Wicksteed's *Essay on the Co-ordination of the Laws of*

Distribution published in 1894. Section III assesses the Marshallian qualities of his 1904 text, *Economic Principles*. The scope of its content, however, considerably exceeded Marshall's own *Principles of Economics*, for assistance to which Flux was thanked in the prefaces of several of its various editions. The final section presents some conclusions.

I

Alfred William Flux was born in Portsmouth on 8 April 1867, the son of a journeyman cement maker. After completing his studies at Portsmouth Grammar School, he entered St John's College (Cambridge) in 1884 as a minor scholar, to study mathematics. In 1887 he was bracketed first in the Cambridge Mathematical Tripos, becoming a Fellow of his College in 1889. While at John's, Flux was befriended by Alfred Marshall and Herbert Foxwell, two Fellows of St John's involved in teaching economics for the Moral Sciences Tripos. This friendship generated an interest in studying economics. Flux attended Marshall's 1888–1889 classes on production and distribution (Michaelmas Term 1888) and trade and finance (Lent Term 1889). He performed sufficiently well in his examinations to be awarded the Marshall Prize, signalling he was listed first in the advanced political economy papers that year. This earned him the sum of £15 to be spent on books.

Flux had attended Marshall's classes in economics while Marshall was completing the text of his *Principles of Economics*, published in July 1890. Flux's quality as a new economics student, together with his substantial skills in mathematics, led to him being thanked in its preface for giving Marshall 'valuable' assistance 'in connection with the Mathematical Appendix' (Marshall 1890b, p. xii). The second edition thanked Flux as one of five friends and colleagues who gave valuable 'help and suggestions' during the book's preparation (Marshall 1891, p. vii), a thanks repeated in the preface to the fourth edition for someone now described as Professor Flux (Marshall 1898, p. vi). In the preface for the sixth edition Marshall acknowledged once more that 'Mr A.W. Flux has also done much for me' during the preparation of this volume (Marshall 1910, in Guillebaud 1961, II p. 60). Although it is not known whether Marshall tangibly recognised Flux's assistance by presenting him with complimentary copies of the various editions of his *Principles*, Flux was definitely sent a complimentary copy of the *Elements of the Economics of Industry* when it was published in 1892 as an abridgement of the *Principles*.

Over the years, Marshall's references to Flux in successive prefaces of the *Principles* indicate Flux's career shifts following his departure from Cambridge. As already mentioned, Flux joined the staff of Manchester University as a lecturer in economics in 1893, becoming its first W.S. Jevons Professor in 1898. Limitations in the scope for teaching and research at Manchester, induced Flux's migration to Canada in 1901 to take up the William Dow chair at McGill University in Montréal. He occupied this position until his return to London in 1908 to become adviser to the Commercial, Labour and Statistics Department.

It may be noted here that most of Flux's academic publications were prepared while he was in academic positions at Manchester and Montréal. Between 1894 and 1909, Flux published no less than twenty-three articles, of which seventeen were published in the *Economic Journal*, three in the *Journal of the Royal Statistical Society* and a further three in the *Quarterly Journal of Economics*. In addition, he published several articles in the *Economic Review* (Fishburn 2008, p. 6). Subsequently, while in the public service and in retirement, he managed to publish a further dozen articles, of which nine appeared in the *Journal of the Royal Statistical Society*, the other three respectively in the *Economic Journal*, the *Quarterly Journal of Economics* and, his last academic publication, in the *Review of the International Institute of Statistics* which had made him an honorary member in 1938. Most of these journal articles dealt with international trade, frequently in the context of specific countries (England, Germany, Denmark, Canada, France) of which Canadian items dominated during Flux's time as professor of political economy at McGill. When Flux entered the world of official statistics, his journal contributions were completely devoted to applied statistical issues, including the preparation of index numbers, the census of production, international statistical comparisons and their problems, indices of industrial productivity, national income, as well as articles on British food supply before and after the First World War, and the preparation of Scandinavian Statistics. The last topic was possibly a reflection of his marriage in 1897 to Harriet Emily Hansen, a Danish woman.

Flux also wrote obituaries for the *Economic Journal* of David Schloss, Harald Westergaard and Clement-Léon Colson, as well as many book reviews. These include his famous review of Wicksteed's *Essay on the Co-ordination of the Laws of Distribution* in 1894, the subject matter of Section II of this chapter.

Flux's marriage explains his residence in Denmark for the ten years of his life in retirement from 1932. He died of pneumonia on 16 July 1942, aged seventy-five, in Fare Ludefluds, Zealand (Denmark), his retirement abode. His contributions were of such quality, that on his death he received no less than three obituaries in leading scientific journals.

Flux's career in official statistics was very distinguished. He became Director of the Census of Production, responsible for preparation of the 1912 and 1924 Censuses and initiating the preliminary preparation of that for 1930. In 1918, Flux was appointed Head of the Statistical Department in the Board of Trade, subsequently becoming Assistant Secretary to the Board. For his services to the public as a government statistician and public servant, he was made CB in 1920 and received a knighthood in 1934. His work on theoretical and applied statistics was recognised by the Royal Statistical Society when it elected him as its president in 1929, and when it successively presented him with the Guy Medal, first in silver, later in gold. Flux was made an honorary member of the International Institute of Statistics in 1938. The University of Manchester, his first academic employer, awarded him an honorary LLD.

Two further matters need to be mentioned in this section on Flux's life and career. The first is a brief resume of his publications in book form; the second relates to his correspondence with Marshall, a tangible sign of their enduring friendship.

Over his lifetime as economist and statistician, Flux published four books. Most significant for the purpose of this chapter, Flux was the author of what Whitaker (1996, I p. xxxii) has described as 'the first Marshallian textbook'. This was his *Economic Principles*, published in 1904 with a revised edition in 1923. After an introductory chapter, it presented the theories of value and exchange, distribution, monetary theory including the theory of prices, international economics including its financial aspects, finishing with chapters on public economics and the incidence of taxation. In true Marshallian style, it concluded with a mathematical appendix containing diagrams and algebraic demonstrations of several economic propositions, including a simplified version of the use of Euler's theorem for solving the problem of general distribution as initially analysed by Wicksteed (Flux 1904, 1923, pp. 296–297). Little more needs to be said about this volume at this stage, since its contents are discussed more fully in Section III of this chapter. In 1906, Flux published a new edition of *The Coal Question* by W.S. Jevons. Flux did so in response to renewed interest in the question of the exhaustibility of British coal supplies, raised in the Report of a Royal Commission set up in 1901 to investigate the matter (Flux 1906, p. ix). In Flux's preface of more than twenty pages, this Royal Commission's findings are briefly compared with Jevons's argument on the subject four decades previously. While statistician, Flux published two further books. One contained his comments on the Swedish banking system given in evidence to the United States National Monetary Commission in 1910; the other, published in 1922, on the foreign exchanges, printed the text of the Newmarch Lectures he had given that year. Flux's Presidential Address on National Income to the Royal Statistical Society of fifty-three printed pages may informally be viewed as Flux's fifth and final publication at book length.

Five letters between Flux and Marshall have survived, four from Marshall to Flux, and one, chronologically last, from Flux to Marshall. In the first, dated 7 May 1898, Marshall touched on the issue of increasing returns and the solution to the 'Cournot problem' he had gradually developed over many years of study, particularly by investigating factories in Britain and elsewhere at first hand. This solution was based on the concept of 'the representative firm' and a growing awareness that it is very dangerous in economics to carry propositions mechanically to their logical conclusions. Its opening reference to Flux's complaint that Marshall had failed to offer him 'satisfaction' on this subject is interesting, as is its diagnosis that Marshall was gradually beginning to view Flux's work as 'becoming more realistic', and hence more likely to be 'valid for future times as well as the present' (Whitaker 1996, II pp. 227–228). Three years later (4 January 1901) Marshall briefly wrote Flux about the latter's decision to leave England for Montréal. Marshall fully appreciated the rationale for Flux's move, but greatly regretted it from the point of view of English economics, which could ill afford the loss of such an able practitioner. However, he also noted that Chapman would probably succeed Flux in Manchester, as indeed he did

(Whitaker 1996, II p. 328). Marshall's third letter to Flux (19 March 1904) records his gratitude for a letter from Flux (not preserved) and for his *Quarterly Journal of Economics* article (Flux 1904b, pp. 280–286) defending Marshall against an American critic on the subject of the laws of returns. He also thanked Flux in this letter for his offer to read the proofs of his new book, *National Industries and Trade*, which in fact did not appear until fifteen years later under the abbreviated title, *Industry and Trade*. Its preface duly thanked Flux for greatly assisting Marshall in preparing an early draft (Marshall 1919, 1932, p. ix). Marshall's final surviving letter to Flux (26 May 1904) mentioned his involvement in festivities associated with the attendance of distinguished European economists (Leroy Beaulieu, Pierson, Lotz and Dietzel) at the British Economic Association Conference to be held later that year. It also lamented the slow progress of his book on industry and trade. Marshall was then about to finish its section on German industry, to commence that on the United States and he was, therefore, still very far away from writing on the subject of international trade (Whitaker 1996, III p. 84). Curiously, the preserved 1904 correspondence makes no reference to Flux's *Economic Principles*. It had been published in February of that year and a presentation copy would surely have gone to Balliol Croft. In any case, the Catalogue of the Marshall Library (1926, p. 29) indicates the presence in that library of no less than two copies of the first edition of this book.

Flux's letter to Marshall (25 January 1923, in Whitaker 1996, III p. 388) congratulated Marshall on completing his *Money, Credit and Commerce*, which Flux had just been perusing. Flux added Marshall's last published book to the references listed with the relevant chapter outlines (that is, Chapters XV and XVIII) in the second edition of his *Economic Principles*, which he was then just completing for publication later that year. It became a standard text over several decades, though references to it are few. It was also not reprinted in the twenty years interval between publication of the first, and of the second, edition.

Other Marshall correspondence mentioned Flux on several occasions. In a letter to John Neville Keynes (2 November 1895, in Whitaker 1996, II p. 133) Marshall referred to Flux as one of his few outstanding 'private' students who made the teaching of economics at Cambridge worthwhile. A letter to Foxwell (8 January 1901, Whitaker 1996, II p. 292) contrasts Flux's 'eagerness' in economic studies with the 'hopeless poverty [in good economics students] of Cambridge' at this time. Four months later, in a letter to Foxwell (24 May 1901, in Whitaker 1996, III pp. 325–326), Marshall named Flux as his outstanding student capable of filling the vacant Birmingham chair, an appointment which, however, did not eventuate. Finally, a letter from Maynard Keynes (7 June 1922, in Whitaker 1996, III p. 313) named Flux (together with Edgeworth, Pigou, Chapman and himself) as the authors of an address presented to Marshall by the Royal Economic Society on the occasion of his eightieth birthday in July.

Flux's solid Marshallian credentials were fully acknowledged by Marshall, given his view of Flux as one of his better students from the first decade of his professorship at Cambridge. The extent to which these credentials are visible in

Flux's economic writings is now explored by examining two major items of that published work: his review of Wicksteed's *Essay on the Co-ordination of the Laws of Distribution* in 1894, and his text, *Economic Principles*, hailed as the first Marshallian text in economics.

II

Alfred Flux published his first contributions to the *Economic Journal* during 1894. Two appeared in its June issue; the third, a two-part article on 'The Commercial Supremacy of Great Britain' appeared in the September and December issues. The first article presented 'extracts from lectures on Jevons and his work', an indication that interest in Jevonian economics was visible early in Flux's work. It contained only four pages, and was shorter than the two reviews he published in the *Economic Journal* for that year. The first of these was a combined review of Wicksteed's *Essay on the Co-ordination of the Laws of Distribution* and Wicksell's *Über Wert, Kapital und Rente*, the second a rather 'inaccurate and unduly critical review' according to Stigler (1940, p. 262n. 1). Since then, Flux's review of Wicksell's book has rarely been mentioned in the literature, in sharp contrast with that pertaining to Wicksteed's 1894 *Essay*.

Flux's book review of Wicksteed's *Essay* became in fact the most famous short economic piece from Flux's pen. In 1968, it was reprinted as item 31 in No. 19 of the London School of Economics series of Reprints of Scarce Works in Political Economy, *Precursors in Mathematical Economics*, edited by William Baumol and Stephen Goldfeld. Before that, its elegant mathematics had been greatly praised by Stigler (1940, p. 335) as 'a genuine improvement over Wicksteed's argument'. Stigler himself in fact heavily used Flux's 'elegant' exposition in his own presentation of Wicksteed's cumbersome discussion of the generalised marginal productivity theorem and solution of the 'adding-up problem' (Stigler 1940, p. 335). With few exceptions, recognition of the significance of Flux's review seems not to have gone much further. This can be illustrated as follows.

When Wicksteed's *Essay* was reprinted in 1932 as No. 12 in the London School of Economics Collection of Scarce Tracts in Economics and Political Science, Robbins' brief prefatory note made no reference to Flux's review. Two years later, the same applies to Joan Robinson when she surveyed the literature on 'Euler's Theorem and the Problem of Distribution' (Robinson 1934, 1960). Schumpeter (1954, p. 831), in the context of Wicksteed's originality, particularly in distribution theory, mentioned that 'even today Professor Stigler is the only economist I know to rate it at its true value' without mentioning that Stigler's 1940 discussion of Wicksteed's *Essay* largely paraphrased Flux's 1894 review. Flux in fact rates no mention in Schumpeter's encyclopaedic history, and rarely features in texts covering the history of marginalist economic thought. An exception is Blaug's *Economic Theory in Retrospect* in its various editions (for example, Blaug, 1962, pp. 418–419; 1996, pp. 123–125). The reasons for this neglect are not clear. A possible explanation is that only Ph.D. students (in this case, Stigler in the 1930s) treat book reviews as part of the relevant material for their literature searches.

In their introduction to the 1968 reprint of Flux's 1894 review, Baumol and Goldfeld as editors briefly indicate its merits. '[I]t provides a more concise mathematical statement of the Wicksteed results and [it] is the place where Euler's theorem apparently made its first explicit appearance in the literature of economics'. These merits convinced them 'to reprint the short and independently noteworthy review 'of Wicksteed's *Essay* by Flux instead of Wicksteed's very long and mathematically cumbersome piece of work, marred by its many printing errors and mathematical slips'.

The opening paragraph of Flux's review neatly sets out the problem as perceived by the literature, and as specified in Wicksteed's *Essay*. First, the theory of rent can be generalised to explain the earnings of other productive agents. Second, this can be proved by the proposition that 'if P be the total produce from L units of land, with appropriate labour and capital, the rent per unit of the land is $\delta P/\delta L$', that is, the rent of land is measured by the marginal product of that land. Third, it then becomes essential to show that when factors of production are paid according to their marginal product, the whole of their product is completely distributed. Flux fully acknowledged that Wicksteed's *Essay* had demonstrated these propositions, but the form of his solution could be considerably shortened and simplified. This was Flux's major objective in his review.

On the assumption of two factors of production, land (L) and the amalgamated unit of capital and labour (C), and $C:L=x:1=1:z$, then $F(x)$ is product per unit of land, $F'(x)$ is the rate of return to the unit and rent is the difference of $F(x)$ and $x.F'(x)$, when x units of capital and labour are employed on the land. That is, rent equals

$$F(x)-x.F'(x) \tag{1}$$

Because $z=1/x$, if x units of capital and labour are used for each unit of land, z units of land are needed for each unit of capital and labour. When z units of land are employed with a unit of capital and labour, then $z.F(x)$ is the product per unit of capital and labour.

If $\Phi(z)$ is this product, then,

$$\Phi(z)=z.F(x) \tag{2}$$

Differentiating this with respect to z gives,

$$\Phi'(z)=F(x)-x.F'(x) \tag{3}$$

where $\Phi'(z)$ is the expression for the rent of land per unit of area. Hence $C.\Phi(z)$ is the product of C units of capital and labour, or

$$P=C.\Phi(z) \tag{4}$$

Now z=L/C when C is fixed and z is variable (a fixed unit of capital and labour applied to different 'doses' of land), and δL=C.δz, and, therefore,

$$\frac{\delta P}{\delta L}=\frac{c.\delta\Phi}{c.\delta z}=\frac{\delta\Phi}{\delta z}=\Phi'(z) \qquad (5)$$

In short, the rent per unit area is δP/δL, the marginal product of that land.

Similarly, $\delta P/\delta C = F'(x)$ and this, together with equation (3) gives:

$$\delta P/\delta L = F(x) - C/L.\delta P/\delta C \qquad (6)$$

or, rewriting this equation,

$$P = L.\delta P/\delta L + C.\delta P/\delta C = L.F(x) \qquad (7)$$

The first part of equation (7) shows that product (P) is sufficient to pay the shares of that product going to land and to the requisite units of capital and labour when these are paid at their respective marginal products.

Flux then discussed the major assumptions Wicksteed made in his analysis: competition, and constant returns to scale in terms of units of satisfaction. The second assumption allowed Flux to introduce Euler's theorem into the argument. This enabled the quick proof that if

$$P = \psi(A,B,C,\ldots) \qquad (8)$$

is of the form where

$$kP = \psi(kA,kB,kC\ldots) \qquad (9)$$

that is, if the production function is homogeneous of the first degree, then the required result follows immediately as a proposition based on Euler's theorem, namely, that

$$P = A.\frac{\delta P}{\delta A} + B.\frac{\delta P}{\delta B} + A.\delta P \backslash \delta C + \qquad (10)$$

Given the simplicity of this argument as compared with Wicksteed's fifty-six pages of cumbersome proof, Flux not unfairly chided Wicksteed 'for delaying to prove a relation [that of Euler's theorem] so well known as this'. Flux then assessed the significance of Wicksteed's result for other economic propositions, in particular its ramifications for implications drawn from the theory of rent by General Francis Amasa Walker and by Alfred Marshall. These related to the treatment of rent as a surplus, the implications of the relative inelasticity of the supply of land for which rent is the factor payment, and the association between rent and the earnings of 'scarce' managing ability and, in the case of Marshall's notion of quasi-rent, between the income of rent and that of productive agents which are in fixed supply only in the short run. Examples are the earnings of certain types of machines and of human skills the acquisition of which need considerable time.

Flux closed his review with a comment on the many printing errors which Wicksteed's booklet contained, particularly dangerous in his view for an argument of this nature. Flux also briefly noted the interesting diagrams used in Wicksteed's exposition, especially its final figure 5 which indicated the apportionment between land (L.δP/δL) and the other factors (C.δP/δC), conveniently amalgamated in capital and labour units. In short, Flux's brief article is a fair and positive review of Wicksteed's contribution.

The Marshallian aspects of Flux's review include a reference to Marshall's extension of the rent concept to ability of management (derived from Walker) and to his innovative short period concept of quasi-rent, applicable to the earnings of machines and human skills which are then in inelastic supply because of the length of time required to produce or acquire them. Marshall himself seems to have liked Flux's review, and cited it in several editions of his *Principles of Economics*. Its third and fourth editions (Marshall 1895, pp. 603–604n. 1; 1898, p. 609n. 1) mentioned Flux's review of Wicksteed's 'interesting *Co-ordination of the Laws of Distribution*', drawing attention in particular to Flux's comments on the various approaches to, and uses of, rent, as summarised above. This note was repeated in the fifth edition, but disappeared from the sixth edition onwards (Guillebaud 1961, II p. 567). Perhaps by that time Marshall thought that such mathematical theorems had only a very limited place in economic argument, and preferred the more realistic and descriptive approach to the subject of distribution as embodied increasingly in the final three editions of his text. However, his remarks in the *Principles* clearly suggest he approved of Flux's review when it was first published, though no other tangible signs of such approval remain. Flux, however, was sufficiently proud of the review to include some of its argument in the mathematical appendix to his *Economic Principles* (Flux 1904, 1923, esp. pp. 296–297). It was a splendid debut for the young economist and mathematician.

III

The specific Marshallian credentials of what Whitaker (1996) described as 'the first Marshallian text', can now be examined. Flux's *Economic Principles* attempted to deal with the whole of economics in an elementary way. It commenced with a brief description of what economics was about: 'the complex organization of communities, the sources of their wealth, the shares claimable by their members, and the allocation of tasks to individuals which result from the choice of occupation freely exercised under the stimulus of the rewards obtainable' (Flux 1904, 1923, p. ix). From this definition, Flux went on to define wealth in its various dimensions, to introduce the concept of value and to review the major divisions of the subject as 'production, distribution and exchange, consumption'. His introductory chapter also mentioned issues of method to depict the historical and the a priori methods as mutually beneficial, before outlining the meaning of the various factors of production and their increase, the laws of returns in production, and the importance of human action to all economic activity. In short, his twenty-page introduction depicted economics as a branch of the science of wealth in its diverse aspects.

There are broad similarities between the scope of economics as outlined by Flux, and that of Marshall's *Principles*. Flux's emphasis on economic organisation, and the role of specific organisations in the operation of a modern economy are quite Marshallian. In Flux's treatment these begin with the family as both a consuming and a producing unit, and include industry, enterprise and the market. The market coordinates wants and efforts through free competition and exchange, not only to provide effectively for society's present wants, but also for those of the future in so far as they can be estimated. In addition, Flux drew attention to what he called the crucial economic assumption of efficiency, which depicts mankind as capable of judging the best means to an end, or the ability of securing desired ends at least cost. However, slavish imitation of Marshall's work is absent in Flux's text. The material is presented quite differently and, in sharp contrast to Marshall, in a very concise and succinct manner. The argument is invariably presented in Flux's words, not in those of Marshall. To repeat, succinct and concise expression are the hallmarks of Flux's style even if the content of the argument varies little from that in Marshall's text. However, economic history and the history of economic thought find no space in Flux's presentation of the principles of economics, in contrast with Marshall's procedure in his introductory material for the *Principles*. Moreover, footnotes are avoided, as are references to the literature. It is substance rather than style which makes Flux's text Marshallian.

Flux's three chapters after the introduction illustrate this to perfection. These deal respectively with demand and value (Chapter 2), exchange and markets (Chapter 3), and supply and value (Chapter 4). Note carefully that this reflects the order in which Marshall dealt with these subjects: things are demanded and consumed, this activity is reflected in exchange and the market, and because goods are demanded, they are produced and supplied. Flux's concise treatment enabled him to deal with these topics in little over forty pages, while Marshall needed the best part of three books of his *Principles*, covering nearly 300 pages. However, in relative terms, Flux's treatment resembles that of Marshall more closely. He required double the space to treat production and supply as compared with dealing with demand and consumption. Flux also resembled Marshall in viewing distribution as part of the theory of value and exchange, in treating supply in terms of its elasticity dependent on time, and of the laws of returns in which increasing returns are discussed in detail, partly by means of a representative producer (rather than firm). Flux's chapter on supply also found room to distinguish prime and total costs. Marshall's substance on these topics is succinctly, and successfully, condensed by Flux into nearly an eighth of the space.

Some special problems in valuation provide the subject matter for Flux's Chapter 5. Its contents resemble that of Chapters 6 and 13 in Book V of

Marshall's *Principles* in dealing respectively with joint demand and supply, and with monopoly. Flux's examples are more apt than those of Marshall in his account of joint supply and demand, and they completely avoid Marshall's use of the theory as a preliminary and formal solution to the problem of distribution, taking the blades and handles of a knife as a rather inappropriate example in this context. Although Flux briefly mentioned Marshall's knife example as a case of joint supply, just as 'a carriage needs horses or a motor' (p. 67), he treated it as a rather simplified case of a complex and important economic problem in the theory of value. Flux's account of monopoly theory is also superior to that of Marshall from both the brevity and completeness of its treatment. However, in combining these distinct problems in value theory as complex cases in that theory, Flux was very Marshallian.

The next five chapters analyse the problem of distribution by looking at factor payments in the following sequence: interest and the share of capital (Chapter 6), rent and the share of land (Chapter 7), wages and the share of labour (Chapter 8) with additional chapters devoted to special problems with wages (Chapter 9), and to the theory of profits as the explanation of the employer's share in the distribution of the national product (Chapter 10). A brief look at the more detailed contents of each of these chapters is warranted.

The chapter on interest discourses at some length on difficulties in the concept of capital including that of distinguishing new capital (defined as a stream of uncommitted resources) and old capital, frozen into a particular form as a machine (for example, Flux 1904, 1923, pp. 81–82). Saving is then described as a flow of uncommitted resources and as a type of postponed consumption for which the payment of interest is the reward (Flux 1904, 1923, p. 83). Capital investment is depicted in Austrian fashion as adopting more roundabout processes of production, deemed to be more productive (Flux 1904, 1923, p. 89). Finally, interest is presented as a price equating the supply of saving made by the public and the demand for new capital, with the concluding comment that savings can never be excessive, since the opportunities for profitable investment of capital borrowed at low rates of interest, is very great (Flux 1904, 1923, pp. 95–96).

Flux's chapter on rent treats it in a very conventional manner on Marshallian if not Ricardian lines. Rent is described as a payment for the differential qualities of land (location, fertility) and as a necessary payment for the indestructible powers of the soil. Surprisingly, little is made by Flux in this chapter of the application of the notion of rent to explain the earnings of other factors, either as a special rent of ability, or as a quasi-rent for instruments of production fixed in supply in the short period, as he had done in the 1894 Wicksteed review. However, Flux (1904, 1923, p. 111) does quote Marshall on quasi-rent as a form of rent applicable in the short run, especially to items of durable capital equipment.

Wages are initially explained by Flux in terms of the diminishing net product of labour, interpreted as the demand side of this pricing problem. The supply side is treated in terms of both the quantity of labour available for work in a particular industry, and in the economy as a whole; the mobility of that labour; while in true Marshallian manner Flux also made comments on the relation of living standards to labour supply, and on the importance in this context of the labourer's standard of life (or the manner in which income was spent by the labourer). Competitive labour markets are presumed throughout, except for the final two paragraphs of the chapter which briefly introduce considerations of monopoly potentially existing in either the relevant factor or commodity market.

Flux next considered what he, following Marshall, called special problems in wages. These include those raised by specific forms and methods of renumeration (Flux 1904, 1923, pp. 136–138); the doctrine of the wages fund as a simple argument linking average wage rates to the (fixed) amount of capital available for the hiring of the given stock of available labour in any particular period (Flux 1904, 1923, pp. 139–140); the operation and effects of trade unions as a matter not treated in any detail (Flux 1904, 1923, pp. 142–143); and the impact of bonuses and other special rewards to 'stimulate special diligence' on the part of the worker (Flux 1904, 1923, p. 145). The chapter ends with a brief discussion of the effects of the growth of the cooperative movement, of profit sharing and of sliding scale wages designed to reflect the economic conditions prevailing with an industry and thereby its capacity to pay (Flux 1904, 1923, pp. 147–149), all again very Marshallian topics.

Profits are discussed by Flux in his final chapter on distribution, largely to indicate whether 'definite principles' can be advanced to determine their amount (Flux 1904, 1923, p. 151). Individual enterprise is distinguished from joint-stock companies; the role of profits as a payment for management is evaluated, as is profit as a source of entrepreneurial income where risk premiums and rent of special ability are introduced as part of the explanation. Flux suggests that net profits eliminate managerial earnings and remain the pure recompense for risk taking and other entrepreneurial skills. By way of conclusion, dividends paid to share holders in joint-stock companies are treated as their share in profits though in this context Flux admits that profits (and losses) can also be made in share price speculation, as is the case in fact with any other speculative activity such as government debt or commodity markets.

The topics shared by Flux's *Principles* and its more famous namesake by Marshall, stop at this stage of the book, a little over the half-way mark. The second part of Flux's text deals with money and monetary problems including the theory of prices and the effects of pronounced instability in the price level. They also cover international trade and the foreign exchanges, free trade and protection, to conclude with two chapters on government intervention. These two final chapters concentrate on the analysis of taxation and its incidence. As already indicated, a mathematical appendix (algebraic and geometrical) completes the work.

It may also be mentioned here that Flux's diagrams are very Marshallian. This applies to both the supply and demand curves in the book and to the offer curves Marshall had developed for explaining aspects of the theory of international trade. Flux's drawings of these curves also tend to follow Marshall's practice of treating price as the dependent and quantity as the independent variable to result in both neater and clearer diagrams. Moreover, Flux's practice of banishing these diagrams to an appendix in principle resembles Marshall's practice of invariably placing them in the footnotes. However, even in terms of relative page numbers for their respective *Principles*, there are far fewer diagrams in Flux's presentation.

More specific Marshallian aspects can be found in Flux's text. Although Flux's book deliberately, and explicitly, avoids cluttering the text with names and references, Marshall's name is a specific exception to this rule. He is quoted twice by name in the text of the *Principles.* One of these occasions (Flux 1904, 1923, p. 111) was mentioned in the context of quasi-rent; the other (Flux 1904, 1923, p. 107) quoted Marshall's 'Ricardian' remark that rent is a payment 'for the use of the original and indestructible powers of the soil'. Apart from these two direct references to Marshall, General Francis Amasa Walker is mentioned on the subject of wages (Flux 1904, 1923, p. 143) while Wicksteed is named in the Appendix (Flux 1904, 1923, p. 296) for his contribution to the marginal productivity theory of distribution. References to the literature, more generally, are strictly confined to the 'authorities' noted (for further reading) at the start of each chapter summary in the table of contents. These cite Marshall's *Principles* as essential for nine of the first ten chapters (the exception is Chapter 8, on wages and the share of labour), and mention chapters in Book III of Marshall's *Money, Credit and Commerce* in connection with Chapters 15 (on the relative values of international currencies) and Chapter 18 (on free trade versus protection). The remaining authorities referred to are either firm favourites of Marshall which he used to set in his classes, or contributions from 'his' Cambridge school, that is, by J.N. Keynes, Nicholson, Pigou, Hawtrey and Walter Layton, or by earlier Cambridge writers on political economy, that is, Fawcett and Sidgwick.

Flux occasionally made use of specific Marshallian metaphors and expressions. These markedly heighten the Marshallian flavour of Flux's book. Flux (1904, 1923, p. 48) used the 'balls in the bowl' metaphor in his discussion of the notion of equilibrium. As previously indicated, he briefly mentioned the knife (blade and handle) example in his treatment of joint supply, and he extensively used Marshallian concepts such as the representative firm and quasi-rent. However, there are also some Canadian examples (Flux 1904, 1923, pp. 113–114, and perhaps p. 66). These remind of the fact that Flux completed and published his book while professor of economics at McGill University.

Flux's *Principles* are therefore quite appropriately called a Marshallian text on a number of grounds. Much of the initial argument on value, exchange, production and distribution is very Marshallian. The Marshallian nature of the material on money, trade and government is less easy to specify in detail, but the authorities cited for this material, as already indicated, suggest a strong resemblance between Flux's views on these matters and those of Marshall, where they can be easily specified.

Flux's tribute to Marshall in the prefatory note to his Principles (Flux 1904, 1923, p. v) says everything that needs to be said on this scope in a very succinct way:

> No Cambridge student of economics in recent years can fail to have gained inspiration from contact with Professor Marshall, and the writer is conscious of a very special obligation to the teacher to whom he owes his chief guidance in economic study.

This note, dated November 1903 at Montréal, remained in the second edition of the text. The preface to the second edition indicated that though Flux had used this opportunity to revise drastically the chapters on money, international trade and the foreign exchanges, much of the 'micro-economics' of value, production and distribution was left as it was. Flux explained this decision by mentioning the advice of friends. This suggested that for these parts of the subjects 'experiences of the last nine years' had confirmed their validity and thereby 'justified a trust in the soundness of the analysis', whose 'principal features' were presented in his book. The intervention of twenty years to 1923 had done nothing to bring the soundness of Marshall's principles of economics into disrepute. This is high praise indeed from a loyal student and adherent to the essentials of Marshall's economics.

IV

What specific conclusions about Flux's Marshallian credentials can be drawn from the two important samples of his work discussed in the previous two sections? The fact that Marshall featured in both is instructive in this context, particularly given the relative brevity of the 1894 Wicksteed review and the very specific nature of its subject matter. The last nevertheless briefly relates the significance of Wicksteed's analysis for the Marshallian notions of rent as a surplus and that of quasi-rent as an explanation of the earnings of productive agents fixed in supply in the short run, is striking in this context. As indicated in Part II, Marshall liked Flux's review, cited it in his *Principles* for the three immediately following (that is, third, fourth and fifth) editions, but dropped it in 1910 from the sixth edition onwards. Whether this was for the reason suggested in Section II cannot be said with certainty. However, if so, this did not deter Flux from using part of his review's arguments in the mathematical appendix of both editions of his *Principles*.

Part III briefly demonstrated the Marshallian credentials of Flux's *Principles*, pointing first to the similarities in the manner in which both he and Marshall outlined the scope of their subject. Flux's imitation on this point is, however, never slavish. For example, he fails to follow Marshall precisely on the definition of the subject. Moreover, similarities in the book do not apply to matters of style. On this score, Flux is clearly the master with respect to concise statement and brevity of expression. Succinct expression occasionally produced superiority of presentation on Flux's part, as in the case of joint supply and monopoly analysis. However, in many other respects, including the construction of diagrams, Flux is decidedly Marshallian. Furthermore, some famous Marshall metaphors intrude into Flux's text; that of the 'balls in the bowl' is a good example. Some of these were updated. The case of blades and handles for knives as an instance of joint supply in Marshall's discussion, in Flux's treatment of the subject becomes that of a carriage needing either 'horses or a motor'. Moreover, the text of the second edition of Flux's book testifies to his belief in the long-levity of the thought of the 'master' at least with respect to the subject of value (supply and demand), exchange, production and distribution. Flux recognised, however, that such durability of Marshall's ideas did not apply to other subjects, particularly money, international trade, and the foreign exchanges. It needs to be noted that Flux said nothing in his *Principles* on the theory of income determination and business cycles.

Flux's experience as economic writer exhibits in one specific way the inordinate influence Marshall exerted over his 'pupils', by frequently 'winning' them for economics despite their original intentions and motivations for studying at Cambridge. Indeed, it can be said that Flux is a particularly good example of the positive influence exerted by Marshall as teacher, since that teaching practice never induced them to become slavish imitators of the 'master'. The two case studies selected from Flux's economic work for the purpose of this chapter, clearly illustrate this. Flux, in short, was an able mathematician 'well caught' for economics, as indicated by both his brilliant review of Wicksteed's *Essay on the Co-ordination of the Laws of Distribution* and, at a very different level, in the neat expository values exhibited by Flux's own *Economic Principles* as a more mature contribution in book form. In this sense, as a future very theoretically competent economic academic, he was a particularly splendid 'catch' for Marshall, even if Flux's academic career as an economics teacher in Britain did not last for a very long time.

4 Charles Percy Sanger (1871–1930)

A brilliant student of Marshall from the 1890s, briefly captured for economics

Charles Sanger took Part II of the Moral Sciences Tripos after completing the Mathematical Tripos as second wrangler. As student of the moral sciences he specialised in advanced political economy, much to Marshall's delight. Marshall wrote to J.N. Keynes in November 1895 that 'Sanger is the only student (man or woman) who has taken up Economics for Part II [of the Moral Sciences Tripos] and was really worth teaching. But one Sanger … is a good recompense for five years work and I am content' (cited in Groenewegen 1995a, p. 537). Sanger finished with a first class result in his examinations, and for a decade or so taught economics and statistics at London University College. While teaching at the University of London, Sanger published a monograph, *The Place of Compensation in Temperance Reform*, a London Study in Economics and Political Science which appeared in 1896, with a second edition in 1901.

Earlier, Sanger had written an interesting paper for the Cambridge Political Economy Club with W.E. Johnson on certain questions connected with demand (Johnson and Sanger 1894, 1968). His first journal article appeared in the *Economic Journal* in 1895 on the subject of recent work on mathematical economics, with special reference to the Italian contributions by Pareto, Barone and Pantaleoni. Over the following decade he published a further six articles in the *Economic Journal*, together with a very substantial number of book reviews. Keynes (1930, 1972) estimated their number at over forty altogether for the *Economic Journal*, often devoted to books published in Italian, French or German, and covering a wide variety of subject matter (see Section III below).

Over these years, Sanger showed himself to be a loyal henchman of Marshall. For example, he served on four occasions (1902, 1903, 1904, 1905) as examiner for the Moral Sciences Tripos; over the years he donated a substantial number of books to the Marshall Library; he was a publicly declared supporter of Marshall in his quest for a separate Economics and Politics Tripos, and was one of ten signatures to the Free Trade Manifesto prepared in 1903 (Groenewegen 1995a, pp. 334, 382, 546, 750).

However, by the second half of the first decade of the twentieth century, Sanger's interest in economics started to wane. His last article in the *Economic Journal* appeared in 1903, though his reviews therein of economics books continued until 1915 with a final two reviews published in 1926, after an interval of eleven years. One of these reviewed *Memorials of Alfred Marshall*, edited by Pigou, which had appeared the year before. As shown in the next section, it contains a brief, but fascinating portrait of Marshall as Sanger remembered him over the years, which supplements the obituary of Marshall he had written two years previously.

Sanger concentrated on law during the final decades of his life, working very successfully as a barrister-at-law. When he completed his legal studies is not entirely clear. He may have taken such studies while teaching at London University College from the late 1890s. Sanger became a noted authority on wills, a subject on which he published several books. *A Concise Treatise on the Construction of Wills* appeared in 1912, *The Rules of Law and Administration Relating to Wills and Intestacy* in 1914 (Whitaker 1987, IV pp. 241–242) with a second edition in 1925. He also published a second edition of *The Law of Charitable Bequests*, which appeared in 1921. In 1915, Sanger published a book, jointly written with H.T.J. Norton (a Fellow of Trinity College, Cambridge), on *England's Guarantee to Belgium and Luxembourg*, in which Sanger described himself as barrister-at-law when taking sole responsibility for the legal aspects of the argument in this topical book.

Sanger also had extensive interests in philosophy. He became a good friend of J.E. McTaggart while studying for the Moral Sciences, and was a close associate for a while of philosophers G.E. Moore and Bertrand Russell (Harrod 1951, pp. 61, 398). This philosophical interest, together with his studies for the Mathematical Tripos in the 1890s and his superb language skills, presumably induced Sanger's translation (completed in 1924) from the Russian, according to Baumol and Goldfield (1968, p. 41), of A.V. Vasil'ev's *Space, Time and Motion*, for which Bertrand Russell wrote an introduction.

Sanger had been a member of the 'Apostles' as an undergraduate, whence arose his later, enduring friendship with Maynard Keynes, assisted by their mutual interests in mathematics, economics, statistics and philosophy. As early as 1909, Sanger presented Keynes with some of his notes for a proposed work on mathematical economics (O'Donnell 1989, p. 206). Sanger also developed a close association with Bloomsbury, in particular with both Leonard and Virginia Woolf. The Hogarth Press which the Woolfs had set up later published several items by Sanger. In 1926, it published a paper that Sanger had read to 'the Heretic Society' at Cambridge on *The Structure of Wuthering Heights*. This talk concentrated on investigating the legal aspects of Heathcliffe's scheming to regain his property, and on commenting on the legal skills of Emily Bronte, Jane Austin and Anthony Trollope, in some of whose books interesting references were made to the 1837 Wills Act and to the Law of Entails. Sanger concluded from his discussion, that the legal complexities contained therein made *Wuthering Heights* a very unusual book. In 1933, the Hogarth Press published a second book with which Sanger was associated. This was Sanger's verse translation of Imre Madàch's *The Tragedy of Man*, though, as can be seen from its publication date, the book appeared after Sanger's death. Publications of this calibre reveal both Sanger's broad cultural concerns, and his enormous skill as a linguist, which will again be noted when discussing this activity as a major book reviewer for the *Economic Journal* in Section III.

This chapter concentrates on Sanger's economic writings, with special reference to its Marshallian credentials. Section I gives the usual biographical overview, with emphasis on his years as student and teacher of economics and statistics. Section II reviews his articles in the *Economic Journal.* Section III surveys the contents and coverage of his book reviews for the *Economic Journal*, while Section IV presents some conclusions on the Marshallian heritage visible in his economics work.

I

Charles Sanger was born in Brighton (England) on 7 December 1871. He was educated at Winchester School, and subsequently at Trinity College, Cambridge. He first took the Mathematical Tripos, becoming second wrangler (second in the first class honours list) in 1893. He was a Fellow of Trinity College from 1895 to 1901. Sanger turned to the study of economics when taking Part II of the Moral Sciences Tripos. Study of economics was successfully completed in 1895 with a first class result. Sanger then returned to London to teach economics and statistics for some years at both University College and the London School of Economics. During these years he was particularly active in the Royal Statistical Society. He was called to the bar in 1896. Work as a barrister was something at which he also excelled; and he was highly regarded within the legal profession. Sanger died suddenly on 9 February 1930, aged fifty-eight, after a short illness (Whitaker 1987b, IV pp. 241–242).

Little other biographical detail is available for Sanger, with two exceptions. Some information has survived about Sanger's experience with Marshall as an economics teacher, largely based on Sanger's own reminiscences thereon, written in 1924 and 1926. Second, considerable detail remains about Sanger's association with the Bloomsbury group. In particular, this is the case with his long friendships with Maynard Keynes and Lytton Strachey, and to a lesser extent that with Leonard and Virginia Woolf. She described Sanger in 1916 in the following terms: 'He is very red-eyed and wizened and overworked but he pumps up the most amazing quips and cracks, and his eyes glow and he looks like one of the dwarfs in the Ring' (cited in Skidelsky 1983, I p. 429).

Only snippets from his life outside these activities remain. These include his marriage by 1904 with the person who became Dora Sanger, and the enduring hospitality of this couple to their Bloomsbury friends. Second, there was Sanger's intellectual brilliance, so well described by Holroyd in his biography of Lytton Strachey, and enlarging on Virginia Woolf's description of him, just quoted: 'Sanger, a gnome like figure, universally loved, with bright sceptical eyes, rather older than Lytton, who had shown exceptional promise at Trinity and was now [circa 1918] a brilliant barrister....' (Holroyd 1971, 1979, p. 169).

> [Sanger] had belonged to that class of men, aspiring yet unambitious, whom Lytton most unenviously admired.... [Sanger] combined great talent with natural modesty, and in his qualities of sincerity, of humour and humility,

> he fulfilled the highest ideas of the Apostles. Sanger was one of the most penetrating intellects and one of the most truly noble characters… [Strachey] had ever encountered.… He was one of those men whose extraordinarily great attributes were never, because of their very greatness, properly appreciated by the world at large. [Strachey attributed Sanger's death to a nervous breakdown from] a long process of over-work, underfeeding, and general discomfort – a wretched business. He had an astonishing intellect; but accompanied by such modesty that the world in general hadn't any idea of his very great distinction. And he was so absolutely unworldly, that the world's inattention was nothing to him.…
>
> (Strachey, cited in Holroyd 1971, 1979, p. 1028)

The many branches of learning to which Sanger contributed during his lifetime, already mentioned in the introduction to this chapter, provide unambiguous evidence of his enormous intellect. Formal studies at Cambridge had covered both the mathematical sciences as then taught at Cambridge, which included the major branches of mechanics and physics; as well as the moral sciences including philosophy, political economy and statistics. Legal studies were part of this formal education to enable his admission to the bar. He subsequently wrote on political economy for publication in the *Economic Journal* (as discussed more fully in Sections II and III), on a variety of legal topics (including international treaties in the book on the British neutrality guarantees to Belgium and Luxembourg, wills and testatory matters, and even on the legal knowledge of some nineteenth century novelists as displayed in their books, with special reference to *Wuthering Heights*). He also translated works on philosophy, on modern physics, and of literature. His qualities as a linguist, visible in these translations, and in his reviews of economics books for the *Economic Journal* (as discussed in Section III), are a further token of his immense intellect. Finally, Sanger's skills as a statistician need to be explicitly recognised. These skills included both statistical theory and practice. In 1921, Sanger reviewed Keynes's work on probability theory for *The New Statesman* (Skidelsky 1992, p. 656), and Keynes thought very highly of Sanger's qualifications in this field. For instance, Keynes wrote to Sir T. Holderness in February 1908 that Sanger

> has a very wide knowledge of theoretical statistics and has also directed practical statistical operations on a large scale. This, and the fact that he has long lectured at University College has made him well acquainted with the younger statisticians, and I think he is an exceptionally good judge of ability.…
>
> (Keynes 1971, Vol. XV, p. 12)

Practical statistical work was carried out by Sanger for the Board of Trade at one stage, in which he was ably assisted by his former student at University College, Walter Layton (Collard 1990, p. 175).

Sanger attended Marshall's classes on advanced political economy from 1893, completing Part II of the Moral Sciences Tripos in 1895 as a special student in political economy. No real details are preserved of the contents of these lectures though, as already indicated in the introduction, Marshall had informed John Neville Keynes in 1895 that Sanger had been the only student who took economics for Part II of the Moral Sciences Tripos who had been really worth teaching. In his obituary of Marshall for the *Nation and Athenaeum* (19 January 1924), Sanger reciprocated that admiration:

> Those who never had the good fortune to be his pupils cannot realize the remarkable qualities of Alfred Marshall. The usual adjectives, such as 'stimulating' or 'brilliant', may be apt, but they fail to express the personal effect which he produced on all who learnt from him. His method was to be at home to pupils several afternoons a week, so that they could ask his advice if they wanted to. The shy undergraduate was shown up into the study – a room with balcony, looking south – and tea was placed on a low stool between him and the professor. The young man asked a question about some point he had not understood in a lecture or a book. The difficulty was often a trivial or a foolish one, but the professor treated it with the utmost seriousness, discussed it with the greatest fairness, and led the youth on till he had solved it for himself. This gave the young man confidence; he began to wish to know more; the professor, with remarkable agility, began taking down books from his shelves which the young man would find it advisable to read; and finally, the pupil went off with the firm intention of reading in the next few days more books than he could possibly read in a month or so. Everything was friendly and informal. There was no pretence that economic science was a settled affair – like grammar or algebra – which had to be learnt, not criticised; it was treated as a subject in the course of development....
>
> (Sanger 1924, 1998, I pp. 31–32)

Sanger singled out Marshall's 'scrupulous fairness' as the quality which particularly impressed his pupils. He also praised the brilliance of Marshall's *Principles*, even if 'his style was rather heavy'. It was also a deceptive book. 'Very often in a short passage or footnote, he managed to say all that was essential about a point to which other writers would devote one or more chapters' (Sanger 1924, 1998, I p. 32). Sanger also noted that Marshall's 'sympathies were with the working classes, but [he] never let sentiment interfere with science'. However, sentiment probably explained his strong opposition to women's degrees at Cambridge, a position on this then controversial subject Sanger did not share. Sanger concluded his obituary:

> Like all great men he had some charming weaknesses, such as a delightful smile when he was going to make a joke. He was interested in all the details of life. He was rather fussy. He would explain to ladies how they ought to dust their rooms and what was the best thing for taking out a stain. But he

> was always sympathetic, encouraging, and eager; his learning never oppressed him; he devoted his life to his work, and a comparison of the state of economics as it was forty years ago with what it is now proves the immense results of that unselfish devotion.
>
> (Sanger 1924, 1998, I. p. 33)

In his review of *Memorials of Alfred Marshall* (Sanger 1926b, pp. 83–84), Sanger stressed some other quirks of his former economics teacher after warning that it was not very easy to give an accurate picture of the man. His enormous originality in economics was now difficult to discern from the style of his writing which avoided controversy, morbidly feared errors, and toned the argument down to fit the 'attitude of his probable readers'. The memorial volume under review, Sanger argued, made a better understanding of Marshall possible. This came from at least three of its qualities. Keynes's memoir of Marshall, previously published in the *Economic Journal*, was one. The selection included of some of Marshall's articles from the 1872 review of Jevons's *Theory of Political Economy* to the 1917 'The Equitable Distribution of Taxation'. Sanger noted the absence of the evidence Marshall had given to Royal Commissions, 'by no means the least important part of Marshall's work' but publication of many of these was by then in progress, as edited by Keynes, in a volume issued for the Royal Economic Society later in 1926. The third part, and the most interesting, were the letters – 'would that there had been more, many more' (Sanger 1926b, p. 83). In his review, Sanger quoted two extracts from this selected correspondence – one dealing with Marshall's strong dislike of the classics and classical studies; the other giving Marshall's favourite dictum:

> Every statement in regard to economic affairs which is short is a misleading statement, a fallacy, or a truism. I think this *dictum* of mine is an exception to the general rule; but I am not bold enough to say that it *certainly* is.

Sanger's concluding paragraph in the review attempted to sum up Alfred Marshall the man, and can be quoted in full:

> The chief characteristics of Alfred Marshall were that his interests were moral rather than intellectual, concrete rather than abstract. Yet he never let his intellectual processes be confused by any moral considerations, nor did his interest in facts ever diminish his remarkable capacity for abstract theory. His attitude to his pupils was one of affection. He took them seriously; he drew them out; he never preached to them; he trusted to their being decent human beings who would try to develop their intellectual capacities for the common good. Above all, he was never dull.
>
> (Sanger 1926b, p. 84)

Sanger's contacts with Bloomsbury came through the friendships he made as a member of the 'Apostles' (the Cambridge *conversazione* society) from the middle of the 1890s. Sanger had been an 'angel' (new member) at the time of Bertrand Russell, G.E. Moore, and R.C. and G.M. Trevelyan, all members of Trinity College. On 24 February 1894, Sanger was recorded as reading a paper to the Society on 'Which Wagner', posing the choice between Richard and Adolf Wagner, or between art and improvement. Sanger, McTaggart and Moore were supporters of the cause of art, despite Sanger's involvement with economics studies at the time. A few years later, the persons who invited Keynes to join the 'Apostles' in December 1903, Leonard Woolf and Lytton Strachey, were both good friends of Sanger. Within a year, Keynes, Woolf and the older Sanger were close enough friends to join each other on a long walking tour in Wales. More important for their intellectual development, they enjoyed philosophical gatherings with George Moore, by then a long time friend of Sanger, to discuss aspects of his *Principia Ethica* published in 1903. Sanger can here be described as forming the bridge between Moore and his three friends among the younger 'Apostles', that is, Keynes, Woolf and Strachey. Sanger's subsequent assistance to Keynes on statistical matters has already been mentioned and this, together with their occasional contact at meetings of the 'Society' and later of the Cranium Club, cemented their lifelong friendship.

It was undoubtedly through Keynes that Sanger continued to write book reviews for the *Economic Journal*, when his interest in writing longer economics articles had ceased by 1903. Both the pressures of his legal work as a highly successful barrister and the growing attractions of other forms of literary work would have assisted in this declining interest in matters economic. However, Sanger's language skills together with Keynes's increasing editorial involvement in the *Economic Journal*, probably made it imperative that Sanger did continue writing reviews for the *Journal*, given the enormous quantity of foreign language matter submitted to the *Journal* for review. These two types of economic contributions by Sanger can now be examined in more detail, starting with his articles.

II

Between 1895 and 1903, Sanger published seven articles in the *Economic Journal*, including a review article, and two short pieces which are more accurately viewed as notes. Given his eclectic and non-specialist nature, the articles covered a wide range of topics. The first, published in the March 1895 issue of the *Economic Journal*, surveyed 'recent contributions to mathematical economics'; the last, published in the 1903 *Economic Journal*, evaluated 'the legal view of profits'. In between, Sanger published an article on 'the fair number of apprentices in a trade' (*Economic Journal* 1895); two notes on the Hungarian zone system for determining passenger railway fares in the 1896 *Economic Journal*; an article on the fairness of the British tax system in the 1899 *Economic Journal*; and a review article of the Report of the Local Taxation Commission in the *Economic Journal* for 1901. Prior to that, in Easter term 1894, Sanger and W.E. Johnson published a short paper on mathematical economics for the Cambridge Economic Club 'On Certain Questions Connected with Demand'

(Johnson and Sanger 1894, 1968, pp. 42–48). Before discussing the contents of the papers published in the *Economic Journal*, the contents of the Johnson–Sanger paper can be briefly reviewed. Sanger, as second-named author, was not necessarily the 'junior author' of the paper, given the fact that at this time he was studying advanced political economy as a special student of Alfred Marshall in Part II of the Moral Sciences Tripos. Johnson, also a former Marshall student, was by then a good ten years older than Sanger.

The Johnson–Sanger paper (1894) briefly discussed four aspects of demand theory as presented by Marshall in the second edition of his *Principles*. In turn, these dealt with maximising total expenditure and the marginal utility of money; a possible relation between total utility and the various commodities upon which a person's income may be expended; a more precise formulation of consumers' surplus; and fourth, variations in the elasticity of demand in association with price variations (Johnson and Sanger 1894, 1968, p. 42). The highly mathematical article (as befitting its authorship by two 'wranglers') briefly discussed these issues to obtain various definitions of the marginal utility of money (Johnson and Sanger 1894, 1968, p. 43); deriving total utility as the sum of the utilities obtainable from consuming different groups of commodities (Johnson and Sanger 1894, 1968, p. 44); the expression for consumers' rent (surplus) as the area of the ordinary demand curve measured in money expressing the difference in total utility between having a specific quantity of the commodity in question and nothing of that commodity (Johnson and Sanger 1894, 1968, p. 45); and, fourth, the proposition that for very low prices, elasticity of demand is very small, while for very high prices, it is initially infinite. From this they concluded that 'it is on the whole more natural to suppose that the elasticity begins by being infinite, and *decreases throughout the entire course of falling price*', a reversal of Marshall's procedure on this point in the *Principles* (Johnson and Sanger 1894, 1968, p. 47, italics in the original). The reprinted version of the paper by Baumol and Goldfeld (1968, p. 47) adds the text of a handwritten note by Sanger correcting some of the mathematics and including a diagram to illustrate the argument that luxury consumption is often price inelastic. It may be noted that Marshall never cited this note in subsequent editions of his *Principles*.

Sanger's first article in the *Economic Journal*, his evaluation of recent contributions to mathematical economics, was, however, recognised by Marshall. Sanger's piece commented especially on recent Italian contributions to mathematical economics by Pareto, Barone and Pantaleoni, with specific reference to their views on marginal utility, and the utility function of money, topics also pursued in the joint paper with Johnson just summarised. From this survey, Sanger (1895a, p. 128) concluded that a good book on pure theory (read mathematical economic theory) was urgently required for the student of economics; that Pantaleoni's text, *Pure Economics*, was 'too elementary'; while the Mathematical Appendix in Marshall's *Principles* was 'too short'. In 1896, Marshall wrote Edgeworth, then the editor of the *Economic Journal* (January 1896, in Whitaker 1996, II p. 265) that Sanger's article appeared 'first rate' to him, even if he had not yet read it. It is, therefore, not surprising that Sanger's article was subsequently cited in the *Principles* from the fourth edition onwards (Guillebaud 1961, I p. 132n. 1; II p. 265) with particular reference to Barone's criticism of Nicholson mentioned by Sanger in the paper (Sanger 1895a, pp. 124–127).

Sanger's second article for the *Economic Journal* dealt with an applied subject, 'the fair number of apprentices in a trade'. It was intended as a modification of supply and demand theory for skilled labour, by investigating more fully the time required to train skilled labour as an ultimate cost for the capitalist or undertaker (Sanger 1895b, pp. 616–617), even though the gain from that training in the form of higher wages accrued to the labourer. Sanger cited Marshall's *Principles*, Book VI Chapters IV and V, which dealt with these issues of training and future labour supply, as well as the factors which influenced the renumeration of skilled labour and the potential for disputes arising therefrom. In his article, Sanger wished to investigate these issues in terms of an actual case, enabling him to examine the problem in a statistical manner. The paper is therefore highly statistical, providing data on the ratio of journeymen to apprentices in the particular case of the action by the Boilermakers and Iron and Steel Ship Builders Union to licence the number of apprentices (Sanger 1895b, p. 618), as well as discussing legal aspects of the matter. Sanger's conclusion from his study is essentially methodological. 'If economics is to be of practical use, it should afford us methods for deriving definite conclusions from definite premises' rather than presenting vague and imprecise arguments on complex issues (Sanger 1895b, p. 636).

During 1896, Sanger turned his attention to a special case in railway economics, a topic to which he claimed British economics had paid far too little attention. A two-page note in the June issue of the *Economic Journal* (Sanger 1896a, pp. 294–295) briefly outlined the details of the Hungarian scheme for determining passenger fares, as presented in a pamphlet by Béla Amrozovics; a topic to which he returned six months later with a further note on the Hungarian zone tariff (Sanger 1896b). This described the details of a journey in Hungary with a fourteen zone ticket in which the low cost of the fare for the long journey was offset by the considerable 'discomfort' of twenty-four hour rail travel in that country. Sanger concluded that zone tariffs as traffic diversions as practised in the Hungarian railway system were a topic worthy of serious study by the economist (Sanger 1896b, p. 632). Sanger's interest in the subject matter of these contributions was also sparked by the possible interest of the tourist wishing to travel in or through Hungary, whether undertaken for business or pleasure.

Sanger's fifth contribution to the *Economic Journal* in article or note form appeared during 1899. It dealt with the question of whether the British taxation system was fair, and whether tax reductions for workers as practised in recent years, continued to be warranted. Sanger departed on this inquiry on the basis of wage data provided by Giffen and Bowley, and from the fairness criteria of taxation embodied in the three 'doctrines' of sacrifice elaborated by Edgeworth (1897) in the *Economic Journal.* These were the tax criteria of equal absolute, equal proportional and equal marginal sacrifice where the application of the last criterion also secured least aggregate sacrifice for taxpayers. Once again a statistical exercise by Sanger, the article attempted to test the available data against the three sacrifice doctrines, from which he concluded that the process of decreasing income taxation of workers should now cease since it had gone far enough, a reference to the increased progression of the income tax rate structure enacted in 1898 (Sanger 1899a, p. 11).

Sanger's next *Economic Journal* article also dealt with taxation issues, this time local taxation. It reviewed the *Report of the Local Taxation Commission* (Cmnd 9528, 1899), and appeared in the *Economic Journal* for 1901. It provided a careful overview and summary of the contents of the report and its findings, and in particular Sanger cited, with much approval, Marshall's views on the subject of site value taxation which he had given in evidence to the Commission (Sanger 1901a, pp. 324–325). Sanger's argument in the review article seems to have been designed to bring the very technical economic issue of site value taxation to the level of very practical politics (Sanger 1901a, p. 333).

Sanger's seventh and final article contributed to the *Economic Journal*, on 'the legal view of profits', appeared in 1903. Its title perhaps suggests that by then legal issues were more interesting and important for Sanger than matters economic, even though there is some economic content in the article as well, drawn from the literature on circulating and fixed capital in authorities such as J.S. Mill and Marshall (Sanger 1903, p. 177). Essentially, the article is intended to inform economists about legal issues for the definition of capital arising in court judgments, in particular a decision by Mr Justice Farwell (in a 1902 case, 1 Chapter 2) which declared that 'leasehold iron ore mines, blast furnaces, and cottages belonging to a steel company were circulating and not fixed capital' (Sanger 1903, p. 177). The articles looks at various views expressed by judges in its first section (Sanger 1903, pp. 177–180); suggests that accounting systems tend to be largely inaccurate on the subject, because their aims are substantially different (Sanger 1903, pp. 180–181); while the third section examines changes to the Companies legislation, which would remove these difficulties (Sanger 1903, pp. 181–185). More broadly, the article seeks to create a bridge between economists and the accounting and judiciary views on capital and profits, a topic in which, judging from some of his remarks, Sanger was particularly interested. Furthermore, the blend in the article between the economic and the legal, in which the legal predominates, acts as a sort of farewell to his economic interests on which he had published for close to a decade. In some ways, this perspective can be substantiated from the years of his book reviewing for the *Economic Journal*.

III

As indicated in the previous sections, Sanger was an ardent book reviewer for the *Economic Journal*, an interest which lasted beyond the eight years from 1895 to 1903 when he published articles in that journal. The books reviewed by Sanger covered very diverse subject matter in a number of languages. To give a clearer idea of this range of Sanger's reviews, a numerical overview of them by language and by type of subject can be presented. First, in terms of language of the book reviewed, Sanger published six reviews each of German and British books, four reviews of Italian books, and three each of books from France and from the United States. Their subject matter was spread over a wide range of topics. Three books were devoted to his main interests in economics, that is, statistics and general economic texts, a further six were on socialism and property rights, and on studies devoted to particular countries. Sanger reviewed two books on the rate of interest and related subjects, on monetary economics and on public finance, as well as one book each on value theory, on distribution theory, the theory of monopoly, the interrelationship between psychology and economics and a book on Homeric geography and the political economy of Troy. Some of these books were by distinguished economists, such as Richard Ely (*Property and Contract in Relation to the Distribution of Wealth*), Irving Fisher (*The Rate of Interest*) and J.B. Clark (*The Problem of Monopoly*).

Sanger's review of the books by three distinguished United States economists can be examined first. J.B. Clark's book on monopoly, Sanger (1904a, pp. 603–604) claimed, was very similar to his earlier book on trusts, published in 1901. The interaction between trusts and tariff policy was rather poorly analysed by Clark in Sanger's opinion, though Clark correctly indicated that free trade (or foreign competition) was the best way to remove the local power exerted by individual trusts. In reviewing Irving Fisher's book, *Appreciation and Interest* (1906), Sanger (1908, pp. 66–69) made two major points. The first related to Fisher's style of writing, and organisation of the book. Although the book as a whole demonstrated 'extreme accuracy of expression and exposition' (p. 66), unfortunately there were occasions of poor organisation of the material, as when important matters were placed in appendices rather than in the text. This is the one, real complaint Sanger had of the book. On contents, Sanger noted that Fisher used time preference as the major explanation of interest, that Fisher was fully aware of the fact that capital values depend on the rate of interest and therefore cannot be used for explaining the rate of interest without arguing in a circle, while Fisher's perceptive discussion of inflation and the rate of interest was matched, in Sanger's view, by that in Marshall's *Principles* (Book VI, Chapter VI from the fifth edition onwards). Last, Richard Ely's book on *Property and Contract* was highly recommended as a veritable 'mine of information', based as it was on both German and British sources, even if the book itself was incomplete.

With respect to the work by fellow 'Marshallians', Sanger (1901b, pp. 193–197) reviewed Bowley's *Elements of Statistics*. The greater part of the review is devoted to a careful summary of the text, prefaced by the remark that this is the first 'elements' of statistics in English, a matter both for congratulations and for gratitude to Bowley. Its clever presentation is particularly noteworthy, because it managed to avoid the use of mathematics completely. The book's main defect, Sanger also observed, is that Bowley too frequently stated dogmatically what can only be properly described 'as a matter of opinion' (p. 197). The second review which falls into this category is that of Pigou's

Memorials of Alfred Marshall, mentioned earlier in this chapter. In this review, Sanger noted the inordinate extent of Marshall's original contributions to economics mentioned in the book; took the opportunity to bestow further praise on Maynard Keynes's marvellous Marshall Memoir; reminded readers that the official papers of Marshall were in preparation as an important supplement to this volume; and deplored the fact that so few letters were included given their very varied nature, so characteristic of the man. The review closed with the remark, it may be recalled from Section I above, that the book fully demonstrated that Alfred Marshall 'was never dull' (p. 84).

The three Italian books Sanger reviewed for the *Economic Journal* were Enrico Montel's *Le Leggi dell' interesse*, Frederico Flora's *Le Finanze degli Stati composti* and Eteocle Lorini's *La Repubblica Argentina e i suoi maggiori problemi di Economia e di Finanza.* The first of these is criticised on the ground that Montel's solution to the theoretical problem posed by the presence of annuities is not very satisfactory (Sanger 1897, pp. 255–256). The second book fared better. It examined a fiscal federalism issue of assignment of local and national taxation. In his review, Sanger illustrated his argument from the tax assignment practice in Germany, Switzerland and the United States and argued that the conclusions reached in this book were relevant to Britain if it decided to create a fiscal federation for the Empire (Sanger 1902a, pp. 71–72). The third Italian book is particularly favourably reviewed by Sanger. He presented it as a valuable addition to the author's earlier treatise on monetary problems, and strongly recommended it to experts on applied monetary analysis (Sanger 1902b, pp. 528–530).

Two of the three French books Sanger reviewed are severely criticised. Landry's *L'utilité sociale de propriété* is depicted as rather out of date and totally unoriginal. There are no proofs offered for the propositions it contains, hence the book is a pure failure as a scientific text. On value and utility maximisation, the book's mathematics is deficient since it failed to make use of the calculus (Sanger 1902c, pp. 69–70). A book by Pierre du Maroussem, *Les enquêtes, practique et théorie* is damned by Sanger as book purely devoted to descriptive economics, a summary of earlier research which heaps up masses of factual information not unlike a novel by Zola (Sanger 1902d, pp. 67–68). A book by de Leener, *Les Syndicats Industrielles de Belgique* is hailed by Sanger as the second edition of a very good, and highly useful book on trade unions in Belgium (Sanger 1904b, pp. 447–448).

Sanger reviewed six German books for the *Economic Journal*, three of them in 1904. In March 1904, Otto Heyn's *Die Indische Warüngs Reform* was described by him as a very good book by a most distinguished author, who treated the subject in the requisite detail. For the June 1904 issue, Sanger reviewed Leo Petritsch's *Zur Lehre von den Uberwalzung der Steuern mit besonderer Beziehung auf den Börsen*, which provided a careful analysis of the incidence of property taxes, fully cognisant of the complexities of this difficult subject. Sanger regretted that lack of space prevented detailed criticism of some aspects of this very interesting work. In the September 1904 issue of the

Journal, Sanger reviewed Stephen Worms' *Das Gesetz der Güter Concentration*, a book strongly recommended by him for social reformers, given its useful information on the very practical subject of unemployment, made very accessible to the reader through the presence of a good index. In March 1908, Sanger reviewed Franz Cuher's *Zur Lehre von der Bedürfnissen*, which provided a fine introduction on the importance of psychology for economics, especially for the economics of consumption. For the June 1908 issue, Sanger reviewed Robert Liefmann's *Ertrag und Einkommen auf den Grundlage einer rein subjectiven Wertlehre*, a very clear and concise work of only seventy-two pages, on profits, production, and aspects of value theory. His last German book review for the *Economic Journal* came in the December issue for 1926. It examined Otto Weinbergen's *Die Grenznutzen Schule*, and described the book as presenting a sound history of this very important school in modern economics.

Finally, Sanger's reviews of English books not so far mentioned, may be briefly noted. In the September 1899 *Economic Journal* he reviewed F.W. Lawrence's Smith Prize-winning essay on *Local Variations in Wages*. This, Sanger (1899b) described as a very useful piece of research, particularly given its agenda for further work on the topic provided by the author as a crucial part of the book. However, its statistical analysis could frequently be faulted, as Sanger demonstrated in the many examples of such errors he provided in the review. In December 1906, Sanger reviewed W.B. Robertson's *Foundations of Political Economy* as a careful study of the work of earlier English economists. However, the book was marred by the fact that its author did not always demonstrate full understanding of the views he attempted to criticise and the book in addition betrayed a lack of awareness of the general interdependence of economic phenomena. In 1913, Sanger reviewed Walter Leaf's *Troy: A Study of Homeric Geography*. Sanger described this as an interesting work which gave a broad analysis of Troy's wealth and economic importance. This had derived in part by Troy's advantageous location for commerce but in the end was destroyed by the effective spread of Greek colonisation (Sanger 1913, pp. 239–241). The final book to be mentioned in this context is H.N. Brailsford's *The War of Steel and Gold*, a brilliant book published before the start of the First World War, hence particularly interesting to re-examine in the light of what actually occurred. Sanger (1915b, p. 243) concluded the review by indicating that the book 'suggests many problems for economists', and that therefore 'everybody ought to read it'. The coverage of topics of the four books mentioned in this paragraph is a fair indication of the generalist position Sanger's broad knowledge allowed him to express in the review columns of the *Economic Journal*, already fully demonstrated in the previous paragraphs of this section.

IV

Sanger's career as 'economist' was rather short-lived. By the early twentieth century Sanger's interest in the subject had been fully swamped by legal topics and by his increasingly busy practice as a barrister-at-law. Economics was more prominent during the second half of the 1890s when he published most of his articles on the subject, of which the first two contributions are by far the more interesting. Later articles for the *Economic Journal* on taxation and on legal aspects of profit were, in any case already more devoted to legal issues rather than to economic considerations. The second of his articles for the *Economic Journal*, on the requisite number of apprentices for a trade, was by far the most Marshallian of these articles, since it tackled the type of applied economic problem which Marshall himself found particularly interesting. Marshall had also claimed great admiration in Sanger's first article for the *Economic Journal* on developments in mathematical economics particularly by the Italians, indicating it was a brilliant piece and citing it in the subsequent editions of his *Principles*.

Sanger was clearly impressed with Marshall as a person and appears never to have regretted his time spent in studying economics as a special student in Part II of the Moral Sciences Tripos. Subsequently, it should be recalled, he acted for four consecutive years as an examiner for that Tripos. His enduring admiration of Marshall the economics teacher is evident from both his obituary of Marshall in 1924 and from his review of *Memorials of Alfred Marshall* in 1926. However, other interests, cultural as well as occupational, became dominant from the first decade of the twentieth century. For Sanger, there was clearly more to be done than just economics, and from that time legal matters captured his imagination far more fully even if his role as economics book reviewer for the *Economic Journal* continued unabated for another decade.

Sanger has not survived well as a figure in the history of Marshallian economic thought or, for that matter, in British history of economic thought. His name cannot be found in the *Biographical Dictionary of British Economists*; is not prominent in the *Elgar Companion to Alfred Marshall*, and fails to make it to Blaug's *Who's Who in Economics*. Yet Sanger was very much respected as both an economics student and a practitioner by Marshall, by Maynard Keynes and possibly by Edgeworth, and he featured among the major book reviewers in the *Economic Journal* for more than two decades. Sanger presents therefore a very interesting case of a truly 'minor' Marshallian, loved by the 'master' as both a very talented student and author, and in turn admiring Marshall for his wisdom and skill, despite all his eccentricities, and, in particular, for the brilliance of the economic system he had created in his major work, the *Principles of Economics*.

5 Sydney John Chapman (1871–1951)

Labour economics, public finance, economic principles and economic history – a Marshall student with great academic distinction

Sydney Chapman was one of Marshall's able, 'mature' students from the 1890s. In 1891, Chapman graduated in history at the University of London. He entered Trinity College, Cambridge in 1894 as a 'miscellaneous' student to study history and philosophy (in the moral sciences) and fortuitously enrolled in a class on economics taught by Marshall. This experience induced Chapman to switch the focus of his studies to economics in preparation of an academic career in that subject. Chapman won both the Cobden and the Smith Prizes for economics and in 1898 graduated BA with first class honours in economics. As a result, Marshall became a lifelong friend, teacher and adviser.

After graduation at Cambridge, Chapman pursued economic research at Manchester, taught economics as a lecturer at Cardiff University College, and in 1901 became Stanley Jevons Professor of Economics at Manchester. Over these years he published major works in economics. These included no less than eight books and close to twenty journal articles. His books included two studies of the Lancashire Cotton Industry, one on Local Government and State Financial Aid, one on United States/United Kingdom Trade, two short elementary textbooks including one for the Home University Library which went through many reprints, and three volumes on *Work and Wages*, updating and expanding the earlier work on this subject by Marshall's friend, Lord Brassey, and his son. In 1918, Chapman published an edited volume, *Labour and Capital after the War*. Chapman's twenty journal articles appeared in both the *Economic Journal* and the *Journal of the Royal Statistical Society*. His last two articles were published in March 1915. By then he was heavily involved in war work as an economic adviser to the Board of Trade. In 1919 he became its Permanent Secretary, in 1927 he was appointed Chief Economic Adviser to the Government, to retire from public service in 1939. The start of the Second World War later that year postponed his retirement for the duration of the war. From 1945 he retired in Ware, Hertfordshire, for half a dozen years. He died on 29 August 1951.

The Marshallian credentials visible in Chapman's published work on economics are the subject of Chapter 5. Three parts of that work were selected for this purpose. These are his elementary text, *Political Economy*, for the Home University Library (Chapman 1912); second, two items on public finance – that is, his study of local government and state aid (Chapman 1899) and his 1913 *Economic Journal* article, 'The Utility of Income and Progressive Taxation' (Chapman 1913, 1959, pp. 3–12); and third, his three volumes on *Work and Wages* (Chapman 1904, 1908, 1914) which continued Brassey's work. Chapman's economic history of the cotton industry is therefore excluded from this study. The chapter starts with a sketch of Chapman's life and work.

I

Sydney Chapman was born at Wells (Norfolk) on 20 April 1871, the son of a businessman. When Chapman was still quite young, the family moved to Manchester. He was educated at Manchester Grammar School and Owen College, before entering the University of London, where he successfully completed a degree in history in 1891. He then taught secondary school for some years, while making up his mind about a future career. At one stage, he seriously thought about entering the Anglican priesthood. In 1894, Chapman decided to continue his university studies, combining further historical work with studies in philosophy. He was admitted to Trinity College, Cambridge, enrolling in history and the moral sciences. While studying these courses, he decided on a whim to take one of Alfred Marshall's economics classes. This experience induced him to specialise in economic studies, as the subject of choice for a future academic career. Marshall became a friend and adviser over the next two decades, as more fully disclosed later in this section.

Chapman was an outstanding student, winning both the Cobden and the Adam Smith Prize, the second a triennial prize for economics to the value of £60 established by Marshall. Marshall later wrote Chapman about the worthwhile investment in good students his Smith Prize embodied, when expressing his pride in Chapman's two books – his monograph, *The Cotton Industry*, and the first revised volume of Brassey's *Work and Wages* – published earlier that year. After proclaiming Chapman's monograph to be the 'best … of the kind … ever published', Marshall continued:

> I am awfully proud of [these] Cambridge products. I bragged indeed and said that there were few Universities which could show as good a series as our Adam Smith Prize lot. First Bowley's which got him the Silver Medal of the Statistical Society at (I believe) an unprecedented early age; next Lawrence's *Local Variations of Wages*; next yours; and there is one good one still to come, that of Pigou on Arbitration and Conciliation, nearly ready for the Press. So I *am* proud of the Cambridge Stables; and I think the quantity and quality of the work you have got through is wonderful. Our best regards to you and Mrs. Chapman….
>
> (Marshall to Chapman, 29 October 1904, in Whitaker 1996, III pp. 93–94)

This picture of the quality of his students as given by Marshall can be combined with the assessment of Marshall as lecturer and teacher provided by

Chapman himself. This comes from his unpublished autobiography preserved at the London School of Economics and can be quoted as follows:

> Was he [Marshall] a good lecturer? Yes and No. I remember at dinner once when during a somewhat formless speech, one of my neighbours, who was a practised speaker, remarked to me, 'there is a technique about these things'. Marshall had no technique, whether in manner, arrangement or illustration. I never heard him give a lecture which he had constructed like a work of art. So I suppose one ought to say that he was not what is commonly called a good lecturer to large or uninstructed audiences. Yet, even then, he could not help making the impression he wanted to make. In the case of small classes of serious students, however, the answer to the question would be emphatically in the affirmative. Marshall's method with them was thinking aloud and not uncommonly on what he had been thinking about in his own work. Consequently, one got the best that could be got from a lecture, not only illumination on a particular theme but also a lesson in how economic theorising should be done. I attended all Marshall's lectures over a period of three years. And I had in addition, after I was definitely committed to economics, the privilege of long talks with him in his study once a week at least, sometimes in connection with one of the essays I had written for him and sometimes in connection with the extensive course of reading he was putting me through. He had most generously given me the run of his library. It was from these talks that I gained most and saw further into his mind.
>
> Whether Marshall was an accomplished lecturer or not, beyond question, he was a great teacher. What constitutes a great teacher, is not easy to define. The best approach to a definition is by way of results. A teacher to be great must inspire, and further he must have the gift of so imparting his ideas that they get rooted in his pupils as if they were their own. How this is done does not matter. It may be done differently by different people, but all great teachers must have individuality.
>
> Marshall certainly had it. I recall in particular his surprising way of putting things, which cracked your shell of commonplace beliefs. How he got to inspire I cannot say – the deepest things in personal relations are the most difficult to fathom – but how he succeeded is evident from the number of economists he created. He certainly made you feel that what you thought mattered a great deal. He was tremendously in earnest.
>
> (Chapman, 'unpublished autobiography', pp. 19–20, as quoted in Groenewegen 1995a, p. 315)

As previously indicated, Chapman's final result in his Cambridge studies in no way disappointed Marshall. He graduated BA with first class honours in economics in 1898. On graduation, Chapman returned to Manchester. He started as research student in Owen College, then went to Cardiff University College as lecturer (where he introduced economics teaching to its syllabus), then, in 1901, he was appointed Stanley Jevons Professor at Manchester. By 1904, he was Dean of its Faculty of Commerce as well. In 1903, he married Mabel Gwendoline Mordey.

These early years of academic success were matched by a flow of publications. By 1904, he had published six articles in the *Economic Journal*, the first in March 1899 on the Trade Union Congress and Federation. In addition, he published the monograph on the cotton industry, and the first of the three Brassey volumes dealing with British and foreign labour, and foreign competition.

Chapman kept in close contact with Marshall and Cambridge during these years. During June–July 1903 Chapman contributed four articles to the *Daily Mail* critical of Hewins' protective views on imperial trade and very supportive of Marshall's free trade position, as Marshall wrote proudly to Brentano (17 July 1903, in Whitaker 1996, III p. 38). Chapman also actively supported Marshall's drive for a separate Economics and Politics Tripos at Cambridge (see Groenewegen 1995a, p. 446) and in 1906 and 1907 acted as Tripos examiner. When in 1908 Chapman was considering whether to apply for Marshall's chair, Marshall told him he would not get his support over Pigou, Marshall's preferred candidate and successor for the Cambridge chair. In the event, Chapman did not apply since Manchester gave him a substantial increase in salary, inducing him to stay for a further six years (Marshall to Layton, 13 January 1919, in Whitaker 1996 III pp. 362–363). Marshall was then asked to suggest a successor to Chapman for the Jevons chair, because Chapman after the war commenced a full-time public service career with the Board of Trade.

This change in direction halted Chapman's flow of publications. His last two journal articles, both joint publications, dealt with the implications of the war for the cotton industry and, more generally, the textile industry (*Economic Journal* 25(1), pp. 109–119; *Journal of the Royal Statistical Society* 78(1), pp. 157–228, both published in March 1915). They were undoubtedly written before the start of the war that previous August. Moreover, since 1904, Chapman had published articles on international competition in the steel trade, on the Report of the Tariff Commission, on cotton supplies, on the laws of increasing and decreasing returns in consumption and production, on the incidence of protective import duties, on hours of labour, on inventions and the rate of interest, on the incidence of land taxes, on the recruiting of employing classes from the ranks of wage earners in the cotton industry, on utility of income and progressive income taxation, on size of business with special reference to the textile industry, and on the tendency of children to enter their father's trade. Labour economics, industry economics, tax incidence and foreign trade, often with a strong Marshallian slant, provided the inspiration for the journal articles (as shown more fully with respect to the article on the utility of income and progressive taxation). They also reveal Chapman's considerable analytical ability applied to questions of general theory, as in the case of his work on the laws of returns and on tax incidence.

Chapman appears to have been an able administrator as well as a good economist. For example, he played a significant role in the lengthy process by which

Manchester gained independent university status. In 1909, Chapman assisted the South African government on labour issues, his first taste of presenting expert advice to government. When the First World War started in August 1914, his services as economist were immediately required by government for the duration of the conflict, initially as adviser to the Board of Trade. The significance of his contributions was recognised by awards of the CBE in 1917 and the CB in 1919. In 1918, Chapman accepted an invitation to join the full-time public service, and succeeded Sir Hubert Llewellyn-Smith the following year as Permanent Secretary of the Board of Trade, retaining this position until 1927. That year he became chief economic adviser to the government. Negotiations with the League of Nations were his major task from 1927 to 1932; he drafted British protective trade legislation in 1932, a major volte-face for the ardent free trader, as was his later appointment as Chairman of the Import Duties Advisory Committee. He retired in 1939, aged sixty-eight. The start of the Second World War brought him back to government service for the duration of the war. Public service and economic advice in the second half of his adult life followed his eminent academic career as economic theorist and researcher in industry, trade and labour economics.

During his early years of public service, Chapman could occasionally find time for his former mentor, though generally in response to initiatives from Marshall. Thus in 1923 Chapman thanked Marshall for sending him a copy of his newly published *Money, Credit and Commerce* (6 March 1923, in Whitaker 1996, III p. 394), a 'kindness' which Chapman had experienced before in connection with other publications after Marshall's retirement from active teaching in 1908. However, the balance in presenting complimentary copies of published books was clearly in Chapman's favour. The *Marshall Library Catalogue* in 1927 recorded no fewer than nine Chapman volumes, two of them joint, plus the three 'modernisations' of Brassey's study on life and labour (Chapman 1904, 1908, 1914).

Chapman's publications also received recognition in Marshall's own books. From the sixth to the eighth edition, Marshall's *Principles* (Guillebaud 1961, I p. 695n. 1) mentioned the text of Chapman's address on 'hours of labour' to the British Association, as published in the *Economic Journal* (1909, 19(3), pp. 354–373). Subsequently, for *Industry and Trade*, Marshall cited Chapman's work on the Lancashire cotton industry three times (Marshall 1919, 1932, pp. 231n., 320n., 601n.), and Chapman's edition of *Labour and Capital after the War* (Marshall 1919, 1932, p. 645n.) once, and his papers with Knoop (Chapman and Knoop 1904, 1906), on anticipations in the cotton market and the market for futures therein (Marshall 1919, p. 801n.).

Marshall's pride in Chapman's work was inspired by both his theoretical contributions and his applied work. This follows from Marshall's considerable citations of his student's work, particularly in *Industry and Trade.* However, on occasions Marshall could be critical of public actions associated with his former student. For example, in response to a report in *The Times* (18 November 1908) of a meeting in Cardiff on business education addressed by Chapman, the discussion was reported to have included a remark from a member of the audience suggesting that 'Oxford and Cambridge graduates were useless as businessmen'. Marshall replied at length in a letter to *The Times* (20 November 1905). This concluded with a statement Marshall attributed to the secretary of the Cambridge University Appointments Board, firmly suggesting 'that the applications to him from leading business firms for men who have received a Cambridge training of one sort or another is large and increasing fast, and that the reports which he receives of their work are as a rule very satisfactory' (in Whitaker 1996, III pp. 118–119 and n. 2). Marshall's letter neither cast any personal aspersions on Chapman nor on the specific contents of his address.

Enough has been said to indicate Chapman's strong, and enduring, association with Marshall, reciprocated by Marshall's considerable appreciation of Chapman's work. The Marshallian credentials of that work can now be illustrated in relation to some of Chapman's specific texts.

II

The first Chapman text to be examined for its Marshallian credentials is his *Political Economy*, published in 1912 for the Home University Library of Modern Knowledge. This book intended to explore 'the fundamental characteristics of economic generalising' by offering 'general explanations' of things economic as they exist in contemporary communities, without attempting to trace their evolution. This summarised the scope of the book. As for method, Chapman intended to use the 'exact analysis' adopted initially by Jevons and Walras, 'perfected and applied' to all economic phenomena by subsequent writers, 'particularly by Dr. Marshall'. Although mathematics was useful for this purpose, Chapman wished to present his outline of political economy without using mathematical language (Chapman 1912, pp. 7–8). Economics is then defined as dealing with all 'facts' which simultaneously relate to people and wealth, where wealth is defined as consisting 'of all the things desired by man which can be attained only by the expenditure of human effort' (Chapman 1912, pp. 8–9).

Chapman (1912, p. 9) noted that economic studies originated both from practical needs and from speculative curiosity. Problems of money and international trade, as well as issues associated with state activity, are good examples. Economic studies therefore need to embrace economic ethics ('what economic actions ought to be in relation to wealth'); economic politics ('or all that politics which has reference to economic facts'); economic art (or the method 'by which given ends can be attained'); while positive economic science seeks to eliminate ethical consequences from the discussion to concentrate on explaining the facts as they are (Chapman 1912, pp. 10–11).

A very brief (and excessively British) history of the science follows. This mentioned Smith and Ricardo as early treatise makers, followed by Senior and the two Mills (James and John Stuart) and preceded by Bentham and Godwin as well as by some seventeenth and eighteenth century writers (Mun, North, Child,

Locke, Petty, Defoe, Hume and Steuart) to end with a discussion of the modern practitioners (Jevons, Walras and Marshall). In this historical survey, Chapman reserved the distinction for Marshall of first realising the far-reaching application of the new ideas embodied in the marginal method, a method Chapman claimed Marshall had 'perfected'. Marshall's innovative work on the concepts and application of supply and demand was a good example of such perfection, and these concepts now formed the basis for the science. Chapman concluded the introductory chapter by stressing the nature and difficulties of scientific explanation in economics. These included the danger and necessity of abstraction in economic argument, the links of its principles with other social sciences such as psychology, the need to view economic generalisations as tendencies rather than settled propositions, and the need to assess their validity over the appropriate time period, short or long.

Chapman warned that the contents of his little book were almost exclusively concerned with long-period results, and that the economic tendencies studied in it were generally measurable in terms of money, as was the case in the real world. Scope and method were therefore elaborated in a very Marshallian manner, justified by Chapman from the enormous contributions Marshall had made to the development of modern economic science.

Chapman's next two chapters dealt with demand and supply. Demand is discussed in terms of utility, an explanation simpler than analysis in terms of preferences, which can only be expressed as ratios and not as whole numbers. After explaining diminishing marginal utility in relation to income and specific commodities, and linking it to the explanation of a downward sloping demand function as a function of price, Chapman illustrated these notions with the example of tea, the very commodity Marshall himself had used in this context in his *Principles* from the third edition onwards. Explanations of the notion of elasticity with respect to demand, including the special case of unitary elasticity, followed. Chapman then introduced the 'law of substitution', indifference, or of equi-marginal returns, as one of the simplest generalisations in economics but one which, nevertheless, had crucial implications for economic analysis. In this, Chapman suggested, it resembled the enormous significance and extraordinary simplicity of the law of the survival of the fittest in biology. Although the law of substitution applied to all economic activity, Chapman confined its illustration to the act of consumption, that is, in terms of maximising its utility by equating the utility attributable to marginal expenditures of special items (bread, tea, milk and clothes, to quote Chapman's examples). However, other factors also explained consumption patterns, such as the 'standard of life' of a member of a particular social class, another concept much used by Marshall. This brought the argument to a discussion of consumer surplus, 'one of the subtlest generalisations wrung by Dr. Marshall out of the facts of experience after analysing them to the last dregs by the marginal method' (Chapman 1912, pp. 47–48). This type of surplus can be measured either in utility or in money terms, and its various dimensions are succinctly outlined together with its applicability to problems of taxation.

Chapman (1912, p. 57) invited the reader to judge whether the application of the marginal method to demand had been worthwhile, particularly in terms of the generalisations reached 'under the guidance of Dr. Marshall in particular'. The demand chapter's final pages define wealth and value. Value of exchange expressed in money is called 'demand price', while wealth is defined simply in terms of the things people want, though this simple perspective can be criticised from an ethical standpoint, as Ruskin had indeed eloquently done (Chapman 1912, p. 60).

Supply in its relation to demand is the subject of Chapter III. Supply is also presented as a schedule linking specific prices to quantities produced at those prices, where an industry is defined as the producing unit consisting of a specific number of firms. Each firm is assumed to have its own cost of production and this information, in conjunction with that contained in the demand schedule, determines the quantity to be produced by each firm under conditions of competition (Chapman 1912, pp. 64–65). The opportunities for specialisation, and variations in cost, are then introduced, partly as a way of bringing Marshall's constructs of increasing, constant, and diminishing returns into the discussion (Chapman 1912, p. 68). The last two of these concepts are considered uncontroversial; the notion of increasing returns as applied to an industry is described as subject to considerable debate. Conceived as abstract relationships between cost and output, the three relationships are correlative: however, they are not easily made realistic by observing actual industrial conditions, yet the two methods of theory and fact finding supplement each other closely. Chapman (1912, pp. 73–77) then shifted to an analysis of equilibrium by combining the data contained in demand and supply schedules. This is straightforward analysis, except for the case where the relevant segment of the supply curve operates under increasing returns. Finally, Chapman noted that cost of production needs to include marketing or selling costs.

To complete the supply theory properly, analysis of the growth of both the firm and the industry needs to be provided. Such growth, generally speaking, presumes that marginal expenses (costs) first fall, and then, for high levels of output, start to rise. This introduced the notion of the optimal size of the firm, a position reached, according to Chapman, when marginal outgoings equal price. Likewise, the relationship explains the growth of an industry since additional firms enter when existing firms in the industry produce at sub-optimal levels. Chapter III concludes with some remarks on factors of production (land, labour, capital and, a very Marshallian touch, organisation) and reminded the reader that the aim of production is to produce the level of output consistent with the level of demand (Chapman 1912, p. 91).

Monopoly is discussed in Chapter IV. It is defined as a market situation 'when competition is absent' and demand and supply play a different role as compared to competition. Chapman first presented the condition for profit maximisation under pure monopoly, implicitly by equating marginal cost and marginal revenue, though this specific terminology is not used by him (Chapman 1912, pp. 95–97). Chapman then analysed discriminative or differential prices, distinguishing in this context individual, trade, and local discrimination. Rail freights are said to discriminate often between trades according to value of bulky outputs, a form of subsidising bulky and relatively cheap commodities such as coal (Chapman 1912, pp. 100–104). Chapman was aware of the risk to monopolists of entry into their monopoly by other firms, a particularly great danger when output is kept deliberately small and prices high by the monopolist. Dumping is described as another form of discriminatory pricing designed to gain market share. Chapter IV concludes with a broad classification of types of monopolies: natural, social, legal and voluntary, where the last is related to associations of firms such as trusts and cartels (Chapman 1912, pp. 112–113).

Chapter V deals with money. It links the purchasing power of money problem directly to the theory of value, and depicts money either as a commodity or as a promise to deliver a commodity in the future. Much of the initial exposition is in terms of the gold standard, and several generalisations are developed in this context. The first is that the value, or price, of money is its purchasing power and that, in a broad sense, the 'true theory of money' is contained in the quantity theory. This theory clearly defined the demand for money, an independent theory had to be found to explain money supply. This is said to depend on the precious metals, as well as on credit levels (Chapman 1912, pp. 120–125). Chapman then introduced credit money, the concomitant need for bank reserves, and for monetary policy including variations in the discount rate. The end of the chapter briefly mentioned the trade cycle (Chapman 1912, pp. 133–137), noting in particular its periodicity and frequent association with good and bad harvests, a Jevonian touch included in Marshall's (1879) treatment of the trade cycle. Implications of the cycle for banking policy and the credit market, and for variations in the price level, are also noted. Steady price falls are a sign of depression, price rises denote periods of 'good trade'. The importance of good statistical data on price movements by way of index numbers is stressed (Chapman 1912, pp. 139–141) and some comments on bi-metallism as a suggested solution to trade and price fluctuations bring the chapter to a close (Chapman 1912, pp. 141–144).

International trade is discussed in Chapter VI. Its essential distinguishing feature from domestic trade is the relative immobility of factors of production between nations as compared to domestic factor mobility. Trade is explained by the doctrine of comparative costs, and is then broadly defined to include international loans and trade in intangible services. The gains of trade are discussed in terms of the increased range of commodities it provides to domestic consumers, and the lower costs of many imports relative to what they would have cost if produced domestically. In this context Chapman (1912, pp. 162–163) reminded his readers of the importance of general exceptions to the doctrine of maximum satisfaction raised by Alfred Marshall. Chapman concluded the chapter by quoting John Stuart Mill's remarks on the civilising aspects of international trade. However, the occasional desirability of regulation or restriction on international trade was deliberately excluded from the discussion, because this was considered to be too large a subject for discussion in a small text book (Chapman 1912, pp. 164–166).

The final chapters all deal with distribution. The first of these (Chapter VII) studies wages, profits and interest. These incomes are determined by marginal productivity considerations on the demand side; the supply side is more complicated governed as it is in the case of labour by long-term factors of population growth and short-term issues such as the responsiveness of hours of work to variations in wage rates. Capital supply is determined by both the power and the inducement to save provided by the rate of interest. Profits are associated with risk and the payment for the skills of industrial organisation. Rent is explained in Chapter VIII as both a return to land (determined by its productivity at the margin) and as a reward for superior abilities of labour or other productive resources. A few practical and applied distribution problems are left to Chapter IX, the final chapter in the book. These include the determination of producers' surplus (Chapman 1912, pp. 220–221), the marginal dissatisfaction of working (Chapman 1912, pp. 222–224), the impact of unemployment whether from the introduction of labour-saving machinery or from deficient demand, though Chapman seems to deny the importance of the second by an implicit appeal to Say's Law (Chapman 1912, pp. 125–126). Other issues raised in Chapter IX are the possibility of a zero rate of interest, the impact of trade union action on wages (Chapman 1912, pp. 230–233), the positive impact on distribution from rapid growth in demand and output, the potential of compulsory industrial arbitration to raise living standards as compared with voluntary conciliation machinery and wage boards, improved organisation of the labour process through the elimination of low paid outworkers, casual labour, and unemployment.

The final pages of Chapter IX (Chapman 1912, pp. 248–253) conclude the book by stressing the value of political economy, the indispensable relationship between fact and theory which had been illustrated in its pages, and its ability to test the practicability of social reform. A note on further reading mentioned useful introductory texts (Flux 1904a and Nicholson 1903a) as well as more specialist literature before recommending Marshall's *Principles of Economics* as '*the* most authoritative treatise on theory' despite its omissions of foreign trade, public economics and finance. This praise, together with a great deal of the specific content of Chapman's *Political Economy* indicates the solid Marshallian credentials of Chapman's Home University Text.

III

Two items of Chapman's work on public economics can now be examined for their Marshallian aspects. The first is Chapman's (1899) contribution to local government finance and state aid. It was written at Manchester in 1897, gratefully recorded assistance from Flux (then professor at Manchester), and succinctly outlined relevant aspects of the local government financing problem associated with its varied expenditure responsibilities, its limited tax powers, and the increased use of central government grants over the course of the nineteenth century. It was therefore an exercise in intergovernmental financial relations, a topic which Marshall had also broached in 1897 when writing on local taxation in his response to a Memorandum and Questionnaire circulated by a Royal Commission on Local Taxation to economic experts (Chapman 1899, Chapter I; Marshall 1897, 1926, pp. 329–364). Marshall is quoted on only one occasion in Chapman's book (1899, p. 5) and then on a general matter associated with the 'fundamental unity of action between the laws of nature in the physical and in the moral world', a matter of some importance. Chapman continued, 'This central unity is set forth in the general rule, to which there are very many exceptions, that the development of the organism, whether social or physical, involves greater subdivision of functions between its separate parts on the one hand, *and on the other a more intimate connection between them* (Chapman 1899, p. 5, quoting from Marshall 1891, p. 300, his italics in the quotation). Chapman's introductory chapter then examines local government institutions in the forms of district or parish, or province, or county, as contrasted with the more complex organism of the nation. Chapman (1899, pp. 7–8) asserted the enormous value of local government in stimulating and educating the political interests of the people, while its presence also ensures that central government is not overloaded with responsibilities. Moreover, local government forms the cradle, Chapman posited, of truly representative government. Chapman (1899, Chapter 3) then discussed rationales for distributing costs between local and national government, and examined reasons why local bodies needed subventions from national government, particularly given the limited taxing power of local government in Britain (discussed in Chapman 1899, Chapter 4). The major local tax, the property tax, is then analysed as to its incidence, its burden, and its equity (Chapman 1899, Chapter 5), a discussion which drew largely on Mill's treatment of the matter as well as mentioning that of Goschen, Thorold Rogers and Seligman. Chapter 6 investigated the causes and degree of differential rating in British local government units, partly on the basis of Cannan's (1895) study of this subject. Chapman (1899, Chapter 7) then tackled the history of central government subventions for local government from their starting point in the 1830s, frequently in connection with the financing of the poor law, but later also of local government responsibilities in sanitation, education and police. The 1888 and 1890 changes made to British local government grants are examined in Chapter 8. These changed the principle on which grants were given to local government from giving grants for specifically designated purposes to general revenue grants, often initially in the form of tax revenue sharing, involving death (probate) duties and later excise revenues from taxing alcoholic beverages. Principles for distributing this revenue to individual local government units were discussed by Chapman in considerable detail. Chapman severely criticised the principles then in force. Allocating the shared revenue from excise according to the number of persons vaccinated was nonsensical; allocating it according to the tax base of rateable value was grossly inequitable (Chapman 1899, pp. 100–103). Distributing shared tax revenue on a simple per capita basis was also unwarranted, because local expenditure responsibilities need not vary with population per se but were more likely associated with the age distribution of that population, or other, more specific, demographic characteristics. As well as briefly discussing the agricultural rating bill, (Chapman 1899, Chapter 9) provided a brief summary of the argument and conclusions. The effect of government grants on the burden of taxation and incidence of local taxation was briefly discussed in an appendix. The Marshallian credentials of this study are not clearly visible. They can only be inferred from the careful nature of Chapman's analysis and the theoretical apparatus used therein, some of which may have been inspired by Marshall's Cambridge lectures attended by Chapman.

The second of Chapman's public economics pieces to be assessed for its Marshallian credentials is his 1913 *Economic Journal* article, 'The Utility of Income and Progressive Taxation'. This article cited only two authorities: the three 1897 Edgeworth articles on the theory of taxation from the *Economic Journal* (Edgeworth 1897), and an undated piece by W.R. Scott. It therefore nowhere explicitly relied on Marshall's discussion of utility and marginal utility in relation to income, or its practical uses, as described in Book III of Marshall's *Principles.* Chapman's discussion of these issues in some respects goes well beyond these foundations. An example can be given from the context of potential discontinuities in the utility of income function when part of that income is devoted to purchasing an expensive, durable good such as a motor car (Chapman 1913, 1959, pp. 3–5).

Chapman's paper explained the nature of the utility of income function by referring to the two empirical and one a priori reasons for arguing that the utility of money income declines for persons as they become more wealthy. Data on work incentives and on spending patterns provide the rationales for the proposition. The a priori argument suggests that urgent necessities (with the highest utility) tend to be satisfied first, so that as income rises, utility from the income when spent declines as commodities of diminishing necessity are purchased for consumption. Chapman then links the phenomenon of declining money income to the rules justifying the adoption of progressive income taxation in terms of equal proportion (but not of equal marginal) sacrifice. However, more pragmatically, Chapman (1913, 1959, p. 12) suggests that equity in taxation is satisfied by progressive taxation since it lightly taxes that portion of income which the rich spend on urgent necessities, while it gradually taxes more severely the income of the wealthy at higher levels, which they spend on items increasingly less essential for sustaining their standard of life.

Neither of Chapman's public economics contributions discussed in this section appears to be very Marshallian. This is not surprising. Marshall published virtually nothing on public economics issues during his lifetime except for references to taxation in his *Principles of Economics* by way of illustration. The separate book on taxation promised for Volume 2 of the *Principles* in an 1887 plan for this book, and that on public economics as part of the projected second volume outlined in 1903, never materialised. However, the material on the utility of money income Chapman published in the 1913 article on progressive taxation never conflicts with Marshall's discussion of the topic in Book III of the *Principles*, even though Chapman's discussion in that article moved well beyond that.

There can, however, be no real doubt that Chapman's public economics material here discussed fits easily into a Marshallian framework, informed as it was by Marshall's theoretical tools and by Marshall's tremendous drive for the necessity of realistic economics when discussing applied topics.

IV

The first volume of Chapman's *Work and Wages* dealt with international trade and its competitiveness. Its opening chapter explains international competitiveness in terms of comparative advantage and the associated free trade. In addition, it drew attention to comparative costs as influenced by relative wage differences. The other nine chapters investigated British international competitivess relative to the United States, Germany, and other relevant countries (largely from Europe) in major industries. These industries included iron ore (Chapter 2), iron and steel (Chapter 3), metal industries including ship building (Chapter 4), the cotton industry (Chapter 5), other textiles (Chapter 6), miscellaneous industries including tin plate, paper, clocks and watches (Chapter 8), commercial methods such as marketing and aspects of dynamic efficiency (Chapter 9) to conclude with railways and other forms of transport and communications (Chapter 10).

All of these industry surveys were statistical and descriptive, drew on sources in various languages (mainly English and German) and, if available, on official publications. The underlying theoretical framework was very much that provided by the Marshallian theory of the firm. This is particularly visible in Chapter 9, where specific issues of industrial competitiveness and dynamic efficiency are discussed. These included cost advantages from large-scale organisation, advantages from 'incomplete development' (excess capacity) or 'half growth' to ensure room for additional output when needed (p. 247), good consumer research (pp. 248–249), access to sound credit facilities (p. 252) and, with special reference to advantages for British firms, the advantages of adopting the metric system, and the benefits of having satisfactory knowledge of relevant foreign languages in the workforce (pp. 251, 254–255). Some of these were not reflected in Marshall's treatment of industrial competitiveness, but most of the more important ones were. Moreover, Chapman drew attention to the advantages of incipient technology such as that associated with electric power and with the adoption of labour saving practices to lower costs such as increased standardisation (pp. 292–294).

Volume 2 was devoted to wages and employment. It was divided into six lengthy chapters and, like its predecessor, contained many international comparisons of British practice with that in Germany, France, the United States and, where appropriate, that in Australasia. Chapter 1 ('Analytical Groundwork') provided a detailed discussion of wages, their relation to employment illustrated by the use of production functions, the laws of returns, and the impact thereon of trade unions and government regulation. Chapter 1 cited Marshall explicitly on no less than four occasions. The first of these citations came from the *Principles* and mentioned the application of supply and demand to explain labour issues (p. 10 n. 1). This was followed by two citations from the chapter on trade unions in Marshall's (1892) *Elements of the Economics of Industry* (pp. 22–23 and n. 1, pp. 32–33) and a quotation from Marshall's 1902 pamphlet, *A Plea for a Curriculum on Economics and Associated Branches of Political Science* on the importance of understanding economics when dealing with social issues (pp. 34–35). The last argument Marshall had considered sufficiently important to reproduce its essentials in subsequent editions of the *Principles*. Chapman's analytical foundations are essentially Marshallian, as is much of the language. Examples are the denial in real life of a stationary state (p. 2), the emphasis on the importance of substitution (p. 7), the difficulties in using marginal productivity theory arising from the laws of returns (pp. 12–13) and the chapter's general emphasis on the importance of always distinguishing long-term from short-term factors in economic analysis (pp. 33–34).

Subsequent chapters dealt with 'the organisation of labour' (Chapter 2) as a comparative study of British, North American, German and French practice; the policies of trade unions (Chapter 3); 'principles and means of industrial peace (Chapter 4), which, among other things, discussed sliding wage scales, and arbitration and conciliation systems especially those used in Australasia (pp. 230–260). It quoted Marshall directly from the fourth edition of the *Principles* (p. 221n. 1) and indirectly from the Labour Commission Report (pp. 277–284). Chapman also frequently mentioned Pigou's work on these topics (pp. 212–219, 287, 293n. 1). Chapter 5 dealt with unemployment both seasonal and general, rejecting technological unemployment as a long period phenomenon and a basically unsound notion. Chapman (1908, p. 320) quoted Marshall's evidence to the 'Gold and Silver Commission', Question 7816, on the link between 'irregular unemployment' and the modernisation of industry, a link Marshall there strongly denied. In this context it is interesting to note that Chapman (p. 322) rejected the applicability to matters of social organisation of *natura non facit saltum* (Marshall's motto from the frontispiece of his *Principles*). Finally, Chapter 6 discussed possibilities for workers' insurance against unemployment and for retirement, treating German and Australasian experiments with old age pensions at considerable length. Marshall's direct impact on the contents of this volume is therefore considerable, as is that of some of his favourite 'pupils', that is, Pigou and Flux (who is cited on pp. 464–465 on Danish experiments with old age pensions). Despite the fact that Marshall addressed few of these matters directly in his own volumes (apart from the material on wages in the *Principles* and the chapter on trade unions in his 1892 *Elements of the Economics of Industry*), Marshall's influence is very visible in various places of Chapman's volume.

The third volume of Chapman's revision of Brassey's *Work and Wages* was devoted to social betterment. Its seven chapters dealt in turn with 'aspects of social progress' (Chapter 1), 'housing' (Chapter 2), 'physical deterioration, mortality and health' (Chapter 3), 'training and children's labour' (Chapter 4), 'conditions of labour' (Chapter 5), 'home-workers and shop assistants' (Chapter 6) and 'public aid' including charities and poor laws (Chapter 7). There are many echoes from Marshall's interests and writings in these chapters, as well as four direct references to (the fifth edition of) his *Principles of Economics*. In addition, the volume also mentions writings by some of Marshall's pupils, including Fay (pp. 215, 222), Pigou (pp. 52, 315) and Clara Collett (pp. 131, 297–301). General echoes of a Marshallian nature in the volume are its references to Octavia Hill's charity work, and to that of Ebenezer Howard on garden cities (pp. 44–45, 68–69, 73) together with criticism of Karl Pearson's then controversial views (p. 98) on declining quality of population from rising reproduction rates of 'lower genetic', working class stock. Quotes from Marshall's *Principles* are confined to Chapters 5 and 6 of the volume. These references are confined to the final chapter of the *Principles* devoted to the theme of economic progress. More specifically, they relate to the proper use of leisure as a crucial element in achieving 'a high standard of life' (p. 237), and to the occasionally undesirable consequences of shift work or excessive hours of domestic industry especially for women workers (pp. 252, 287, 312 and n. 1). In this context, it is interesting to note, Marshall subsequently (*Principles of Economics*, sixth edition, 1910, p. 695n. 1) also cited Chapman, that is, his Address to the British Association on working hours in the *Economic Journal* (Chapman 1909). This is no coincidence. Chapman's interests, as revealed in this article, and in the contents at large of the third volume of *Work and Wages*, embrace many of the themes discussed in the final chapter (Book VI Chapter XIII) of the *Principles*, from its fifth edition onwards.

Enough has been said to indicate that the three volumes of *Work and Wages* prepared by Chapman as updates of Brassey's original book on the subject fully demonstrate Marshall's considerable impact on this work by a former pupil. Marshall's works are sporadically cited in its pages, including extracts from successive editions of his *Principles*. Works by members of the Cambridge school Marshall had created, in particular by Pigou, but also by Fay, Flux and Clara Collett, are cited as well. Perhaps the fact that Chapman had chosen the extensive task of updating Brassey is itself a bow in the direction of his 'economics master'. After all, Brassey's book had been somewhat of a favourite with Marshall from its original publication in 1873. Moreover, its careful international comparative content and empirical work made Chapman's work precisely the sort of work Marshall liked his former students to do, and which made him proud of the products from his 'Cambridge stable'. All this is of course rather speculative, since Marshall left no specific comments on this substantial part of Chapman's published work.

V

Before concluding on the material presented in the previous sections, it is useful to recall briefly Marshall's admiration for, and use of Chapman's work. In the first place, that work was cited on no less than five occasions in Marshall's first companion volume to the *Principles*, that is, *Industry and Trade*. It may also be recalled that the printed *Catalogue* of the Marshall Library at Cambridge (1927) contained eight items by Chapman as sole author and two joint works (with J.S. Hallsworth on *Unemployment in Lancashire* and with A.N. Shimin on *Industrial Recruiting and Replacement of Labour*).

Marshall's continuing familiarity with Chapman and his work is also attested to by references to Chapman made by Marshall in his correspondence with others between 1897 and 1922. This was quoted in Section I. Moreover, in 1922 Chapman was among the signatories to the Address Marshall's former pupils presented him with on the occasion of his eightieth birthday. In the year 1897 Marshall's correspondence with J.N. Keynes recalls Chapman as one of the few promising economists Marshall was then teaching, while a letter in 1901 mentioned Chapman as a potential replacement for Flux on his departure for Manchester (in Whitaker 1996, II pp. 193, 199, 328).

The Marshallian credentials of Chapman's published works were illustrated in the three preceding sections. Chapman's *Political Economy* was a particularly good illustration of this, given its praise of Marshall's method, its complete acceptance of Marshall's position on the scope of economics, the organisation of its analytical contents in terms of supply and demand, emphasis on the laws of returns in its cost analysis, its inclusion of 'organisation' as an agent of production, and the contents of its chapters on distribution.

Chapman's material on local government and taxation is less obviously Marshallian. However, his book on local government more than likely drew on Marshall's views on the subject as given in his evidence to the Royal Commission on Local Government Finance, while Chapman's 1913 article on taxation principles was in line with Marshall's utility theory in the *Principles* in so far as this went. Last, but by no means least, Marshallian flourishes are very clear in the three volumes of Brassey's *Work and Wages* which Chapman prepared, while the spirit of that undertaking was very much within Marshall's research programme. In short, without implying anything about Chapman's considerable originality, his association with Marshall as student and junior colleague is clearly imprinted on the pages of his later published work.

6 John Harold Clapham (1873–1946)

A Marshallian Cambridge economic historian?

John Clapham, the very important early Cambridge economic historian dedicated the first volume of his *An Economic History of Modern Britain*, published in 1926 by Cambridge University Press, to 'the memory' of Alfred Marshall and William Cunningham. The rationale for this double dedication – not repeated, incidentally in later editions – was explained in the final paragraph of its preface:

> I have ventured, with the consent of those entitled to give it, to dedicate this volume to the memory of two Cambridge economists of very different temper and outlook. One of them told me, twenty-five years ago, that it was my business to write something of the sort. The other first taught me economic history.
>
> (Clapham 1926, p. xi)

The sequence of the reasons for the dedication follows the order of names in the actual dedication, but more than a quarter of a century had passed from when Marshall first wished Clapham to become a Cambridge economic historian working on the modern era. Marshall indicated this in letters to Lord Acton (13 November 1897, 19 November 1897, in Whitaker 1996, II pp. 206–207, 212) where Marshall suggested that:

> Clapham has more analytical faculty than any thorough historian whom I have ever taught; his future work is I think still uncertain; a little force would I think turn him this way or that. If you could turn him towards XVIII and XIX century economic history, economists would ever be grateful to you & I am sure you would have no cause to regret.

Marshall added, Clapham 'is looking over the papers done by my "general" class; & I see much of him. I think he is a splendid fellow….' (Marshall to Acton, 13 November 1897, in Whitaker 1996, II p. 206). Two years earlier, Marshall wrote Oscar Browning (21 November 1895, in Whitaker 1996, II p. 138) that Clapham was the best 'historical man' he had ever taught in Cambridge.

Much of this, and more, is indicated in Phyllis Deane's splendid entry on Clapham in *The New Palgrave* (Deane 1987, I pp. 427–428). She there also concisely stated:

> What Clapham had learned from Marshall was that economics is the study of mutually interacting quantities and that it was the function of the economic historian to put the key quantitative questions to the historical record – for example, how large? how long? how often? how representative? – when spelling out the chains of cause and effect linking economic events. He [Clapham] made it his business to demolish, or qualify, facile generalizations that did not stand up to the available statistical evidence …

The Clapham–Marshall relationship was therefore not straightforward. Clapham, for example, criticised the highly theoretical nature of the 'new' (1903) Economics and Political Tripos when this was under public discussion at Cambridge, even if, as Phyllis Deane (1987, p. 427) suspects, Marshall had probably been instrumental in gaining his appointment as Professor of Economics at Leeds in 1902.

Marshall did not live to see the publication of Clapham's first volume of his monumental modern British economic history. However, he would have received Clapham's comparative study of the economic development of France and Germany (1815–1914) on its publication in 1921. This book, together with Clapham's 1897 monograph, *The Causes of the War of 1797* and his 1907 study of *The Woollen and Worsted Industries* were present in the Marshall Library (Marshall Library of Economics 1927, p. 16), as indeed were two copies of the first volume of *An Economic History of Modern Britain*. Marshall's admiration and praise of Clapham's ability are also clearly indicated in other parts of his correspondence. Moreover, Clapham's work was cited in Marshall's *Industry and Trade* (1919, pp. 62n., 71n., 232n., 707n.) and in the *Principles* from the fifth edition for a comment on railways (Guillebaud 1961, I p. 747n., II p. 732). Clapham cited *Industry and Trade* on two occasions in his comparative study of French and German economic development in the nineteenth century (Clapham 1921, 1951, pp. 310n. 1, 393n. 1). An investigation of the Marshall–Clapham association is therefore of considerable interest, with special reference to Clapham's Marshallian credentials.

These credentials are examined as follows. Section I presents a biographical sketch of Clapham with special reference to his association with Marshall at Cambridge. Sections II investigates the Marshallian credentials of some important economic history pieces by Clapham, while Section III reviews the implications of Clapham's famous paper 'Of Empty Economic Boxes' on this score. The final section presents some conclusions.

I

John Harold Clapham was born on 13 September 1873 at Broughton, Salford, in Lancashire. His father was John Clapham, who worked as a silversmith in

Manchester; his mother, Mary Jane Chambers, was his father's second wife. From his father, John Clapham inherited Yorkshire yeoman stock and later probably admiration for that spirit of enterprise which induced his father to set up as jeweller in Manchester, a massive break with family tradition.

Clapham's early schooling began near his home at Prestwick. At fourteen he was sent to Cambridge's Leyes School, where he was influenced by its headmaster, Dr Moulton, and especially by its senior history master, George Green. Green prepared Clapham well for university studies, by giving him the freedom to study for himself under his tutorial supervision, a form of training which enabled the young Clapham to win an Exhibition for study at King's College, Cambridge. Successful scholarship was not the only quality which marked Clapham's years at school. He was also a senior prefect, and a distinguished sportsman, performing particularly well on the cricket pitch and as a distance runner in athletics. Clapham became a prominent member of the school's debating and literary society, his skills in the last activity still visible in the several papers he produced for the school magazine (biographical details for this, and the next paragraph, from King's College, 1949).

In 1892, Clapham entered King's College. He continued to excel there both in sport and in his historical studies. He became Scholar in History in 1894, and gained first class honours in the 1895 History Tripos examinations. 'The three Cambridge teachers who most influenced Clapham's mind in these formative years were Acton, Cunningham and Alfred Marshall. He became 'equally interested in economics and history' (Trevelyan 1946, p. 23). Clapham took economics in Part II of the Moral Sciences Tripos following his successful results in the History Tripos, though earlier (1892–1893) he had taken some economics when enrolled for the History Tripos as part of a cohort of six 'History men' in that year attending Marshall's classes. During this period, Clapham distinguished himself sufficiently as a twenty-year-old undergraduate for Marshall to record on Clapham's registration card for this class, 'shows force' (cited in Groenewegen 1995a, p. 327).

Until 1902, when Clapham went to Leeds as Professor of Economics 'at the instigation of Marshall' (Trevelyan 1946, p. 23), Clapham had taught 'economic history' for the History Tripos and assisted Marshall by marking his 'general essays'. This had its problems, as Marshall complained to Foxwell (14 May 1901, in Whitaker 1996, II p. 320) because it 'raised a division' between him and his students. In addition, Clapham lacked full qualifications for this job, because his 'turn of mind has always been dominantly historical'. Perhaps this is why Marshall was eager to send Clapham to Leeds in 1902, although he enthusiastically welcomed Clapham back to Cambridge in 1908. From then on, Clapham's main role at Cambridge was teaching modern economic history for the History Tripos, for which, Marshall claimed, he was almost uniquely qualified (Marshall to Clerk of Girdlers Company, 2 June 1909, in Whitaker 1996, III p. 226). In between these years, while Clapham was at Leeds, he had continued to assist Marshall in various ways.

Two forms of this assistance may be specifically noted. In 1903, Clapham informed Marshall he would have greatly liked to support as a signatory the Free

Trade Manifesto initiated by Edgeworth but actively encouraged by Marshall (Groenewegen 1995a, p. 382). Second, Clapham was a signatory to the Memoir in support of the Economics and Political Science Tripos which Marshall had circulated to members of the Cambridge University Senate in May 1903, despite his criticism of its 'excessive' theoretical nature mentioned previously (Groenewegen 1995a, p. 546). When Clapham returned to King's College in 1908, his teaching responsibilities included a set of lectures on modern economic history to first year History Tripos students, a course he continued to teach until 1935.

While at Leeds, Clapham in 1907 published his first major economic history study, *The Woollen and Worsted Industries.* At Leeds he also married Margaret Green, a marriage which lasted a lifetime and which resulted in the birth of their four children, one son and three daughters. In 1921, Clapham published his comparative study of *The Economic Development of France and Germany, 1815–1914.* This was followed by his *magnum opus* in three volumes, *An Economic History of Modern Britain.* The first of these volumes, *The Early Railway Age 1820–1850*, was published in 1926. In 1932, Volume II (*Free Trade and Steel, 1850–86*) followed, and the work was completed in 1938 with the third volume, *Machines and National Product 1887–1914.* Clapham's final book, published posthumously, was *A History of the Bank of England (1694–1914)*, commissioned from him by the Directors of the Bank itself, a major sign of his distinguished reputation as British economic historian from the 1920s and 1930s.

During the First World War, Clapham worked at the Board of Trade, a war service which gained him the CBE. In 1928, he became the first Professor of Economic History at Cambridge. In 1933, he was appointed Vice-Provost at King's College, a position from which he only retired after a decade's service. Students acknowledged him as an excellent supervisor and teacher, and his lectures attracted substantial crowds. Further honours followed. In 1940, Clapham was elected as President of the British Academy; in 1943 he was knighted. During the Second World War, Clapham was very active as Chairman of the Society for the Protection of Science and Learning and, at the end of the war in 1945 he became Chairman of the Committee of the International Congress of History Sciences, a position he held until his sudden death, aged seventy-two, on 29 March 1946.

His personal association with Marshall can now be further elaborated, largely by way of Marshall's correspondence, including the few letters he exchanged with Clapham which have been preserved. A letter from Alfred Marshall, in 1912, mentioned a conversation he had with Clapham on university reform and discussed German doctorates in that context (Whitaker 1996, III pp. 294–295). A letter from Clapham (12 October 1912, Whitaker 1996, III p. 299) accompanied a presentation copy for Marshall of his book on Abbé Sieyès, even if it was not a work on economic history. (As implied earlier, it therefore did not make it to the Marshall Library and is excluded from its 1927 Catalogue). A third letter from Marshall to Clapham (4 November 1912, Whitaker 1996, III pp. 301–302) further mentioned university reform and noted Marshall's inability to attend a meeting thereon. It also mentioned Marshall's firm belief that economics was a subject unsuitable for teaching at schools, and that he did not believe that it should be studied at Cambridge by very large numbers.

As shown earlier, some of Marshall's correspondence with others mentioned Clapham, generally in a very favourable light. A further example of this is in a letter to John Neville Keynes (13 December 1908, in Whitaker 1996, III pp. 214–215) in the context of Marshall's support for Pigou as his successor. This letter also indicated that if a second chair in economics was created, Marshall would support Clapham for the position and not Foxwell. He added, that '[e]ven if Foxwell were still in his prime, I should hesitate to put him on the same intellectual level with Clapham'. There is therefore little doubt about Marshall's enormous admiration for Clapham.

The manner in which some of Clapham's work from the 1920s and after reciprocated that admiration, can now be looked at. One item of mature criticism on Clapham's part may be noted in this context. In 1936 Clapham published a note on 'Marshall and Dutch Shipbuilding' (Clapham 1936, pp. 212–213). This indicated that the material thereon in *Industry and Trade* (Marshall 1919, Appendix B, §3, pp. 694–695) had:

> conflated two chapters in the *Considerations* [i.e. *Considerations on the East-India Trade*, chapters XI and XII which, according to Marshall attributed the division of labour to Dutch shipbuilders]. Such an inference was clearly unwarranted [from the text], only one chapter of which, and that not the one apparently dominant in Marshall's mind, refers explicitly to the Dutch.
>
> (Clapham 1936, p. 213)

It hence greatly overstated the degree of Dutch supremacy in industrial specialisation at the end of the seventeenth century. Clapham was therefore clearly a *critical* Marshallian, something further demonstrated in Section III below.

II

It is appropriate to start an assessment of Clapham's Marshallian proclivities with an examination of some of his early work on economic history. This was, after all, his major research area and the field which Marshall himself had encouraged his very talented pupil to pursue. Three pieces of Clapham's writings have been selected for this purpose. The first is his comparative study of French and German economic development (Clapham 1921, 1936) which, as indicated already, was cited twice in Marshall's *Industry and Trade*. Second, the first volume of Clapham's *Economic History of Modern Britain* (Clapham 1926) is assessed in this way. As a volume dedicated to 'the memory of Alfred Marshall (and William Cunningham) it is particularly appropriate for this purpose. As third piece, Clapham's entry on 'Economic History as a Discipline' for the

Encyclopaedia of Social Sciences (Clapham 1931, V, pp. 327–330) seems a suitable item, given Marshall's stress on the importance of the subject as a branch of economic study to which Clapham should devote his skills as historian. Each of these is examined in turn in this section for evidence, if any, of their Marshallian credentials.

Clapham's second book on economic history was a comparative analysis of the economic development of France and Germany from 1815 to 1914. In alternate chapters, it examines agricultural conditions in the two countries before the railway age (that is the middle of the nineteenth century), then their respective industrial conditions for 1815–1848, then (in single chapters), the communication and commerce systems in the two countries, their money and banking arrangements, and then the making of their first railway and telegraph networks between 1830 and 1869. The next six chapters repeat this cycle of alternate examinations of agriculture and industry for the two countries from 1848 to 1914, followed by two single chapters on communication developments, and their money and banking systems for these years. A short epilogue reviews the rise in living standards ('wealth') of the common man for the century of economic development in Western Europe covered by the book.

Apart from the two Marshall citations already mentioned, the book contains only a few Marshallian flourishes. The following examples can be given. The surveys of development in France and Germany stressed changes in productive organisation over the century (Clapham 1921, 1936, pp. 53, 398–401), as Marshall had done in his *Industry and Trade*. The book also in particular noted cooperative aspects of European agriculture as an important factor in its development (Clapham 1921, 1936, pp. 185–189, 221–227), a stress which would have pleased Marshall as an active cooperationist. Moreover, it dwelled on significant growth in the scale of manufacturing production, with special reference to the role of cartels in Germany in fostering the concentration of industry (Clapham 1921, 1936, pp. 309–310), again a view strikingly endorsed by Marshall. Its concluding section, as indicated in the previous paragraph, emphasised the significant impact of development 'on the living standards of the common man' (Clapham 1921, 1936, p. 402) undoubtedly another very Marshallian aspect of its general thrust, given his emphasis on rising living standards for all as a major consequence of economic progress.

On the methodological side, Clapham showed extreme caution in drawing anything resembling very precise conclusions, largely because of a lack of precision in the necessary statistical evidence. To give an example, 'statistical discussions about the rise or fall in the size of average holdings [in French agriculture] are [said to be] full of pitfalls' (Clapham 1921, 1936, p. 165) while elsewhere Clapham claimed that 'statistics will not measure exactly the growth of the retail stores', including their cooperative segments especially significant in parts of Germany (Clapham 1921, 1936, p. 226). Clapham (1921, 1936, p. 186) also showed himself very conscious of the difficulties inherent in trying to formulate very precise definitions. On another note, Clapham's (1921, 1936, p. 134) appreciative references to Brassey's liberal and advanced labour practices based on the adage that in construction work 'a man who would work well, must eat largely' may also have been Marshall inspired given Marshall's great admiration for Brassey's attitudes to labour (see Groenewegen 1995a, p. 178). However, Clapham's preference for using the word 'entrepreneur' rather than 'undertaker' (e.g. Clapham 1921, 1936, pp. 86, 288) was somewhat un-Marshallian. Unfortunately, Marshall left no comments on this modern economic history work even though Clapham had almost certainly presented him with a presentation copy on its first publication in 1921.

Despite its dedication to Marshall, there is little explicitly Marshallian in the first volume of Clapham's *Economic History of Great Britain* (*The Early Railway Age 1820–1850*) even if it could be considered as another instalment of the sound economic history work Marshall had hoped for, if not demanded, from Clapham during the 1890s. The book itself is divided into two parts: a general introduction of eight chapters providing an overview of the state of Great Britain on the eve of the railway age in which the first chapter acted as an introduction to the introduction. Subsequent chapters discuss population (Chapter 2), communications by road and canal (Chapter 3), agrarian and industrial organisation (Chapters 4 and 5), organisation of commerce (Chapter 6), the financial sector (money, banking and insurance) and special commercial organisations (Chapter 7) to conclude with an overview of economic activity by the state (Chapter 8).

Book II, *The Early Railway Age*, introduced the topic announced by the title of this first volume. Railways and railway policy were therefore appropriately the topic of Chapter 9; Chapter 10 introduced the technical requirements for early railway construction: that is, iron, coal, steam and engineering; Chapter 11 discussed the impact on agriculture; Chapter 12 overseas trade and commercial policy; Chapter 13 examined changes in money, banking and other financial markets; while the final Chapter 14 reviewed life and labour in industrial Britain at considerable length.

Alfred Marshall (and his economics), unlike two other Marshalls – John Marshall and William Marshall – was not mentioned in Clapham's book. Neither are there real and easy to spot Marshallian flourishes present in the book's contents. Economic theory also rarely obtrudes in the book and, when it does, most frequently mentions that from the economists of the 1820s (e.g. Clapham 1926, pp. 334–335). There are occasional references to monopoly price theory (Clapham 1926, p. 416), to the concentration of the cotton industry (Clapham 1926, pp. 442–443), to the impact of railway demand on demand in the home market (Clapham 1926, p. 427) as well as general references to 'supply and demand' in the context of exploring the life and living standards of the labourer over the period (e.g. Clapham 1926, pp. 549–550, 599).

An emphasis on the facts, and on the frequent difficulty of finding adequate statistics are methodological issues preserved in this work by Clapham as it earlier was in his study of French and German economic development. Finally, and as also implied in the previous section, Clapham, acting very unMarshallian in this respect, followed Volume I of his British economic history with the projected Volumes II and III within a decade. He thereby showed himself far more disciplined a writer than his acknowledged general source of inspiration for the task, Alfred Marshall. However, no matter with how much pleasure Marshall would have greeted this book on publication, a matter prevented by his death in 1924, there is little perceptible influence of Marshall's work visible in that of his 'historical' pupil.

The same can very much be said with respect to Clapham's entry on 'Economic History' for the 1930s *International Encyclopaedia of the Social Sciences.* At the start of his article, Clapham announced that economic history 'is a branch of general institutional history' or 'a study of the economic aspects of the social institutions of the past'. Economic history needs to rely heavily on quantitative analysis, that is, statistics, and this is its major distinguishing feature, methodologically speaking, from history in general. Absence of appropriate statistical material makes economic history often unachievable, even the most simple quantitative questions in economic history can frequently not be answered because of lack of statistical data (Clapham 1931, 1948, Vol. V, p. 327). Where records are relatively abundant (as in the Domesday Book, to take Clapham's example, 1931, 1948, p. 328), quantitative historical method works well. Statistical abudance is particularly the case for 'modern' economic history, which increasingly can rely on official statistics including decennial census data. However, historical analysis must always ask, 'how representative' are the data at hand and hence, how useful are they for settling specific historical questions. It cannot operate satisfactorily in the absence of satisfactory statistical data.

Clapham's entry took issue in particular with the economists of the German Historical School who tended to build substantial stadial schemes out of very weak statistical raw material. This made him dismissive of those 'parts of economic theory [which] purport to be generalizations from history' (Clapham 1931, 1948, pp. 328–329).

Hence the relationship of economic history to social history is much closer for Clapham than that with economic theory. Representativeness remains a key issue, but for the historian and the economist these problems increase as individual disciplines specialise more and more to the neglect of studying related disciplines (Clapham 1931, 1948, p. 330). However, and this is Clapham's concluding observation in his entry, 'it is at the overlapping margins of disciplines that the most important discoveries are often made' (Clapham 1931, 1948, p. 331). The substantial reference list which follows the entry includes no work by Alfred Marshall nor does there appear to be any room for Marshall's views on the nature and necessity of economic history in Clapham's authoritative overview of the subject for a major international reference work in the social sciences.

Clapham's survey did draw attention to a potential deficiency in economic theory in either resting on over-generalisations from the all too often unrepresentative facts, or in ignoring the facts altogether and implicitly presenting their categories as figments of their imagination totally unrelated to the actual situation in which they exist in the world. This was a situation in contemporary economic theory which Clapham himself had publicly diagnosed as early as 1922, when he wrote his famous complaint of that theory by noting that this all too frequently could only present 'empty economic boxes' (Clapham 1922a, 1953). As indicated in the introduction, Clapham's 1922 criticism is sufficiently important in the context of this chapter, to be discussed in its next section.

III

Clapham's short piece 'Of Empty Economic Boxes' targeted several concepts in economic theory which seemed to have no easily recognisable factual counterparts in the real world of industry. The concepts on which it concentrated were the laws of returns – increasing, constant and diminishing returns – their association with the theory of monopoly and, at a further remove, the inspiration which these concepts gave to identifying welfare efficient rules for the conduct of taxation policy. The dominant school at which this criticism was directed was that of Cambridge (England), singling out its two eminent leaders, Alfred Marshall (still alive but in retirement) and Pigou (Marshall's successor to the Chair of Economics since 1908). More specifically, Clapham's criticism is directed at their two major books, respectively the *Principles of Economics* and *The Economics of Welfare.* The second of these first appeared in 1920 as a replacement of Pigou's 1913 *Wealth and Welfare.* Clapham also mentioned Marshall's other great book, *Industry and Trade*, but its almost 900 pages are said to have only two

> references to Constant Returns – one in a footnote – and a handful of references to Diminishing and Increasing Returns *im allgemeinen* [but] not ... in close relation to the facts of those British, French, German and American industries of which the great book has taught him so much.
>
> (Clapham 1922a, 1953, p. 120)

Subsequently, Clapham (1922a, 1953, p. 127n. 4) mentioned this 'great book' once in a footnote dealing with the desirability of Chancellors of the Exchequer to tax only commodities produced under diminishing returns and not those produced under conditions of increasing returns.

Marshall's more theoretical *Principles of Economics* (the page references are all to the definitive 1920 eighth edition) escaped Clapham's criticism less easily. That criticism, as the title of the piece proclaimed, was to investigate whether the theoretical boxes labelled constant, increasing and diminishing returns were easily identified (filled) with specific industries after deciding the appropriate concept of industry to use for this purpose. Marshall's, and Pigou's views on the nature of the laws of returns and, more specifically, the examples they used in the context of explaining these laws, were therefore carefully scrutinised by Clapham. This was done by way of examining a hat factory, and its study by a member of the dominant school of economics as to whether it is part of an industry operating under increasing, or constant, or diminishing returns and the ease by which such an examination can be conducted. Clapham indicated that Pigou's *Economics of Welfare* is no real help in this task. It failed to give illustrations of actual industries in its discussion of the matter. The definition offered by Pigou in terms of the increment of product associated with an additional unit of resources states nothing about the nature of this product (such as, for example, its divisibility), or the measurement of a unit of resources when, as is usually the case, more than one resource is employed in production. Nor, Clapham (1922a, 1953, p. 120) notes, is it easy to clearly define industry in this context in terms of a specific example of output produced by the industry.

Marshall's *Principles of Economics* dealt more fully with these aspects but, Clapham emphasised, not in a very rigorous or satisfactory manner. This can be illustrated in terms of Clapham's example of hats, or by using commodities (outputs) selected by Marshall in his book such as coal, wool, wheat, timber and rubber or, in connection with the various raw materials used in the production of hats, 'coal, rabbits' fur, shellac, leather for the inside band and pulp for the box' (Clapham 1922a, 1953, p. 121).

Of this list of inputs, coal seems relatively easy to classify in terms of laws of returns. However, as Marshall (1920, pp. 167–168) had warned, to claim that coal operated invariably under diminishing returns was 'misleading'. Clapham debated this issue at some length. For example, were the improvements made to Yorkshire coal mining before the start of the First World War designed to bring increasing returns or 'merely to keeping constant the yield of coal "per unit of resources"' (Clapham 1922a, 1953, p. 121)? But if, to risk a generalisation, British coal is produced under diminishing returns, did this also apply to coal produced in Silesia, or in South Africa, or in parts of the United States? This is a matter of some importance 'when the world is fast becoming a single market for coal' (Clapham 1922a, 1953, p. 121). Rabbit fur, in many ways, is an equally difficult case, not to mention the fact that it is a complex joint product as well. The organisation of rabbit fur production (as in Hampshire, Belgium and the Australian outback) is 'elusive', especially with respect to its 'internal and external economies' (Clapham 1922a, 1953, p. 122). Shellac production probably operates under conditions of diminishing returns but, Clapham asked, is there such a thing as 'cultured shellac' where the conditions of production may be assumed to be quite different? Whether the same applies to wood pulp, is more difficult to say in Clapham's (1922a, 1953, p. 123) view. Hence, discovering under what conditions of returns in production the hat industry operates, entails a very complex calculation. In short, the economist will have to 'leave the [hat] factory with no formed opinion about the proper economic box for hats' (Clapham 1922a, 1953, p. 123).

Clapham then conceded that if it was suggested that hat production was not a typical form of industry, other, more suitable examples in such a classification, were easily found. He admitted that some industries – his example is the car industry – operate under increasing returns, but whether this proposition applied equally to textile machine production or locomotive manufacturing would, in his view, be more difficult to decide. The present extensive availability of raw materials in the world, Clapham indicated, made diminishing returns unlikely for such 'mechanical industries' especially since 'a strict interpretation of diminishing returns, as we know [from Marshall's *Principles*] excludes the mineral stocks'. He then invited his reader to consider 'wool' or, more specifically 'combed wool "tops"' (Clapham 1922a, 1953, p. 124). In that context, it needs to be recalled that fifteen years earlier, in 1907, Clapham had published a monograph on the British woollen and worsted industry, so that it was an industry with segments of which he was quite familiar.

Woollen tops, Clapham indicated, came largely from Australia, with occasional supplies from New Zealand or Argentina. That is, therefore, it was all 'new country' wool, provided that is, if Australia could still be correctly classed as a 'new' wool producing country. As Marshall indicated, diminishing returns 'has almost exclusive sway in an old country' (Marshall 1920, p. 319, cited in Clapham 1922a, 1953, p. 124). The Australian districts in which fine merino wool is grown are likely to operate under diminishing returns, since increased demand for this commodity at the present time induced little supply response according to Clapham. On the basis of what Marshall wrote long ago about the production of blankets, it seemed likely, Clapham suggested, that 'Botany wool is in fact produced today under conditions of slightly diminishing returns [and] conceivable that 64s Botany tops are being turned out very near … constant returns, *but we do not know*' (Clapham 1922a, 1953, p. 125, my italics in the quotation). In this context, Clapham also warned that constant returns, being always a 'mathematical point', must necessarily fall into the category of an 'empty box' (Clapham 1922a, 1953, p. 125).

A further qualification is in order, Clapham suggested. In the context of his blankets example, Marshall had argued that increasing returns resulted from improved organisation and not from technical innovations. An increase in the aggregate volume of production is all that is required (Marshall 1920, pp. 318–319; Clapham 1922a, 1953, p. 125). Further ambiguities in the use of these concepts were suggested by Clapham. Addressing particular returns in the coal industry raises difficulties from the measurement of 'units of inventiveness' and units of 'normal managerial' capability, which are required in this context. If this is regarded as pedantic nit-picking, or raising practical difficulties in fixing standards clearly irrelevant to the requirements of theory, Clapham posited various counter-responses to this charge. First, it makes translating theory into facts impossible; second, it depends on the values underlying such translations; and, third, it relies on a person's view about the consequences of economic analysis 'outrunning [its] verification' (Clapham 1922a, 1953, pp. 126–127). Unless the boxes can be filled, they remain empty. There are other grave dangers in Clapham's view in establishing 'hypothetical conclusions' on matters of the fiscal policy of determining taxes and bounties, and hence on the application of 'a practical science such as Economics' (Clapham 1922a, 1953, p. 127).

At this point, Clapham invoked the frequent Marshallian assumption that many economic propositions for their validity require the condition, '*other things being equal*' (Clapham 1922a, 1953, p. 127, Clapham's italics). This conditional clause applies as well when imposition of a tax or bounty is proposed with respect to diminishing and increasing returns industries. Rules developed under these conditions are therefore a very 'unsafe guide' for actual tax and bounty policy.

By way of conclusion, Clapham suggested the following. First, in broad comparisons of costs over centuries, rough estimates can be given on the increasing returns derived from invention and organisation. This is the point of his Christopher Wren comparative example over two and half centuries (Clapham 1922a, 1953, p. 128). Second, for some raw materials, broad generalisations may be made as to whether they are produced under conditions of diminishing returns while the same applies to increasing returns if its impact is confined to that arising from improved organisation and not from invention (a hard yardstick to apply in actual situations, Clapham warned). Furthermore, the reality of increasing returns need not be denied: Clapham's criticism concerned the possibility of actually measuring increasing returns under these simplified conditions, unless only broad historical comparisons are intended (Clapham 1922a, 1953, pp. 129–130).

Clapham's 'negative' piece on the laws of returns is therefore very critical of some aspects of Marshall's theory, and even more of Pigou's exposition of these issues (see especially Clapham 1922a, 1953, p. 122). As the good economic historian he had fully become, Clapham tended to seek verification of theoretical propositions from their proximity to the facts. If such propositions had no such resemblance to reality, then they needed to be seen as nothing but *empty economic boxes*, irrelevant to, and inappropriate for, serious economic analysis. Diminishing returns and increasing returns are clearly such empty economic boxes from his examination of the literature. If they were to be 'filled', immense care had to be taken in selecting the type of investigation for which they are to be used. Building practical fiscal policy recommendations in the assignment of taxes and bounties on their foundations seemed highly dubious practice to Clapham.

Clapham's paper on empty economic boxes started a wider debate than he had perhaps intended, particularly when it moved into other areas of economic theory such as the precise nature of the competitive firm (Winch 1969, 1972, pp. 48–49; Seligman 1963, pp. 625–627, esp. p. 626). Whether this is what Clapham wanted is difficult to say. His response to the initial stages of the debate in the pages of the *Economic Journal* does not suggest this. Clapham's rejoinder, published three months later (1922b, pp. 560–563) was essentially addressed to Pigou and showed him unrepentant about the value of his original remarks and of his ability to assess whether the 'boxes' were in fact empty or capable of being filled in the present. Moreover, the fact that he launched this criticism in the first place clearly demonstrated that he was a Marshallian who felt himself completely free to criticise 'the master' when this seemed necessary and desirable.

IV

In his long association with Marshall and his work, Clapham revealed himself as a critical Marshallian. He was an admirer of Marshall and his many contributions but considered him as an economist, nevertheless, whose opinions, if untrue, would have to be clearly and assuredly challenged. This makes the Marshall–Clapham relationship far from straightforward, as Phyllis Deane observed in her 1987 *New Palgrave* entry on Clapham (as cited in the introduction of this chapter). For a start, it was not a master–pupil relationship in any lasting sense. Clapham was indebted to Marshall as a teacher of, and adviser on economics, and Clapham probably respected Marshall's views on many other subjects as well. However, if Clapham thought Marshall was wrong, he never hid that view under a bushel. Such differences of opinion could be on small points – such as Clapham's correction of a minor factual matter in an Appendix of *Industry and Trade*, or a major critique as that Clapham made of the manner in which the Cambridge economists used the laws of returns in their theorising in his justly famous 'empty economic boxes' article of 1922. Furthermore, Clapham's major economic history research published in the 1920s and 1930s undoubtedly made him realise how poor an economic historian Marshall actually was even if he knew a great deal that was useful to the economic historian. This both explains the dedication to Marshall (after Acton and Cunningham) in the original first volume of his British *Economic History* and its removal for the later volumes and editions.

There is little clear indebtedness to Marshall visible in Clapham's economic history work. The encouragement Marshall had given to turn Clapham into an economic historian was initially acknowledged, and may in fact have been crucial to steer Clapham in that direction. Much method and theory in general was probably imbibed from Marshall and his *Principles* during the second half of the 1890s, the period when Marshall was at his intellectual peak as teacher. The importance of facts and of realistic theory was probably one of the major views Clapham absorbed from Marshall during that period of teaching. In any case, it was certainly greatly reinforced by Clapham's formal study of economics with Marshall and his later contacts with him. It should not be forgotten that historian Trevelyan in his 1946 obituary stated clearly that Marshall, together with Acton and Cunningham, constituted the major influences on the young historian, and it may be suggested that in this context the last named is not necessarily the least. How much more practical learning experience came through Clapham's acknowledged assistance to Marshall during the construction of *Industry and Trade* will never be known with precision.

There was also other personal assistance to Clapham on Marshall's part. Marshall had probably done a lot to get Clapham appointed to the chair at Leeds and earlier had given him valuable teaching experience in general classes at Cambridge as considerable personal cost to himself (as he told J.N. Keynes in the letter quoted above in Section I). Moreover, significant book lending from the substantial Balliol Croft Library, perhaps especially of German economic texts, probably also took place. Of social contact there was probably little, and the surviving correspondence is surprisingly small. Two episodes may be mentioned in this context. One is the reference to Marshall's intention to finance the keep of 'half a Belgian' refugee during the First World War, a promise which involved the Claphams (in Groenewegen 1995a, p. 641); the other, implying considerable personal contact, took place later during the war when Clapham was assisting Marshall in completing his *Industry and Trade.* However, it seems fair to say on this score that Clapham never featured in Marshall's life at this stage in the manner of the young Maynard Keynes (for a discussion of this, see Groenewegen 1995b, esp. pp. 132–133); a different opinion on Marshall's association with Clapham is presented by Kadish 1994, esp. pp. 225–229).

The major point in this association was that Clapham did what Marshall had desired of him during the late 1890s. He became Cambridge's major economic historian during the 1920s and 1930s, producing work on 'modern' economic history covering the major European industrial nations – Great Britain, France and Germany – for much of the nineteenth century. By the time these contributions appeared, Marshall was no longer capable of appreciating their significance for establishing economic history studies at Cambridge on a sound footing. Had Marshall lived to the end of the 1920s he may have patted himself on the back for the foresight in selecting Clapham as the economic historian for Cambridge. For Marshall, Clapham was the ideal teacher of this important segment for the new Economics Tripos syllabus he had created at their Alma Mater in 1903. In this sense, and irrespective of Clapham's well targeted criticisms of Marshall, Clapham played a very important role in the Marshallian enterprise of Cambridge University economics education in the twentieth century, and from this perspective alone has to be seen as an important, even if 'minor', Marshallian.

7 David Hutchinson MacGregor (1877–1953)

A 'favourite' student of Marshall and an innovative Marshallian industry economist

MacGregor, after gaining an honours degree in philosophy at the University of Edinburgh, went to Cambridge to study economics under Marshall, gaining a first class honours result in the Moral Sciences Tripos in 1901. At this time, he became one of Marshall's favourite students, perhaps because he already by then showed a willingness and aptitude to follow Marshall's method of carefully blending theory with the facts, and maintaining a firm hold on realism in his work. In 1905, he joined the small teaching staff of the new Economics Tripos, teaching 'English and American Trade from 1800' in 1905; and 'Economic Development of England from 1800', in 1906. Both of these courses combined economic history with an account of theories of progress and development. MacGregor was a Tripos examiner in 1907 and 1908. He left Cambridge in 1908, the year of Marshall's retirement, to succeed Clapham as professor of economics and economic history at Leeds. In 1919, MacGregor went to Manchester University as professor of economics; in 1922 he was appointed Drummond Professor of Economics at Oxford, the academic position he held for the remainder of his life, that is, until his retirement in 1945. He died in an accident in 1953.

MacGregor concentrated his economic research on industry economics, especially industrial combinations. He also wrote on employment policy and on taxation. A monograph, *Industrial Combination*, based on his 1904 Fellowship dissertation, appeared in 1906, and was reprinted in 1938 (and again in 1966). In 1911, MacGregor published *The Evolution of Industry*, a general study of industrial growth and development. A research monograph on *International Cartels* by MacGregor appeared in 1927 following a study on the subject he had conducted for the League of Nations. In 1934, MacGregor published a collection of essays, entitled *Enterprise, Purpose and Profit*, an effective summary of much of his work on industrial organisation. MacGregor's last book, *Economic Thought and Policy*, appeared 1949. On the centenary of Marshall's birth in 1942, MacGregor wrote a perceptive assessment of Marshall's economics, 'Marshall and his Book', which was published in *Economica.* Other journal articles by MacGregor appeared from 1907 to 1943: the vast majority (nineteen) in the *Economic Journal*, one in the *Journal of Political Economy*, one in the *Oxford Institute of Statistics Bulletin* and two further papers (that is, in addition to the Marshall centenary assessment) in *Economica.* Some of these papers dealt with competition; that in all competition, there was an element of monopoly' (introduction to 1938 reprint of *Industrial Combination*, reprinted without page numbers in MacGregor 1906, 1966). The preface of the 1906 edition thanks Marshall, Foxwell and Sanger for their constructive criticism; its final sentence pays his 'tribute of thanks to Professor Marshall, to whom I owe my guidance in economic study, and whatever may be of value in my work (MacGregor 1906, 1966, p. vi).

MacGregor's book to a large extent explores these aspects of competition, with special reference to the monopolistic elements which intrude in competition through combinations, amalgamations, cartelisation and other forms of business organisation. The monograph can therefore be said to constitute a specific contribution to an important aspect of Marshall's economic research agenda in industrial economics.

Not surprisingly, this first book by MacGregor has strong Marshallian characteristics in its general style and approach. First of all, its eight diagrams (MacGregor 1906, 1966, pp. 83–85, 104–105) are firmly placed in footnotes, rather than in the text. The same is the case with its one example of mathematical equations, drawing on those from Cournot's argument (1838, Section 44; MacGregor 1906, 1966, pp. 196–197n. 2). Second, MacGregor makes considerable use of some of Marshall's specific analytical apparatus. These particularly include the representative firm (MacGregor 1906, 1966, pp. 3n. 1, 168); consumer surplus analysis (MacGregor 1906, 1966, pp. 213–214) with the appropriate reservations about its inadequate statistical basis; and, third, the 'particular expenses curve' (MacGregor 1906, 1966, p. 85n. 1). Much use is also made by MacGregor of other Marshallian economic tools including internal and external economies as well as increasing returns and falling supply price. Marshall is one of the major authorities used, as indicated by the number of citations from his work. These include the *Principles of Economics* in its fourth (1898) edition; the *Elements of the Economics of Industry* in an early, unspecified edition; as well as Marshall's 1890 Presidential Address to Section F of the British Association, 'Some Aspects of Competition', and Marshall's 1897 *Quarterly Journal of Economics* article, 'The Old Generation of Economists and the New'.

Before looking at these citations in more detail, an outline of the structure of MacGregor's book can be given. It is divided into three parts, respectively entitled 'The Factors of Competing Strength', 'Trusts and Cartels, and their Relation to Trade Unions', and 'National Aspects'. The four chapters of Part I deal with 'productive efficiency', 'risk', 'bargaining strength' and 'resource', with an appendix on 'fair price'. There are three chapters in Part II: 'general causes', 'comparative causes and structures', and 'industrial combination and labour combination'. The final part contains only two chapters: 'national effects of combination' and 'public policy and industrial combination'. There is an introduction called combination as 'representative method'. Marshall citations occur in all three parts.

MacGregor's (1906, 1966) citations from Marshall's work can now be looked at in more detail. The first citations are used by MacGregor (1906, 1966, p. 3) to summarise Marshall's depiction of the representative firm. Its

> structure is typical of a period of economic development ..., has access to all the normal economies of that period, and is of the size which is suited to their most efficient use. It has had a 'fairly long life, and fair success', is 'managed with normal ability', while its size takes account of 'the class of goods produced, the conditions of marketing them, and the economic environment generally'.
>
> (Quotes within the quote are directly taken from Marshall's *Principles*, fourth edition, 1898, p. 397)

As MacGregor (1906, 1966, p. 16) explains, the notion of 'representative' applied to 'combinations' plays a major role in his analysis. Another broad reference to Marshall (1898, Book IV Chapter X, section 2) is to his views on the importance of internal economies to the localisation of industry (MacGregor 1906, 1966, p. 22n. 1). On the next page (MacGregor 1906, 1966, p. 23) Marshall is praised for his exposition of internal economies without giving a reference to a specific part of his *Principles.*

MacGregor (1906, 1966, pp. 25–26) mentions Marshall's concise presentation of the

> proposition that, where marketing is easy, the production is routine, and in such productions a business of moderate size realises all the economies which are due to localisation and concentration, but where increasing return acts between wider limits, marketing is more difficult, for the goods are such as depend on individual tastes and fancies.

The source is here undoubtedly the *Principles* but no precise reference is given by MacGregor. Another citation from the *Principles* (Marshall 1898, p. 358) is on the high capital cost associated with the application of new inventions in actual production processes. Such an investment is not open to weak and small firms, unless they can be assured that their investment will secure them an immediate prospect of profit (MacGregor 1906, 1966, p. 30 and n. 1).

MacGregor (1906, 1966, p. 31 and n. 1) next briefly cites Marshall's 'Old Generation of Economists and the New' (Marshall 1897, 1925, pp. 307–308) on the potential disadvantage of 'salaried' managers as against 'owner-managers' where 'salaried' managers who experimented 'would take all the odium of failure and only part of the reward of success'. This would induce a languishing of invention, and was seen by MacGregor as part of the analysis of combinations and efficiency, and the growth of business enterprise to secure the realisation of the best possible economies in production.

MacGregor's Part I, Chapter II on risk starts with a linking of risk with industrial organisation, and the issue of whether the risks of a 'representative firm' are static, or dynamic, or both. Not surprisingly, MacGregor (1906, 1966, pp. 46–47) considered the dynamic risks associated with change to be the most important. Determining the risk of the representative firm is the subject matter of the chapter. In this context, MacGregor (1906, 1966, pp. 51–52) drew attention to the factor of competition in assisting 'the less direct operation of Natural Selection between … firms', drawing on analysis in Marshall's *Elements of the Economics of Industry* (Marshall 1892, p. 321). Marshall's *Principles* (Marshall 1898, p. 338, but not pp. 337–338 as MacGregor wrongly indicated), are then cited on the facility, and smallish cost, of transforming a watch factory into a sewing-machine factory, provided that nobody in the new factory is put to work on a job requiring a 'higher order of intelligence than that to which he was already accustomed' (MacGregor 1906, 1966, pp. 55–56 and n. 1). Subsequently, MacGregor (1906, 1966, p. 85n. 1) mentioned Marshall's *Principles* (1898, p. 521n. 1) as the source of the 'particular expenses curve' for analysing surpluses under decreasing costs. Finally, on the last page of Part I of MacGregor (1906, 1966, p. 112), there is a reference to the fallacy of a 'fixed work fund', an expression first introduced by Marshall (1890b, p. 733).

At the start of Part II, Chapter II, MacGregor (1906, 1966, p. 138), cast doubt on the relevance of the 'method of historical evolution' for showing how forms of combinations succeed each other; a method of 'lateral comparison' is preferred, a remark which could be taken to imply a criticism of Marshall's belief in the effectiveness of examining historical change by evolutionary apparatus. Individualism is then taken as an important factor for understanding American industrial combinations given the fact that there 'the individual counts for much more … than in English economic movements' (MacGregor 1906, 1966, p. 140 and n. 1, citing Marshall's (1890a), 'Some Aspects of Competition', p. 266). This paper is mentioned again by MacGregor (1906, 1966, p. 141) on the next page, and backed by a long quotation therefrom:

> Traditions and experience are of more service and authority in an old country than in one which has not yet even taken stock of a great part of her natural resources.… In England the dominant force is the restless energy and versatile enterprise of a comparatively few very rich and able men who rejoice in that power of doing great things by great means which their wealth gives them.… They strive to dominate it [the Joint Stock system] not be dominated by it.
>
> (Marshall 1890a, pp. 266–267)

At the start of Chapter III of Part II, MacGregor (1906, 1966, p. 168) reiterates the importance of the 'representative firm' to his analysis. Later (MacGregor 1906, 1966, p. 181) approvingly quoted Marshall's *Elements of the Economics of Industry* (Marshall 1892, p. 321) for its remarks on the fact that 'business undertakers' constitute a 'class of their own', a statement MacGregor (1906, 1966, p. 52) had cited previously. At the end of his chapter on labour combinations, MacGregor (1906, 1966, p. 186) cited Marshall's *Principles* (1898, Book V Chapter XI, §2, esp. p. 512) on 'two equivalent propositions' describing employment as unique and not a simple case of demand and supply, and proclaiming the firm rather than the individual to be the efficient economic unit.

At a later stage, MacGregor (1906, 1966, p. 196) cited Marshall's *Principles* (1898, p. 469) on the competitive struggle between two rival producers where 'no free play is allowed to the normal action of economic forces, and it can [therefore] hardly be said to have a normal supply curve'. Such a situation is compared by MacGregor to Cournot's analysis of the contest between two monopolies, the only instance, as was mentioned previously, in which mathematics occurs in MacGregor's book. In the context of 'price discrimination' MacGregor (1906, 1966, pp. 213–214 and n. 1) mentions the possibility of using static consumer surplus analysis to estimate the losses suffered by consumers when prices are raised, and the gains for consumers 'who now buy at low prices elsewhere what they formerly did not buy at all', a situation more valuable to the poorer consumers. The final chapter of the book on public policy (MacGregor 1906, 1966, p. 228n. 3) contains only one reference to Marshall's *Principles.* It cites Marshall (1898, p. 303n.) on the importance of very large public investments for mitigating poor business conditions in explanation of the fact that the 1902 German industrial crisis was 'much alleviated by the demand for labour on the national railways'.

Given the close proximity of MacGregor's first published book to his undergraduate studies and subsequent close association with Marshall as a teacher for the Economics Tripos on industrial development, it is not surprising that Marshall was quite influential in its preparation. Apart from being the original inspiration for the topic of MacGregor's first research project, its actual construction was aided in two different ways by Marshall's work as suggested by the references to Marshall's work in the book. First of all, it used specific parts of Marshall's tool box for its analysis, including the representative firm, consumer surplus, and internal/external economies. Second, it drew on Marshall's writings for facts, and for selective opinions of use in bringing certain facets of the analysis to the fore. In this manner, MacGregor underscored the general, broad acknowledgement to Marshall at the end of the original 1906 preface to the book cited in the opening paragraph of this section.

III

In 1934, MacGregor published a volume of 'essays on industry', called *Enterprise, Purpose and Profits.* The last three of these had appeared first in the *Economic Journal*, Essays 5 and 6 both published in 1930, Essay 7 in 1933. Essay 5, 'Some Aspects of Rationalisation', was also MacGregor's Presidential Address to Section F of the British Association, given at Leeds in 1927. Essays 3 and 4, on 'Enterprise and the Trade Cycle', and on 'Risk of Enterprise', were, as MacGregor (1934, p. vii) put it in the preface, all that he could salvage from his revisions of his book, *Industrial Combination*, 'of which the manuscript was accidentally lost'. The 1938 reprint of this volume, first published in 1911, was examined in the previous section.

The contents of the book reflect Marshall's approach to economics. They contain no mathematics (if the formula for the general index of insolvency on pp. 91–92 is ignored). The contents are highly descriptive, and combine facts with the theory through the extensive use of statistics particularly in the last three essays. Graphs are also used occasionally, and the essays pay considerable attention to the historical background of the problems being analysed. Many of the references are to official sources and are international in range, since MacGregor drew on German, French, United States, as well as British and Commonwealth (especially New Zealand) publications. They also rely to a degree on earlier work of MacGregor himself. An example is his 1929 *Economic Journal* article on 'Joint Stock Companies and the Risk Factor', which is used (and occasionally corrected) in Essay 4 of the volume on 'Risk of Enterprise' (MacGregor 1934, p. 98n. 1).

The topics covered in the volume, dealing as they do with 'different aspects of the rationalization of industry' (MacGregor 1934, p. v) fall well within the Marshallian research programme, given their emphasis on 'organisational' features of the theory of the firm such as amalgamations, its impact on competition, and the economics of private enterprise. Although discussion of the economics of socialism was much in the air during the late 1920s and early 1930s, its problems are largely ignored by MacGregor with the exception of the first essay and a long note at the end of the fourth which, among other things, comments on the lack of need for centralised planning in order to regulate a modern free enterprise economy. The concomitant problem of competition and large-scale industry, as approached at the time in the continuing contributions to the 'cost controversy', also played no real role in this volume. MacGregor's interests are in the theory of the large firm, the product of amalgamations, and its association with both the trade cycle, and the reduction of risk. Rationalisation of industry and economic progress would be another way of describing the contents of this volume, even if the 1930s depression during which the book was largely written, made economic progress in the Marshallian sense a less visible phenomenon at the time.

Since the basic aim of this section is to assess the direct Marshall content of MacGregor's 1934 volume, its citation of Marshall's views needs to be examined with care. There are no less than ten references to works by Marshall, not only to his *Principles*, but also to *Industry and Trade* and to *Money, Credit and Commerce*. Some of MacGregor's references are critical of Marshall, including the first in this volume. In the context of industrial rationalisations, MacGregor (1934, p. 43) mentions the role of biological analogies, 'freely used by Marshall' but these cannot provide a proof or the sanctioning of industrial rationalisation. 'In economics, survival does not show fitness without further argument', and biology as the mecca of the economists has its problems in real life.

In the context of the risk of enterprise, Marshall's treatment of this subject in the *Principles* is criticised. With reference to the representative firm in this context, MacGregor (1934, p. 96) is also sceptical of Marshall's occasional view that these firms may actually have 'existed and could be indicated' in real industrial settings but, as shown below, not consistently so (Marshall 1920, p. 318). MacGregor (1934, p. 97) also criticised Marshall's view (Marshall 1890b,

p. 658; 1920, p. 621) that 'the risks of trade are on the whole diminishing rather than increasing' because contrary to his promise, 'as we shall presently see', no explanations of this generalisation were given by Marshall over the eight editions of his *Principles.* Finally, Marshall (1920, p. 622 and n.) is criticised for a misinterpretation of a statement by Leroy-Beaulieu because Marshall failed to point out the limitations imposed thereon by its author (MacGregor 1934, pp. 97–98).

MacGregor (1934, p. 66) discussed the notion of 'normal prices', depending on what is actually 'normal' in the conditions in which they occur. Marshall is not explicitly cited in this context, but it is the Marshall conception of 'normal' as applied to prices which MacGregor brings here into play. There are also references in MacGregor (1934) to both Marshall's *Industry and Trade* and his *Money, Credit and Commerce.*

MacGregor's (1934, p. 55 and n. 2) first reference to *Industry and Trade* relates to 'elasticity of demand for supplies of a particular business ... [and] the general elasticity of demand which need not be different'. The reference is to Marshall's discussion of the market, including that of a particular market gained by individual suppliers in a segment of the market as a whole for the commodity in question (Marshall 1919, p. 182). The second citation arises in the context of MacGregor's (1934, pp. 82–83) remark that 'enterprise ... has the priority at times of change in the cycle', a statement based on Marshall's (1919, p. 334) view that 'most promotions of new companies, and reorganisations of old companies, are made in the years just before an inflation of credit and prices reaches its bursting point'. It is interesting to note here that MacGregor (1934, p. 83n. 1) substitutes 'formations' for 'promotions' in the Marshall quote, to make it fit his argument better.

The first reference to *Money, Credit and Commerce* (Marshall 1923, pp. 249–251) relates to MacGregor's (1934, p. 64) remark that Marshall was a 'contingency theorist', linking increases in credit to a 'particular contingency' which then feeds into the cycle. This is indeed the impact of the section of *Money, Credit and Commerce* (Book IV Chapter III, Section 3) to which MacGregor referred when dealing with the turning points of the cycle in relation to the availability of credit. Two further references to *Money, Credit and Commerce* follow (MacGregor 1934, pp. 88 and 89). The first quotes Marshall's (1923, p. 245) observation that credit can be granted unwisely by the financial system 'to business ventures that are somewhat lacking in administrative capacity, or in foresight'. The second remark links Marshall (1923, p. 251) to the view that there is 'a detonating' influence of insolvency about the time of highest prices (MacGregor 1934, p. 89), more specifically to Marshall's view that when the price level is very high, people start to expect a 'downturn in prices' (and activity levels), and act accordingly.

There are also some citations of Marshall for which MacGregor (1934, pp. 107–108) gave no specific references. One of these mentioned Marshall's argument that 'implicit and explicit co-operation of producers' may operate in bad times to prevent the spoiling of the market', something which he claimed had happened in 1890, perhaps a reference to *Money, Credit and Commerce* (Marshall 1923, p. 262).

A long note to the essay on 'the risk of enterprise' (MacGregor 1934, pp. 120–124) discussed Marshall's approach to 'orders, systems, plans and arrangements in theory' because Marshall, after all, 'is the most admired and criticised of modern economists'. Marshall's concepts of control rely on 'substitution' and the 'representative business'. The extent to which these concepts succeed as regulatory factors, MacGregor argued, enables discussion of a 'co-operative order' as a working account of competition. In the following pages, MacGregor (1934, pp. 122–124) discussed Marshall's views of the interaction of substitution as between enterprises in both its lateral and vertical forms. This account focuses on the work of management, a class set apart by Marshall, because its labour is non-specialised and depends greatly on natural qualities. MacGregor cites Marshall's *Principles* in support (that is, Marshall 1920, pp. 313, 606, 613, 663). Supplementing the vertical influence of substitution is its lateral influence, partly through the competition of enterprises, partly through the strength of efficiency interactions which put business ability in command of the necessary capital to give it scope. This mechanism includes business management's control over price cutting to prevent it from spoiling the market (Marshall 1920, p. 374; 1919, p. 326). The representative firm plays a role in this analysis as well, MacGregor (1934, p. 124) points out. It brings reality into the argument, by selecting the actual firm in this position through surveying the firms in the industry (Marshall 1920, p. 318). In this way, co-operative order in the market does away with any need for central planning, a topic more closely examined in MacGregor's (1934) second essay in the context of socialism and business enterprise.

MacGregor's general judgement of Marshall as 'the most admired and criticised of modern economists' quoted earlier in this section, also indicates his general position on Marshall's economics by the early 1930s. As shown in the next section, in MacGregor's 1942 appraisal of Marshall and his book, criticism of Marshall mixes easily with admiration for his work. As shown in this section, such an opinion also applies to MacGregor's position on Marshall as a source in contemporary industry economics. But even if Marshall was therefore not always right – a conclusion all too easily drawn from the copious literature on the cost controversy of the 1920s and early 1930s – his work, at least for MacGregor, still contained far too much valuable insight into business behaviour and practice, for it to be unceremoniously dropped. In this sense, the various references to Marshall's work in MacGregor's (1934) volume of essays, point to a loyal, albeit occasionally critical, student of Marshall.

IV

MacGregor's 1942 paper commemorating the centenary of Marshall's birth is, on his own account, a 'personal recollection' combined with some observations on Marshall's great book, *Principles of Economics*, arising from the many years

MacGregor used it both as a student and as a teacher of economics. As shown later in this section, many of MacGregor's observations on the economics of Marshall's *Principles* reflect on the aspects of its contents which he himself had found most useful in the context of his own research. Other observations relate to the book's obsolescence with respect to the views of contemporary economists, and here MacGregor's views coincide somewhat with the sentiments expressed by Hicks, and later by Harold Wilson, when they attended MacGregor's lectures at Oxford.

The second paragraph of the article starts with MacGregor's statement that 'the *Principles* was the first book on economics I ever read'. From the previous two sections, it can also be deduced that he studied virtually all of its successive editions – the first and fourth editions being cited in his first book, the 1922 printing of the eighth edition being the version cited in his 1934 volume of essays. MacGregor (1942, 1982, p. 114) then adds that there were no real 'steps up to it through any other literature, not even by the [1879] *Economics of Industry*' or, for that matter, the 1892 summary provided in Marshall's *The Elements of the Economics of Industry* which MacGregor cited in both his 1906 *Industrial Combination* book and his 1934 volume of essays. An account of Marshall's lecturing style follows, part of which was quoted in Section I above. It reiterates that when MacGregor was an undergraduate student at Cambridge from 1899 to 1901, 'there was no other book you had to know but the *Principles*' (MacGregor 1942, 1982, p. 115).

After indicating some major problem areas in the theory of value of the *Principles* for him as a student (that is, consumers' surplus, short period value, and quasi-rent), MacGregor (1942, 1982, pp. 115–116) neatly identified the logical structure in which Marshall's *Principles* were constructed.

> The *Principles* is written in a logical order. Things are wanted (Bk 3), so they are produced (Bk 4), and are then exchanged (Bk 5), and the price is divided. It is like the development of a plot. The most fundamental idea is consumers' benefit, from its explanation in the third Book to the climax in the fifth, where the good monopolist or the public authority comes in to maximise it.
>
> (MacGregor 1942, 1982, p. 116)

At the end of his paper, MacGregor (1942, 1982, p. 126) draws attention to Marshall the 'socialist', sympathetic to all classes in society, pointing to the need for both understanding and imagination in economics, and the greater array of possibilities now open for those wishing and working to advance social and economic progress for every member of society. These possibilities may induce some curtailment of the 'rights of private property', through taxation and public expenditure, more specifically, some public investments at the local level in transport, roads, education, and the provision of other local services (Marshall 1920, Book I Chapter 4, p. 48).

In elaborating on aspects of his concise summary of Marshall's *Principles*, MacGregor (1942, 1982, pp. 116–118) first notes the absence of psychological underpinnings to Marshall's theory of consumption as presented in Book III; utilising in this context the views of some of the originators of the concept, 'elasticity of demand' (that is, De Quincey, Lloyd, Cournot, Dupuit and especially Whewell). MacGregor then suggests that time and elasticity are the ultimate focus of Marshall's discussion of demand in the *Economics of Industry* (1879) with a much wider treatment of 'demand and supply' in the *Principles of Economics*.

MacGregor (1942, 1982, pp. 118–121) also examines the origins, nature and importance of consumers' surplus. Origins are attributed to both De Quincey and Dupuit, as well as to Malthus to a lesser extent. Its various meanings in the *Principles* are then discussed, before an attempt is made to assess its validity. Here MacGregor distinguished three cases, partly to further explain the nature of Dupuit's originality vis-à-vis Marshall. Two of these cases are indicated as 'same commodity, same use, different buyers', or that of a rich man purchasing a cheap edition for poor buyers; and second, that of 'same commodity, same buyer, different uses'. These cases, MacGregor (1942, 1982, p. 119) argued, were both first investigated by Dupuit. Marshall, MacGregor added, concentrated on the most difficult case where buyer, commodity and use are all the same. This followed the 'marginal construction' of Marshall's demand curve, with constant total market value for any buyer. When Marshall took the analysis commodity by commodity, he opened it up, according to MacGregor, to a monetary misinterpretation but one which, nevertheless, was also the only completely valid use of the concept.

Consumer surplus is used in Book V of the *Principles* to express an aim in public policy, 'where the test of the policy is its effect on surplus'. MacGregor (1942, 1982, pp. 119–120) suggests this is different from the consumer analysis of Book III, where the consumer as presented by Marshall aims to maximise the total and not the net return on expenditure. Why the net expenditure is not important to the consumer, is explained by MacGregor in terms of the interaction between consumers' welfare in consumption, and his total environment, a topic which Marshall himself had tackled in Appendix K of the *Principles.*

MacGregor (1942, 1982, pp. 121–125) examines problems encountered in Marshall's Book IV on production. These arise from his two laws of returns, whose construction relies on quite different types of theory. These are diminishing returns (a natural phenomenon) and increasing returns based on internal and external economies in production. The last has relevance for Marshall's theory of competition which always has an element of monopoly contained in it and where equilibrium requires that average cost equals price and not the equality of marginal cost and marginal revenue. The concept of perfect competition for Marshall implied that firms in the industry were so numerous that no producer can influence price by his own actions. In this context, MacGregor (1942, 1982, pp. 122–123) reintroduced the notion of the representative firm. For Marshall, MacGregor argued, 'this was not an abstract idea' but an empirical reality, a position supported by MacGregor's own experience at Leeds and Manchester. The representative firm reflected the reality that in most markets it was possible, generally speaking, to point to the firms whose costs were price determining. This approach was also verified for MacGregor from his personal experience on many public commissions and inquiries into industrial price behaviour. Moreover, he argued, the same could be said for the idea inherent in Marshall's 'particular expenses curve', as shown in Appendix H of the *Principles*. This, according to MacGregor (1942, 1982, p. 123) was clearly accepted in reports of various Coal Commissions, the Colwyn Committee and in several United States' Price-fixing Commissions, with which he was familiar. By this stage of his centenary assessment of Marshall's *Principles*, MacGregor had therefore vindicated what he saw as its three principal analytical tools: consumers' surplus, the representative firm and the particular expenses curve.

MacGregor commented negatively on the findings of the cost controversies. Decreasing costs for MacGregor did not necessarily imply the instability of competition in the sense that the firm which is a cost leader must inevitably become a monopoly. This is far too simplistic a picture of the consequences of falling costs, the reality of the situation is much more complex. However, MacGregor (1942, 1982, p. 124) admitted that the business structure analysed by Marshall was somewhat out of date, even if there were occasional references in his *Principles* to joint-stock companies, trusts and cartels as forms of business organisation.

The final pages of MacGregor's centenary assessment return to the concepts of surplus and their relationship to maximum welfare. MacGregor here emphasised again its potential breach with a pure private enterprise society since the tax/bounty model Marshall (1920, pp. 467–470) had put forward, required state action to achieve maximum welfare. Furthermore, in advocating taxation of diminishing returns industries in order to subsidise increasing returns industries with bounties, MacGregor questioned whether the taxing of extractive industries (the realistic counterpart of diminishing returns industries) to subsidise the manufacturing sector was justifiable given that the manufacturing sector invariably required inputs from the output of extractive industries. Marshall's brief exposition of the tax/bounty policy left too many ambiguities which needed to be resolved to be useful. Such ambiguities were also abundantly present in much of the public policy content of the two final chapters of the *Principles of Economics* on economic and social progress, a topic on which MacGregor did not give more detail.

MacGregor's final paragraph raised the paradox that there may be many ideas in a book which do not come out of it, apropos the main treatises of Marshall, Marx and Smith. Smith's *Wealth of Nations* contained so many things, that it was possible to get out of it anything you wanted in support of your argument. This is not the case with Marx or Marshall according to MacGregor (1942, 1982, p. 126). They both used work from earlier writers to transform their ideas and make them part of their own system. For MacGregor, and with this part of his paragraph it is easy to agree, 'Marshall unified and integrated the economics of enterprise'. The ending of MacGregor's article completes a strong defence of the continuing importance of Marshall's contributions to economic analysis, though not with special reference to the use MacGregor made of the surpluses, the representative firm, and the particular expenses curve, as crucial parts of that system Marshall's *Principles* had created.

V

The sample of MacGregor's writings explored in the previous three sections indicates that his research systematically utilised some special aspects of Marshall's *Principles.* Apart from the three items identified once again in the previous paragraph, that is, the doctrine of the surpluses, the representative firm, and the particular expenses curve, MacGregor drew especially on Marshall's view of competition which for him inevitably included monopolistic elements; economies of scale and decreasing costs as an important feature of contemporary industry, and the varied use Marshall made of the notion of elasticity which, from the way he used it, he virtually made his own. MacGregor also favoured, and adopted Marshall's partial equilibrium approach to economic analysis, since for him there was no realistic way to study the complexity of an economy as a whole with its manifold forms of productive structures.

The combination of fact and theory when presenting economic analysis and priciples was also something that MacGregor had fully imbibed from Marshall. This made him a true Marshallian. Theory had to match the facts, and had to be realistic in both its formulation and its application. No artificial constructions for MacGregor in the writing of economics: analysis of real situations in industry and elsewhere is the hallmark of his economic research in industrial economics. As indicated in Sections II and III especially, MacGregor's references to Marshall's work in both his 1906 book and his 1934 volume of essays were invariably of both a theoretical and a factual nature.

Moreover, MacGregor's general approach to the writing of economics was, as shown above, quite similar in form to that of Marshall. The use of mathematics was largely avoided, and the few diagrams used in MacGregor's analysis were placed in footnotes and not in the text. It can also be said that MacGregor's research programme fitted in neatly with Marshall's enunciation of the aims of economics with respect to its scope, as expressed in his final lecture (quoted above in Section I). These included the study of competition in relation to monopoly, amalgamation of railways and in enterprises associated with other forms of transport, the analysis of trusts and cartels. Collectivism and socialism also fell within the Marshallian research programme, but were an aspect less frequently addressed by MacGregor in his work. They were, however, not totally ignored by him even if he was a self-confessed analyst of private enterprise capitalism. The same applies to the analysis of consumer surplus, as Marshall himself had identified it, 'within a demand curve of rapidly changing elasticity', while MacGregor implicitly accepted the view that the doctrine of consumers' surplus and its application to economic problems was described by Marshall as one of his more enduring contributions, the value of which would outlive both him and his initial generations of students.

MacGregor could also be quite critical of Marshall. For example, he appears to have never been greatly taken by Marshall's advocacy of using the tools of biology and more broadly evolutionary theory. Second, he accepted the fact that Marshall's realistic preoccupations implied that his economics would rapidly grow out of date in many important ways, since the facts of industrial life were continuously changing. His own field of economic combination, trusts and cartels was a good illustration. Although Marshall had recognised the existence of these specific organisational forms of modern industry, he had never really analysed them in his economic work, not even in *Industry and Trade*, his supplementary volume to the *Principles.* Recognising this aspect of Marshall's economics had nothing to do with MacGregor's loyalty to Marshall as his former student; perhaps it can be said that admission of the potential for wider application of Marshall's work to date was a important feature of that loyalty, since Marshall had frequently implied this himself. Furthermore, other broad parts of Marshall's legacy such as his insistence on the realism obtained from blending theory and facts, and the usefulness of some of his specific theoretical conceptions, would endure to a much longer extent.

MacGregor is therefore an important Marshallian. Not only had he studied under Marshall in the decade following the publication of his *Principles*, he had been a colleague of Marshall for some years as teacher and examiner for the Economics Tripos. Subsequently, although there was little apparent direct contact between teacher and student in the years after 1908 when MacGregor went to Leeds, he carried the Marshallian message with him, as he did in his subsequent moves to Manchester and especially, Oxford. This is demonstrable not only from his published work, but also from his lecturing and seminars, as evident in Hicks' specific complaint about the contents of his Oxford lectures as too much 'old-fashioned' Marshall. MacGregor's early adoption of Marshall's economic research programme clearly made him a 'favourite pupil'.

8 Frederick Lavington (1881–1927)

An able Cambridge monetary theorist cut off in his prime, and a very loyal Marshallian

Frederick Lavington graduated in 1911 with a first class honours result in Part II of the Economics and Politics Tripos, the same year as Gerald Shove. He was part of the brilliant student cohort of pre-1914 graduates, including Hubert Henderson and Dennis Robertson, trained by Keynes and by Pigou as the successor of Marshall. Lavington subsequently concentrated on topics in monetary theory associated with the rate of interest, uncertainty, and speculative activity, subjects on which he published three articles in the *Economic Journal* in three consecutive years (1911, 1912, 1913). Of these three, his brilliant 1912 article, 'Uncertainty in Relation to the Rate of Interest', established him as a major Cambridge monetary theorist within a year of graduation. During the 1920s he published two books. *The English Capital Market* was published in 1921, with a second posthumous edition in 1929; the far shorter and quite unoriginal *The Trade Cycle*, appeared in 1922. Both were reviewed in the *Economic Journal* (Lemberger 1921 and Cannan 1922). A further article, on the topic of 'Business Risks', appeared in two parts in the *Economic Journal* in 1925 and 1926. He also published a lengthy book review in the *Economic Journal* (Lavington 1923) and three articles in *Economica* (Lavington 1924, 1926b, 1927), the last two dealing with topics in what would now be called the theory of the firm. They established his reputation as a sound Marshallian economist, specialising in the wider area of financial economics.

On graduation, Lavington first worked in the newly formed Labour Exchanges section of the Board of Trade (1912–1918). Lavington was appointed Emmanuel College Lecturer in Economics at Cambridge in 1918. Two years later, in 1920, he obtained the Girdler University lectureship in economics, a position he held until his premature death in 1927. He thereby became part of the major Cambridge monetary school of the 1920s, that included Maynard Keynes, Pigou and Robertson, who all published on monetary theory and on economic fluctuations and the business cycle. Lavington was, however, never greatly involved with Maynard Keynes, even if he can be ranked among Keynes's economist friends. A single letter (from 1911) between the two economists survives, while Keynes's appointment book records only one occasion with Lavington, that is, a meeting for dinner on 30 April 1922 (Moggridge 1992, pp. 433–434).

Lavington's lectures at Cambridge were initially devoted to topics in finance and the capital market. From 1920 onwards, he also lectured on the structure and organisation of industry, and published two articles on this subject in *Economica* during the last two years of his life. When appropriate, Lavington's work on industrial organisation was reflected in his work on financial institutions.

Lavington's Marshallian credentials are discussed in detail in what follows, even if his personal contacts with Marshall were very limited. Lavington, it may be noted, was among the many economists who received a complimentary copy of Marshall's *Money, Credit and Commerce* in 1923, for which he thanked Marshall cordially in the one letter to Alfred Marshall which is extant (Whitaker 1996, III pp. 388–389). As was the case with so many of these 'thank you' letters in connection with *Money, Credit and Commerce* (see Groenewegen 1995a, pp. 724–725) Lavington like them expressed the pious wish that Marshall live to complete his book on progress, which he for so long had been contemplating as the third companion volume to the *Principles* and which had been announced as such in its later prefaces. Moreover, as a very orthodox Marshallian economist in his published writings, and a staunch believer in the literal inspiration (Wright 1927, p. 504) of Marshall's *Principles of Economics*, Lavington is credited with the saying, 'It's all in A. Marshall'.

The remainder of this chapter is divided into six sections. Section I provides biographical background on Lavington, with special reference to his studies and teaching in economics. Section II evaluates the early articles he published in the *Economic Journal* before 1914. Section III examines the argument of his book, *The English Capital Market* and his two-part article on risk, published in the *Economic Journal.* Section IV looks at his book on *The Trade Cycle.* Section V reviews the contents of Lavington's three *Economica* articles, the first of which cited by Pigou (1927, p. 252n. 1). The final section draws conclusions, with special reference to the Marshallian influences on his work.

I

Frederick Lavington was born in 1881. From 1897 to 1908 he was employed in the Capital and Counties Bank, a sign of things to come. In 1908, the year at the start of which Marshall had retired from his Cambridge chair, Lavington entered Cambridge as a mature student. In 1909 he obtained a Fellowship from Emmanuel College, the college with which he was associated for much of the remainder of his life. As a student in his later twenties, Lavington was considerably older than his fellow undergraduate students and even, by two years, than one of his lecturers on economics, Maynard Keynes.

Charles Fay (1927, pp. 504–505) later recalled that Lavington:

> came up from a London Bank with two passions, one for the academic life of discussion and analysis, the other for the pulsating romance of the London Money Market. His essays on the latter in Part I of the Economics Tripos extracted from us the unusual mark of 90 percent.

Fay added that as an undergraduate Lavington tried to gain maximum value from his tutorial classes. He always chose the time slot of 12.00 to 1.00, 'so that there should be no one to follow'. Fay also mentioned two problems in Marshallian economics which particularly intrigued Lavington. These were the nature of the 'particular expenses curve' and 'the validity of consumer surplus'. Neither was answered to his satisfaction by Fay until Fay 'had been on a special mission to Madingley Road', to get the definitive answer from Alfred Marshall, the creator of these valuable tools of applied economics. No wonder that in 1910 Lavington was placed in the first class of Part I of the Economics Tripos, followed by another first in 1911 when he completed Part II. At this time, Lavington also successfully entered an essay, 'The Agencies by which Capital is Associated with Business Power' for the Adam Smith Prize. As already indicated, he published three articles in the *Economic Journal*, in 1911, in 1912, and 1913; the first not long after he had completed Part II of the Economics Tripos.

His university education completed, Lavington found employment in 1912 in an administrative post in the new Labour Exchanges established by the Board of Trade, after a short spell of lecturing at Cambridge on the capital market (Collard 1990, p. 197). Little is known of the six years he spent at the Board of Trade. Whether his visit to Russia before the start of the First World War (recalled by Lavington in 1926) was associated with Board of Trade work is not clear. It mentioned the complete loss of every child born in a single year in a particular Russian village. Harvest failure and the associated famine, due to the tremendous isolation of Russian villages from other towns and settlements at this time, were the cause. This was a matter of interest when Lavington discussed arbitrage possibilities in food and other organised produce markets in the second part of his article on business risks (Lavington 1926a, p. 192). Collard (1990, p. 179) also indicates that 'an illness associated with the pancreas kept him out of the war'.

In 1918 Lavington returned to Emmanuel College as college lecturer in economics. In 1920, Lavington obtained the Girdlers lectureship as the successor of Keynes, the position he occupied at the time of his death in 1927. The 1920s were marked by ill health, assisted by a tendency to overwork himself in his activities as university don, including the arduous task of examining for the Tripos. Apart from his teaching and research (he produced his two books, a review article and the two-part article on risk for the *Economic Journal* in these years, together with three articles in *Economica*), he played an active part in life at his college, and in wider university activities. He contributed considerably to college administration, helped in the drafting of new statutes arising from the suggestions thereon contained in the Report of the Royal Commission on Oxford and Cambridge; presided over the College Hockey Club, and was prominent in the lively discussions of the Emmanuel Economic Society. Fay mentioned 'he was an excellent supervisor', a quality which probably owed much to his own love of tutorials and supervision while an undergraduate.

Lavington, as both Fay (1927) and Wright (1927) indicate, was far more dogmatically devoted to Marshall and his economics than were his colleagues in the Faculty of Economics and Politics generally. Lavington:

> seemed to believe in the literal inspiration of Marshall's *Principles.* His own work on the English capital market was designed to fill in the details of one corner of Marshall's broad picture, but Lavington insisted that the work of economic analysis had been practically completed, once and for all, by Marshall, and that only the application of that analysis to practical problems remained to be done. 'It's all in Marshall, if you'll only take the trouble to dig it out', was one of his favourite dicta; and Marshall's lightest word on any economic point would carry extraordinary weight with him. Thus, in writing of economic subjects, he had something like an inferiority complex, and deliberately adopted an arid and pedestrian style. There is no trace in his books of his vivid personality, his keen appreciation of literature, or the vivacious wit and humour which lent colour to his conversation.
>
> (Wright 1927, p. 504)

Fay made the same point more concisely:

> Marshall was his hero, as of all of us; and there was in both of them that completeness of devotion and rigour of standards which are perhaps the greatest gift that a teacher can bestow on those who sit around him.
>
> (Fay 1927, p. 505)

The subsequent sections of this chapter examine these Marshallian affiliations more fully by a careful investigation of Lavington's published work. Unfortunately, there are no accounts in the public arena of the quality of Lavington's teaching or of his 'brilliant conversation' with reference to his regular participating in the Emmanuel College Economic Society.

Wright's obituary ends with a further indication of Lavington's intellectual hero worship, which on occasions tended to be rather dogmatic. This was his admiration of Herbert Spencer's philosophical work, perhaps gained as a student in the Economics Tripos (Wright 1927, p. 504). It clearly is another sentiment which Lavington shared with Marshall (cf. Groenewegen 1995a, pp. 167, 412, 417, 591).

Lavington died in 1927 at the early age of forty-six. His life during the 1920s was plagued by ill health, described in Wright's obituary as a 'long triumphant fight against physical disabilities' to which he eventually succumbed. However, he achieved much during the thirteen years he was involved in economics as an undergraduate student, lecturer and researcher. His work on finance was important, changing Cambridge views on the demand for money, and on the determination of the rate of interest. It greatly expanded the scope and depth of this topic as treated by Marshall in the introductory part of his monetary theory as published in *Money, Credit and Commerce* (Marshall 1923, Book I). However, few of his contributions were directly acknowledged by his Cambridge colleagues who worked on monetary theory. They were simply absorbed within their theoretical frameworks, as indicated briefly in the final section of this chapter. As previously noted, an exception is Pigou's (1927, p. 252n.1) citation of Lavington's first *Economica* paper on long-term and short-term interest rates.

II

Lavington published three articles in the *Economic Journal* in three successive years – 1911, 1912, 1913 – following his completion of Part II of the Economics Tripos. These articles laid some of the theoretical foundations for his 1921 study of the English capital market and developed from his understanding of the monetary literature in English and in German which he had been reading as part of his economic studies. They may also have reflected his preliminary banking experience with the Capital and Counties Bank before he commenced his university studies. In turn, these articles dealt with 'The Social Importance of Banking' (Lavington 1911), 'Uncertainty in its Relation to the Rate of Interest' (Lavington 1912) and 'The Social Interest in Speculation' (Lavington 1913).

As previously indicated, the 1912 article earned him a considerable reputation as a new monetary economist, and was quite influential. His 1912 and 1913 articles, it is interesting to note, were mentioned by Frank Knight (1921, p. 199n. 1) as two of the half dozen or so contributions to the economics literature on uncertainty which by then had appeared in the United States and Great Britain.

Lavington's first article, consisting of only eight pages, presented his thoughts on the social importance of the banking system, through its facilitation of capital mobility, its provision of currency and its other objectives, all of which greatly contributed to the social welfare of the community. The article explains how banks, as part of the system of financial intermediations, carried out these functions under the then still existing gold exchange standard. Banks have the power to create money through their ability to offer current (chequing) accounts, the use of which by banking customers affects the size of the money supply (Lavington 1911, pp. 54–55).

Lavington also used the article to discuss whether banks were operating under free competition, or whether they exerted some monopoly power, given their above normal profitability (Lavington 1911, pp. 55–56). However, Lavington dismissed the view that banking profits constituted a 'social evil'. Bank profits, after all, were distributed to a substantial body of shareholders. Moreover, with the boards of the banks fully elected by these shareholders, the self-interest of a competitive banking system was very similar to the public interest (Lavington 1911, p. 57). Free competition was maintained in banking despite the growth in size of trading banks and the establishment of branch banking. Moreover, growth in size carried with it certain economic and social advantages. Some of these resembled the benefits accruing to all large-scale enterprises from economies of scale. Moreover, size of the business increased the security banks could offer to deposit holders; while the local knowledge of branch managers was not necessarily inferior to that of the by then dying breed of small private bankers (Lavington 1911, p. 57).

Developments in modern banking, Lavington argued, provided currency in a superior way, gave money supply greater elasticity to meet changes in demand from business and the public over the course of the business cycle, though there could be harmful consequences from this monetary flexibility for changes in the price level. A brief discussion of the operation of the money multiplier of the gold reserve in the creation of new bank deposits, indicated this (Lavington 1911, pp. 58–59). Bank rate variations were useful for controlling these changes in the quantity of money, while common action of the banking system on discount rates regulated currency supplies effectively (Lavington 1911, pp. 59–60), thereby guarding against over-issue, and discouraging speculation and the associated inflation of the currency. The conclusion reiterated these points, leading Lavington to the proposition that the self-interest of competing banks enhanced the material welfare of society, which recent (but unmentioned) changes to the banking system, had also encouraged (Lavington 1911, p. 60).

Lavington's second article in the *Economic Journal* addressed the problem of uncertainty in relation to the rate of interest and, more generally, issues in financial intermediation. Lavington (1912, p. 398) started his investigation by stressing the fact that the future can only be imperfectly foreseen, and that 'the cost of imperfect foresight is a continuous maladjustment of resources'. Moreover, 'imperfect knowledge' about the future was claimed by Lavington to lower productivity and to enhance the social costs of production, while its consequences enhanced the level of risk in rational business decision making, hence raising the necessary 'compensating probability of exceptional gain'.

In a diagram showing 'the curve of prospective net returns', for which Lavington acknowledged his indebtedness to Pigou, he illustrated how any demand for resources under conditions of uncertainty, required an additional return. Alternatively, Lavington argued, 'uncertainty is a disutility for which payment must be made in addition to the net rate of interest' (Lavington 1912, p. 399). Following J.B. Clark on the subject, Lavington associated uncertainty with a particular form of ignorance present in most forms of business decision making (Lavington 1912, p. 400). Business uncertainty was also the consequence of financial insecurity, preventing the 'close investment' of capital, since locking in resources, and the concomitant increase in their immobility, greatly raised uncertainty. As an important conclusion to his article, Lavington therefore suggested that uncertainty can be considerably reduced at the cost of creating a financial reserve for the firm in question (Lavington 1912, p. 401). More generally, uncertainty can be lowered through the creation of new forms of specialised business organisations, for example, insurance companies. Financial institutions could further assist the reduction of risk by the types of securities they issued. Examples were riskless government bills, which carried low rates of return, as well as business bills of exchange, which invariably carried greater risks and therefore needed a higher rate of return (Lavington 1912, pp. 403–404). The availability of such financial instruments is affected by the degree of organisation of the bill market and the variety of specialised financial instruments it was able to offer (Lavington 1912, p. 405).

The final pages of Lavington's 1912 paper expressed some overall results on uncertainty and the rate of interest. 'Costs of insecurity are at a maximum in the case of capital invested in an irredeemable security with a narrow market', a very uncertain type of investment needing a high return. Moreover, Lavington (1912, p. 406) argued that the same type of bank loan would invariably be associated in the financial market with the same interest charge. Organisation in the financial market lowered imperfections in the availability of certain types of capital and hence in security premiums embodied in the appropriate financial charges (Lavington 1912, p. 407), while the presence of appropriate financial institutions lowers uncertainty, enables increased closer investment of capital, thereby raising productivity and, subsequently, national income levels (Lavington 1912, p. 409).

Lavington's 1913 article discussed the social value of speculation, within a setting of the need to develop specialised financial institutions to take advantage of the efficiency gains from this increased division of labour. Appropriate speculative machinery, Lavington argued, was an essential aspect of the circulation of goods in an organised market. This also applied to the capital market bringing savings and investment decisions into balance, despite the different motivations underlying these two activities. Saving provided uncommitted productive resources by the act of foregoing their present enjoyment, while investment was command over capital resources and their employment enabled by the act of saving. These were simple propositions of saving-investment analysis firmly established by Marshall in his *Principles of Economics* (Lavington 1913, p. 36).

In modern economies, the process of placing saved resources in the hands of productive investors, was the task of the capital market, made up of the financial operations by the banking system, the stock exchange and trade credit, effectively the definition Lavington used in his 1921 book on that market. Lavington (1913, pp. 36–37) described the type of securities created in their transactions as an efficient manner of risk spreading, a role in which speculative activity in security prices played an important part. Referring back to his 1912 paper, which had analysed the impact of uncertainty on rates of return, and the need for financial intermediation in this process, the stock exchange could be said to make the securities in which it traded more marketable, thereby lowering the insecurity associated with holding these types of financial assets. Speculators by their activity tended to equalise rates of return on what could be described as equivalent investments, hence enhancing the degree of competitiveness in financial markets, always a good outcome (Lavington 1913, pp. 45–49). From this analysis, Lavington concluded that competitive financial markets enabled prices to move close to investment values, lowering cost of production from the more productive use of resources whose supply price was lowered from the presence of this type of financial intermediation. From these productive aspects, speculation, in short, was useful by making a positive contribution to human welfare, a proposition about the positive impact of some types of speculation also presented by Marshall.

Lavington's three articles reviewed in this section represented his position on the nature, the advantages and modus operandi of the financial system as it existed in the decade before the start of the First World War. Banking played a crucial role in this system as the major creator, and effective regulator of currency supply, best carried out by large, competitive banks earning profits. Uncertainty reduction was another matter in which the financial system could assist by enabling firms to create the necessary financial reserves as a safeguard in preserving their security. The last of Lavington's three articles reviewed the positive role of speculation in stimulating the saving-investment mechanism, thereby raising productivity through increased capital intensity in production and lowering production costs. As shown in the next section, Lavington's detailed study of the capital market in England, revisited most of this territory and explained it in considerably more detail.

III

According to Fay (1927), Lavington's work on the capital market was designed to fill in the details of 'a corner of Marshall's broad picture' not effectively completed by him. A significant part of the book drew on the material published in Lavington's three *Economic Journal* articles published before the war, and also commented on the subject of risk, the topic Lavington was to address in a two-part article in the 1925/1926 *Economic Journal* and discussed at the end of this section. In a note on sources for the book, Lavington acknowledged his general indebtedness to Marshall's and Pigou's economic work (Lavington 1921, 1929, p. 283). Looking at the references cited in Lavington's notes, none were dated after 1920. The fact that the 1929 printing only contains a preface for the original 1921 edition, suggests that it probably was a reprint, corrected for small errors only. As Lavington had died two years before its publication, this is not very surprising.

The structure of *The English Capital Market* is as follows. The book is divided into four, very uneven, parts with respect to size. Part I presents 'Leading Ideas' by way of a short introductory chapter, a discussion of the market in relation to money and capital, and trade credit, concluding with an overview chapter which presents 'a general view of the market'. Part I introduces the capital market as part of the specialisation practised under the division of labour in a modern economy, designed to provide credit efficiently to business. Part II presents an outline of the theory of money in its six short chapters.

Chapter V introduces the quantity theory as a supply and demand theory of the value of money. The demand for money is explained in Chapter VI, while Chapters VII to IX analyse the supply factors. The final chapter (Chapter X) presents an overview. Part III of the book is devoted to 'the Transport of Capital'. Its eight chapters analyse 'the Flow of Resources into Investment

(Chapter XI), the 'Influence of the Market on.... Waiting' (Chapter XII), and on risk (Chapter XIII) including that from 'imperfect knowledge' (Chapter XIV) and the immobility of invested resources (Chapter XV). Chapter XVI looks at the marketing of securities, Chapter XVII at the influence of the market on the demand for capital, before closing with a review of marketing operations (Chapter XVIII). Part IV, well over half the size of the book, devotes its twenty-five chapters to the types of institutions of which the English capital market consists. Its first nine chapters (Chapters XIX to XXVII) discuss the banking system and its role in the provision of currency as an essential feature of the capital market which assists the circulation of capital in a modern economy. The next fifteen chapters (Chapters XXVIII–XLII) discuss the stock exchange as a market for long-term securities, including the role of the speculator in that market, both in general and in terms of the specific operations of the London Stock Exchange. Chapter XLIII reviews the important role of trade credit as another aspect of the English capital market. The last chapter (Chapter XLIV) presents brief conclusions.

Some general features of the book need to be highlighted. First, the presentation of its argument is largely within the setting of the pre-war Gold Standard, with bullion stocks the major reserve underpinning the note issue. Second, the book is frequently internationally comparative, with reference to German, French and United States' practice. Third, despite the year of initial publication, 1921, much of the factual material included is pre-World War and often end of the nineteenth century. These data are largely derived from *The Economist*, from official inquiries into the monetary system and from reference works equally divided between English and German language titles (shades of Marshall) and, to a lesser extent, French and North American sources.

Lavington's broad acknowledgement of Marshall's and Pigou's work has already been mentioned. This probably referred more to their teaching than to their writing. For Marshall, references are confined to his *Principles* (cited in Lavington 1921, 1929, pp. 23, 69, 275 and also pp. 55–56), Marshall's 1887 evidence to the Gold and Silver Commission (cited on pp. 27, 33), his *Industry and Trade* (cited pp. 176, 270) and his 1887 article, 'Remedies for Fluctuations of General Prices' which is referred to indirectly on at least two occasions (Lavington 1921, 1929, pp. 55, 152). Special references to Marshall relate to his saving-investment analysis in the *Principles,* his distinction between net and gross interest, and his stress on the factor of 'organisation as a fourth agent of production'. Pigou is only cited once for his work in *Wealth and Welfare* (Lavington 1921, 1929, pp. 87–88) in the context of analysing aspects of risky investments by means of the only two diagrams included in Lavington's book. It may be noted that Pigou's (1917/18) essay on 'The Exchange Value of Legal Tender Money', published in the *Quarterly Journal of Economics*, was not directly mentioned by Lavington even if its detailed consideration of the quantity theory as a supply and demand explanation of the value of money could have assisted him in preparing Part II of his book. In addition, there are two references (Lavington 1921, 1929, pp. 212, 213) to Foxwell's work on issue-houses in the *Economic*

Journal. In the context of price stability, Lavington mentioned the plans by Jevons, Fisher and Goschen, together with the already mentioned plan in Marshall (1887a, 1926).

Part II of *The English Capital Market*, containing an outline of the theory of money, is essentially a discussion of the theory of the value of money based on supply and demand. The algebraic form of the theory presented by Lavington is the Fisherine form of the quantity theory,

$$P = T/MV$$

where P is the price level, T the volume of transactions, M is the quantity of money and V the average velocity of its circulation, though it should be pointed out that Lavington's equation substitutes $n \times r$ for the MV of the Fisherine form, where 'n' is the practical equivalent of M ('number of units of money') and 'r' that of V (the average velocity of its circulation). Lavington explicitly viewed his theory as a specific form of the theory of supply and demand since his argument on the previous page identified P with D/S where relevant demand factors explaining the value of money are indicated by T, the volume of transactions; while the relevant supply factors are the effective quantity of money, MV (Lavington 1921, 1929, pp. 23–24).

The next chapter explains the demand for money in terms of the distinction between 'the yield of convenience' in holding money, and 'the security' associated with this action. Moreover, money's 'marketability' (Lavington's term for what would now be called its 'liquidity') or general acceptability is part of its return for the holders of money, and explains why money is so attractive an asset to hold (Lavington 1921, 1929, pp. 30–31). In this chapter or, for that matter, in the book as a whole, there is no explicit reference to what became known as the Cambridge cash balance equation where the demand for holding money was related directly to the level of income of the holder, and inversely to the rate of interest. Lavington (1921, 1929, pp. 36, 37) simply explained the supply of money by the instruments capable of acting as money (notes, coin, bank deposits in cheque accounts, bills of exchange drawn on secure borrowers or, as was the case before the First World War, gold reserves and stocks of gold coin as a significant part of money supply).

Lavington (1921, 1929, pp. 65–66) then examined the role of the capital market from the perspective of Marshallian saving-investment theory. Lavington (1921, 1929, pp. 75–79) identified the terms 'waiting' with both saving (postponement of, or waiting for consumption) and investment (waiting for output from production). He devoted much space to the risk involved in these activities. Risk is explained by imperfect knowledge and uncertainty, a discussion in which Lavington (1921, 1929, pp. 87–89) referred to both Pigou's discussion of this subject in *Wealth and Welfare* and to his own analysis in Lavington (1912). Moreover, risk is enhanced for specific investments by their degree of immobility. Marketability is therefore a valuable quality of an investment since it lowers risk for individual investors, and is an important service which the capital market institutions render to investors by reducing risk. The supply price of capital is then explained explicitly by Lavington (1921, 1929, p. 101), once again in a quite specific Marshallian manner as comprising net interest, the price of risk bearing, and other costs of moving capital not specified by Lavington. How to reduce these costs is a specific task Lavington ascribed to the capital market, the analysis of which occupied the remainder of the book.

In this discussion as well, there are various implicit Marshallian touches. For example, in the concluding chapter on the banking system as part of the capital market, Lavington (1921, 1929, p. 177) warns of the crucial importance of keeping explanations of the market always 'close in touch with ordinary business language and ideas'. The discussion then shifts to examination of the role of the stock exchange in the capital market and the functions served therein by the speculator in the form of arbitrage, of estimating future values, and of enhancing the marketability of securities and thereby increasing their mobility. In concluding his analysis of this part of the market, Lavington (1921, 1929, pp. 255–256) indicated in summary:

1 speculation with special knowledge establishes truer prices and hence is efficient;
2 skilled speculation in security market with variable/uncertain values distorts markets by their ambiguous, destabilising effects;
3 unskilled speculation lowers the efficiency of the market by distorting prices;
4 unskilled speculation governed by irrational herd impulses provides waste.

The final segment of the market Lavington discussed is trade credit. In explicit contrast to John Stuart Mill and Thomas Tooke, Lavington (1921, 1929, p. 270) did not view trade credit in principle as destabilising, although '[L]ocal changes' in trade credit may, however, be responsible for destabilising prices in that area. The same can happen in raw produce markets, especially ores and coal, but futures trading, a form of trade credit in Lavington's view (1921, 1929, pp. 270–271) has positive features in this regard. Trade credit can be said in general to boost economic activity, a valuable contribution to national output and to economic welfare (Lavington, 1921, 1929, pp. 272–273).

Lavington concluded the book on a solid Marshallian note. The capital market, he argued, can be depicted as part of that important additional agent of production which Marshall called 'organisation'. Moreover, the capital market's significant role in enhancing supply also raises welfare from its positive influence 'on the national dividend'. However, the boundaries of the money market are flexible, so that statistical evidence on its aggregate effects is difficult to obtain. However, that flexibility is itself an important attribute which needs to be stressed in any record of this very important part of the modern economy (Lavington 1921, 1929, Chapter XLIV).

To conclude this section, Lavington's 1925/26 analysis of risk published in the *Economic Journal* needs to be reviewed. Lavington (1925, pp. 186–187) introduced risk as an indication that there is no 'perfect knowledge' in the world as is, so that 'complete calculation' is impossible in business decision making. Undertakings of future events which by definition are uncertain, are filled with risk or 'the unrelieved probability of loss'. Following J.B. Clark (in an unspecified source), Lavington (1925, p. 194) identified three costs associated with uncertainty, namely:

1 expenditure of organising capacity by which these losses [of uncertainty] are reduced;
2 reduction in real incomes of producing parties as a result of the imperfect use of their productive resources;
3 a reduction in the efficiency of using individual incomes as a result of their uncertainty.

Lavington (1925, p. 194) then examined payment for the bearing of risk and uncertainty, using an analytical apparatus developed by Pigou. This allowed him to argue that growth of the firm tended to lower the costs attributable to uncertainty and risk; that stock prices set in the market reflected the cost of risk; that risk reduced efficiency in using productive resources while uncertainty lowered the efficiency in which income can be used (Lavington 1925, pp. 195–198). Insurance cannot lower risk, only uncertainty for the insured, while costs attributable to risk can be said to fall on both producers and consumers alike (Lavington 1925, p. 199).

In the second part of his paper, Lavington (1926a) appraised the following aspects of risk and uncertainty. Certainty of supply whenever that can be achieved, considerably enhances consumers' surplus. Lavington (1926a, p. 192) illustrated this topic by an event he had witnessed during a visit to Russia (already summarised in Section I above), and which so strikingly had displayed the opposite. He then argued that while losses arise from the incalculability of uncertainty, the additional expenses from specific risks are quite estimable. Moreover, much of the entrepreneurial task arises from problems associated with risk. Business risks are then identified with the possibility of war, insecurity of property, variable standards of value and unstable tariff policies (Lavington 1926a, p. 200). Technical risks are simply defined as the possibility of destruction, transport difficulties and accidents (Lavington 1926a, p. 201). Lavington (1926a, pp. 202–203) illustrated this argument with a wheat/potato example, where fluctuations in output tend not to be offset (or neutralised) by opposite price changes. This phenomenon tends to make farmers' incomes unstable, or as stable as if prices of these commodities had been stable at their average level. The paper on risk was Lavington's final publication in the *Economic Journal*. His *Economica* articles are discussed in Section V.

IV

The contents of Lavington's second book, *The Trade Cycle*, are now examined. Its subject matter is covered in nine short chapters which treat both the social and the economic aspects of the phenomenon. In the preface, Lavington (1922,

p. 7) acknowledges that 'most of the leading ideas [for the book] have been drawn from the writings of Dr Marshall, Professor Pigou, Mr D.H. Robertson, and from the great work on business cycles by Professor W.C. Mitchell of California. The facts and subsidiary argument have come from a wider range of sources, including the writings of Mitchell and those of Aftalion, to whom inadequate acknowledgement is made in the text.

Lavington (1922, p. 9) added that he was also indebted to H.D. Henderson 'and other Cambridge friends' for valuable criticism and suggestions, while his use of the records of the Board of Trade, Lavington's former employer, are also acknowledged.

The introduction to the book recognised that 1921 was a crisis year, with much 'unwilling unemployment' and 'ample resources vainly looking for employment'. Price uncertainties, preventing reliable business forecasts, high protection costs limiting the ability of industry to successfully compete in foreign markets, and growing distrust in the labour market hampering appropriate wage settlements, are all part of the crisis picture (Lavington 1922, p. 10). The cycle, Lavington (1922, pp. 11–12) adds, is a recurring phenomenon, as indicated by a century's history of prosperity and depression, the major causes of which need further investigation.

The second chapter of Lavington's book evaluates the nature of the business cycle. It suggests growth occurs in waves, whose rhythmical character demands an explanation. From peak to peak, the average cycle is estimated to last eight years, and is marked by three stages: rising activity, the peak (followed by the crisis and panic), and then declining activity. Wholesale prices follow a similar pattern, as does the rate of change in capital goods production (Lavington 1922, pp. 14–16). Lavington ends the chapter with the claim that the cycle is the major cause of unemployment in modern industrial society, before rejecting sun spots, or other natural phenomena *à la* Jevons, as explanations for the cycle.

Chapter III elaborates on the broad economic underpinnings of the contemporary business situation which generates cycles. Entrepreneurs make business decisions either in private firms, or in partnerships, or in joint-stock companies, engaged either in manufacturing, in wholesale or in retail trade (Lavington 1922, pp. 18–19). Modern production takes time, resources have to be invested to meet future demand, hence expectations about the future have to be formulated. Given this pattern, investment goods production tends to fluctuate more widely, but there is nevertheless considerable interdependence among all classes of producers. Incomes generate production, and indicate the prevalent volume of demand, which in turn influences output decisions. The pattern of the income–output cycle is also reflected in the price level, adding monetary factors to the recognised influences on cyclical patterns of the production process. Moreover, movements in this price index reflect the state of actual market decisions (Lavington 1922, pp. 23–25). Another way of stating the problem is that business decisions determine activity levels, and hence the cycle. The state of business confidence is therefore a key factor in cyclical behaviour (Lavington 1922, pp. 27–28).

It is, therefore, not surprising that business confidence is examined in Chapters IV and V. Lavington (1922, pp. 29–30) suggests that business estimates of future market conditions are influenced by waves of optimism and pessimism which can collectively, and cumulatively, rise or decline. In a planned and regulated economic world, Lavington (1922, p. 31) argued, such waves of confidence would have little influence on decision making in business. It is catching. This tends to exaggerate business reactions in both the upswing and the downswing, partly though their impact on purchasing power and money supply, which follow activity levels. As Lavington (1922, pp. 36–37) put it at the end of Chapter IV:

> When markets are rapidly expanding, and prices rising, the most efficient entrepreneurs find business easy and profitable; rationally based confidence gives way to optimism – judgements are infected by a general error; many businesses are extravagantly managed, many ventures are undertaken with no reasonable prospects of success; and causes are set in motion whose effects, in the form of realised business error, destroy the confidence from which they arise and bring the period of prosperity to an end.

In the second chapter on business confidence (Chapter V), Lavington adds the pertinent aspects from price influences on business confidence, thereby introducing the role of money in explaining the trade cycle. Rising confidence during an upswing is reflected in rising market expectations, rising output, and eventually rising prices. Initially, an expansion of output tends to lower prices but its impact falls also on money supply as bank deposits are more actively used as business improves. Monetary growth after some time outstrips output growth, putting pressure on prices on quantity theory grounds (Lavington 1922, pp. 47–48). However, rising prices gradually shift income increasingly towards entrepreneurs, lowering income levels for landlords, capitalists and especially wage labourers. Rising entrepreneurial incomes gradually induce errors in business forecasts from over-optimism, eventually bringing the upswing to an end. Price rises also gradually affect the availability of purchasing power as monetary growth slows with the burst of activity (Lavington 1922, pp. 50–51).

Chapters VI, VII and VIII present a discussion of the course of the business cycle. They quote Mitchell's study of business cycles on the view that it is difficult to identify the definite starting point or finish of the cycle (Lavington 1922, p. 53). In addition, Pigou's *Economics of Welfare* is cited on the association between good harvests and prosperity in the United States (Lavington 1922, p. 54). Lavington's account of the cycle starts with the downward phase of 'dull business'. As it proceeds, 'the minds of business men' gradually turn towards the future and its possibilities, armed with the thought that no depression is ever permanent. Confidence gradually starts to increase, assisted by other promising features in the economic situation: lower wages, reduction in stocks to very low levels, rising bank reserves and low interest rates, and the fall in wholesale prices comes to an end. Sooner or later the view takes holds that the end of the depression is near, and with this sentiment, business confidence rises further. Repair work is recommenced, it generates growth in purchasing power and renewed consumer spending. The process of recovery becomes cumulative and confidence grows with its acceleration. Although Lavington (1922, pp. 60–61) admits that the reasoning behind his theory is still speculative, the fact that it was accepted by economists such as Marshall and Pigou is a clear indication of its value. Lavington summed up the argument on the upswing at the end of Chapter VI, as a lead in to Chapter VII which reviews the eventual downturn in economic activity and spread of depression. As Lavington (1922, p. 65) put it:

> During the upward swing of a business cycle we have, then, a development of these conditions: a marked extension of capital plant whose completion and entrance into operation are likely to result in the exposure of error in some of the business forecasts which called it into being; the employment of resources in exceptionally risky ventures whose success depends upon the continuance of unusually favourable conditions; an expansion of credit, leading on the one hand to a great increase in business commitments based on a precarious extension of confidence, and on the other to a drain upon banking reserves; and finally an encroachment of costs upon the margin of business profits.

Are these conditions sufficient, Lavington asked rhetorically, 'to explain the transition to the following phase of apprehension and declining trade'? His answer is given in Chapter VII, dealing with 'the period of apprehension', and Chapter VIII, 'the growth of depression'. Chapter VII indicates that as the upswing gains force, it needs to be accompanied by monetary expansion, an expansion which is ultimately limited by bank reserves in the form of gold stocks and treasury notes, both inelastic in the longer run.

Furthermore, investment at the top end of the boom proceeds too quickly, the requisite levels of saving do not keep up with it, causing pressure on both investment yields in a downward direction, and upward pressure on the structure of interest rates. Lavington (1922, p. 69) attributed this part of the theory to Robertson's (1915) study of business fluctuations. As the boom further progresses, expected yields from new investments are not realised, this eventually lowers the demand for new capital, then lowers investment itself, and then the general level of demand for output. This fall in demand makes a depression inevitable (Lavington 1922, pp. 70–73, 78–79).

In Chapter VIII, Lavington (1922, p. 80) attributes the path to depression to 'a period of rising confidence, … rises into optimism, and … as a result of the business errors to which it gives rise, [the] precipitated … apprehension.' What turns apprehension into depression is part of the story told in Chapter VIII. The explanations are both real and monetary. As the situation is transformed gradually into one of declining confidence, optimistic expectations start to disappear and transform both the monetary and the savings-investment situation. Money is increasingly formed into hoards to enhance security for the businessman; savings thereby gradually come to exceed investment (Lavington 1922, pp. 82–83). This fall in demand reverses the progress of prices into price falls, hence lowering profits, and becoming 'a tax' on entrepreneurs making it virtually impossible for them to continue expanding their business.

At the end of Chapter VIII, Lavington (1922, pp. 88–92) presents a summary overview of the analysis in which the emphasis is on entrepreneurial expectations and the state of confidence on which they are based. Expectations of yields (from rising to falling), growing monetary tightness and rising interest rates, can trigger the change from general optimism to overall pessimism among businessmen. These cause the downward phase of the cycle, frequently via a spectacular crash. Lavington's (1922, p. 92) final paragraph in the chapter admitted the theory to be both 'too simple and too dogmatic' but it did contain many of the inferences which can be drawn on the matter from general economic theory and which appear to be in reasonable agreement with the facts. The facts are, however, more or less absent in this short discourse on the cycle. Lavington's study simply asserts that the 'rhythmical character of these changes arise from variations in the level of business confidence'.

In his final chapter, Lavington assessed the social conditions of the trade cycle. These are set in the background of a growing economy deriving much from both free trade and free entry, in which real wages are growing considerably and income distribution favours the middle classes and, to a lesser extent, the working class. These perspectives were drawn from studies by Clapham and Bowley. With respect to the growth of middle class incomes, Lavington's facts drew on the fifth edition of Marshall's *Principles* (Marshall 1907, 1925, p. 687). This is not to state that business cycles have no harmful effects over the longer run. Their impact on unemployment, for example, was considerable, as shown by William Beveridge's study, *Unemployment.* But then, as Marshall (1907, 1925, pp. 687–688) also suggested, even 'medieval artisans had inconsistent employment', so that the problem was an old one, not necessarily exclusively confined to contemporary developments (Lavington 1922, pp. 94, 96–97, 98, 99, 101). Social reorganisation, Lavington also argued, cannot really provide a cure. However, the banking system, Lavington (1922, p. 109) suggested, had done much to mitigate the extent of the cycle, and in particular had reduced the incidence of panics. Moreover, the policy of public works, particularly that of spacing the incidence of public works to fall into depressed periods, was spreading as a remedy for cyclical unemployment (Lavington 1922, pp. 109–110). Greater flexibility of wages and prices could also assist the speedier revival from periods of depression and unemployment. 'Checking the excessive growth of business confidence' by greater control over price changes would likewise mitigate and limit 'the extravagance of the boom and the intensity of the following period of depression' (Lavington 1922, p. 113). Remedies for the adverse consequence of the cycle, in Lavington's view, were necessarily related to the fundamental causes of the business cycle.

As Lavington himself came close to admitting, there was little originality in his treatment of the business cycle. The essentials of its position were very similar to Marshall's brief treatment of the subject in *Economics of Industry*

(Marshall and Marshall 1879, Book III Chapters 1, 2). It also considerably resembled Pigou's discussion of cyclical fluctuations in Part VI of *The Economics of Welfare* (Pigou 1920, 1921). Finally, the publication of Robertson's *A Study of Industrial Fluctuations* in 1915 had greatly assisted Lavington, and was directly acknowledged for its underlying saving-investment analysis. Lavington's main contribution was the book's emphasis on the financial market and the uncertainty faced by businessmen when making financial and investment decisions. Furthermore, the book was a neat little volume, clearly setting out business sentiments and fluctuating confidence explanations of the business cycle, so popular in the 1920s. Lavington's study was quite critically reviewed by Cannan (1922) who noted a number of errors in the argument. It was, however not mentioned in Haberler's (1937, 1952) classic survey of the literature on *Prosperity and Depression* nor, earlier, in Pigou's (1927) study of *Industrial Fluctuations.* Robertson, as mentioned in the previous section, did, however, defend Lavington's and Marshall's position on the rate of interest, and more generally, their saving-investment analysis, against Keynes's criticism in the *General Theory* (Presley 1978, pp. 207–209).

V

Lavington published three articles in *Economica* in the 1920s. The first (Lavington 1924) looked at the interconnection between long and short rates in the money market. After stating the general principle that interest rates tend to be higher, the longer the duration of the loan (Lavington 1924, pp. 292–293), Lavington indicated that security markets transform long borrowings into short, highly marketable loan instruments, the case for both the bill market and the stock exchange. Lavington provided data on three months bill rates and the yields on consols, suggesting that these rates generally move together, but not always (Lavington 1924, pp. 295–297). However, the data on long and short rates showed no normal relationship in which long rate changes are invariably those appropriate to corresponding short-term rates (Lavington 1924, pp. 298–299). Examination of the data suggested the following conclusions to Lavington (1924, pp. 202–203). Organised markets facilitate a relationship between long-term and short-term interest rates, though the financial implications from the war seem to have destroyed the conformity of movements in these rates revealed by pre-war averages. However, the profitability of business, greatly influenced by movements in the general price level, by its influence on the demand for capital, seem to have a stronger impact on rate changes in the market. As previously mentioned, this article was cited in Pigou (1927), a rare sign of recognition of Lavington's work by his Cambridge colleagues.

Lavington (1926b) discussed the role of monopoly in preserving business stability, in particular the even output strategies visible in monopolistic behaviour as compared with that of competitive firms (Lavington 1926b, p. 136). In general, this monopoly action is seen as less beneficial to the consumer as the alternative, less stable output policy of the competitive firm. However, Lavington (1926b, p. 147) suggested in concluding his argument that there may be a substantial benefit to the public from this stable monopolist output strategy if it increased continuous employment of appliances and labour. It probably also raised supply of the commodity in question as compared with the outcome under competitive conditions. Lavington's first excursion in print into an aspect of the theory of the firm did also preserve strong links to his discussion of the evils of unemployment raised in the context of the social consequences of the trade cycle, as discussed in the previous section of this chapter.

Lavington's final journal article was devoted to a topic completely within the theory of the firm. Moreover, it was explicitly related to Marshall's treatment of this topic in *Industry and Trade.* Under the title, 'Technical Influences and Vertical Integration', the paper, more specifically, examined the proposition that the more restricted the variety of processes undertaken by a single form, the more simple is the management task of direction (Lavington 1927, p. 27). This 'higher specialisation' was described by Marshall as 'uniform continuous process', combined with more 'powerful appliances of production', constituting the 'dominant technical economies of modern means of production' (Lavington 1927, p. 28). Marshall had illustrated this phenomenon in his *Industry and Trade* by the operation of the German Dye Trust and the United States steel industry where generally techniques induced the aggregation of business. Individualism in production was here sacrificed for the sake of standardisation, with only high quality goods (in the motor vehicle and in the woollen textiles industries) preserving individuality in production (Lavington 1927, p. 34). Lavington (1927, pp. 35–36) concluded his discussion with the following propositions. Form and size of business was influenced by love of power and the desire for monopoly, not just by economic efficiency. However, given the complexity and volume of tasks involved in a single business, such aspects of the specialised production process had consequences for the efficiency and organisation of the managerial task. Following Marshall's position, as expressed in *Industry and Trade*, Lavington urged that the dominant technical economies are those attainable from the application of modern continuous process and powerful appliances, but that the pressure to attain this situation required vertical integration and lateral disassociation of processes. There is only a small range of appropriate processes but considerable promise of large output, modifying pressure for vertical integration in modern business, as shown in the modern steel industry with its strong need for 'balanced plant'.

The three *Economica* articles published by Lavington can be interpreted as a switch in research interests on Lavington's part, in line with his teaching responsibilities at Cambridge. The second and third of these articles were both devoted to topics related to the theory of the firm, even if the first of these articles stressed the highly desirable 'macro-economic' policy objective of stability in the employment of both labour and capital appliances. Such macro-economic considerations are totally absent in the 1927 article, devoted to vertical integration and the benefits of economies of scale. Lavington's death that year meant that this new research endeavour could not be further pursued and that Lavington's explorations of Marshall's industry economics ended with the 1927 *Economica* article. Further conclusions follow in the final section.

VI

As a mature age student, with employment experience in banking before graduation, Lavington entered Cambridge late, to take Parts I and II of the then still fairly new Economics Tripos, gaining first class honours on both occasions. Lavington's attendance at Cambridge was too late for him to have had Marshall as a teacher. He was, however, taught by two of Marshall's more eminent students, Pigou and Maynard Keynes, keeping intellectual contact with Pigou as professor, as an academic and, as shown by some of his publications, gaining specific advice from Pigou on treating certain analytical problems. There is little direct evidence of much contact with Keynes after graduation, and the commentators (Bridel 1987; Eshag 1963; Patinkin 1965, 1976) treat Lavington as a strict Marshallian and Pigovian, and therefore part of the Cambridge old guard in so far as Keynes was concerned. This picture is not completely accurate. Lavington's articles for the *Economic Journal*, which Maynard Keynes would definitely have seen as one of its editors, frequently discussed themes which were to become of importance for some of Keynes's own monetary research. This is discussed later. It is emphasised here that Lavington's early death – in 1927, at just forty-six years of age – facilitated the treatment of him in this way, when these commentators were chronicling the road from Marshall to Keynes's *General Theory*.

Furthermore, the commentators just mentioned effectively treat Lavington as the author of one book even though they often formally acknowledge that he published a second book, *The Trade Cycle.* In other words, Lavington's importance, historically contemplated, rests on his study of *The English Capital Market* published in 1921 with what probably is best perceived as a corrected reprint, posthumously published in 1929. References to his eight journal articles – five in the *Economic Journal* and three in *Economica* – occur most infrequently. Nor is it generally recognised (Collard 1990 is an exception) that Lavington may have started to switch his teaching and research interests to questions of industrial organisation – the subject of his final two articles for *Economica* and, to a lesser but still significant extent, in his second *Economic Journal* article (Lavington 1912). Lavington specifically related this interest to Marshall's work, especially his emphasis on 'organisation' as a new, important, fourth agent of production in addition to labour, land and capital. However, it is fully recognised in the commentary literature that Lavington was a staunch if not dogmatic, Marshallian, enormously devoted to the system of the 'master'. His remarks that 'it is all in Marshall' are frequently quoted in this context, even if Lavington had virtually no direct association whatsoever with Marshall (and see in this context Fay (1927) on Lavington's tendency in tutorials to seek full and 'authorised' explanations of the various analytical components of Marshall's system).

There is a peculiarity in this devotion to Marshall by Lavington if seen purely as a monetary economist. Marshall himself had published little on money during his lifetime. As already indicated, there was Marshall's evidence to official inquiries, particularly to the 1887 Gold and Silver Commission; a few journal articles, and a chapter or two in the 1879 *Economics of Industry*, purely attributable to him even if the book in which they appeared, was jointly published with his wife. *Money, Credit and Commerce*, the volume specifically desgned to set out Marshall's position on monetary issues, did not appear until 1923, a decade after Lavington's early *Economic Journal* articles on banking, on uncertainty and the rate of interest, and on speculation. As mentioned earlier, two of these articles were noted by Knight (1921) as part of the small but growing literature on risk and uncertainty, both crucial features in Lavington's depiction of the monetary and financial system as it was developing in the second and third decade of the twentieth century. Lavington's contributions to risk and uncertainty, as recognised early on by Knight, are interesting for at least two reasons. First, they show the importance of not ignoring Lavington's journal articles but treating them as complementary elaborations on the depiction of the English capital market given in his 1921 book. Second, the 1912 paper on uncertainty and the rate of interest, the 1913 on the importance of speculative activity to the operation of the market, and the 1925/26 two-part paper on risk in this context, clearly indicate that risk and uncertainty in financial transactions were part of the research agenda on both sides of the Atlantic in the early decades of the twentieth century.

Furthermore, as shown earlier in this chapter, Lavington was very clear on the importance of uncertainty, particularly in the context of the rate of interest, and in the matter of investment choices whether in 'real capital', in securities, or in bank balances. The banking system is in fact depicted by him as mitigating uncertainty in business and in other investment activity by facilitating the creation of appropriate financial reserves. Moreover, Lavington devoted Chapter XIV in his *The English Capital Market* to matters associated with uncertainty on the costs of, and returns to, risk bearing. This discussion, it can also be noted, benefited from Pigou's assistance in designing an appropriate set of diagrams for analysing the matter (Lavington 1921, 1929, pp. 87–88). Skidelsky's recent claim in his new book, *The Return of the Master*, needs therefore some correction unless it embraces the Cambridge input to Keynes's emphasis as a key factor in his theory, of 'the existence of inescapable uncertainty about the future' (cited in *The Economist*, 31 October 2009, p. 80). The investigation of uncertainty was very much in the air at Cambridge in the 1920s, with special reference in the case of Lavington to the rate of interest and the price of liquidity.

In this context, Lavington's Marshallian credentials may be briefly reiterated. In the first instance, these reveal that Lavington designed his work as additions to material not fully treated by Marshall himself and within a basically Marshallian framework of analysis. That analytical framework for Lavington consisted of both the *Principles of Economics* and *Industry and Trade* but, with monetary economics and the analysis of the trade cycle specifically in mind, also of the

1879 *Economics of Industry*, some specific articles by Marshall on such topics, and his evidence to Royal Commissions. This comes out clearly in the Fay and Wright obituaries of Lavington, and from the text of Lavington's books and articles. Specific parts of Marshall's work to which Lavington explicitly adhered include his acceptance of 'organisation' as a very important agent of production, the general cost analysis, the theory of the firm under competition and monopoly and the overall saving-investment analysis in relation to the rate of interest. Moreover, Marshall's judgements on the growth of the middle classes in contemporary society, on medieval unemployment, and on the theory of management, were 'uncritically' accepted by Lavington as important 'truths'. This in no way detracts from Lavington's originality in his work on money and financial institutions, under uncertainty and risk, much of which cannot be found in Marshall's own writings and, as pointed out in the previous paragraph, anticipating Keynes's contribution in some respects. Schumpeter (1954, pp. 895, 1084) appreciated Lavington's originality in these matters, because Lavington, together with so many of his Cambridge colleagues, 'developed Marshallian teaching … on lines of their own'.

9 Walter Layton (1884–1966) on *The Theory of Prices* (1912) and *The Relations of Capital and Labour* (1914)

Marshallian texts *pur sang*?

After completing the new Economics and Politics Tripos at Cambridge University with first class honours in 1906, Walter Layton taught economics at Cambridge from 1908 to 1914 under Pigou as the new professor. During these years as economics teacher, Layton published two monographs. The first, *An Introduction to the Theory of Prices*, was published in 1912; the second, *The Relations of Capital and Labour*, appeared in 1914. This chapter evaluates the Marshallian credentials of these books in the usual manner. Section I provides a brief biographical sketch of Walter Layton, emphasising his personal contacts with Marshall during his lifetime. Sections II and III then succinctly examine the contents of his two books, emphasising their Marshallian credentials in particular by way of Marshall citations or of the similarity of their contents to Marshall's pronouncements on these topics in his published writings or elsewhere. Section IV presents the conclusions.

I

Walter Layton was born in London on 15 May 1884. He grew up in a musical and cultured upper middle class household. Layton was initially educated at the King's School, London, and the Westminster School; he then attended University College, London, where he gained a third class honours result in history in 1903. Subsequently, he entered Trinity College, Cambridge, as a graduate student, taking the second part of the Economics Tripos, which he completed with first class honours in 1906. While a student in 1905, he was treasurer in the recently revived Social Discussion Society. Layton won the Cobden Essay Prize in 1907 with the subject, 'Relative Wages'. Along with Keynes, he was appointed assistant lecturer in economics at Cambridge in 1908, the year that Marshall retired. His position was paid for from Pigou's own pocket, Marshall's successor as professor of economics at Cambridge. Layton was elected Fellow of Gonville and Caius College in 1909. That year, he was also appointed Newmarch lecturer in economics at University College, London. He became lecturer in economics at Cambridge in 1911. In 1910, Layton married Dorothea Osmaston, a marriage resulting in seven children.

While an academic at Cambridge and London, Layton published his two books on economics, that is, in 1912, his *Introduction to the Theory of Prices*

(1912, second edition with an additional chapter, 1922) and his *The Relations of Capital to Labour* in 1914, the usual date assigned to its publication. Earlier, he had published several journal articles: a paper on 'Argentina and Food Supply' for the 1905 *Economic Journal* and one on 'Changes in the Wages of Domestic Servants' for the 1908 *Journal of the Royal Statistical Society.* Subsequently, in 1914, he published a review article in the *Economic Journal* on the land question and, in 1939, a paper on 'British Opinion on the Gold Standard' in the *Quarterly Journal of Economics*.

Layton's promising academic career was cut short by the outbreak of the First World War in 1914 and the necessity to engage in war work. After a short period with the Board of Trade during the early months of the war, Layton joined the Ministry of Munitions, part of a team selected by Lloyd George to run the new ministry. Among other intellectuals, this team included William Beveridge. On the Munitions Council, Layton worked closely with both Lloyd George and Winston Churchill (under whom he was to serve in a similar capacity during the Second World War). In early 1917, Layton accompanied the Millner Commission to Russia. This had been appointed to discover how long Russia was capable of staying in the war on the side of its west European allies. Here Layton predicted privately that Russia's position as an active military participant was not likely to last long, given the imminent threat of a revolutionary uprising. In 1919, after rejecting a knighthood for his war services, Layton was named Companion of Honour.

At the conclusion of the war, Layton decided to build a career in economic journalism instead of continuing his academic career. He became editor of *The Economist* in 1922, and editorial director of the *News Chronicle* and *The Star* in 1930. With financial assistance from various friends, he was able to buy *The Economist* in 1928. Layton served as its editor for sixteen years (1922–1938) and was chairman of its board of directors from 1944 to 1963. In this context, the historian of *The Economist* (Edwards 1993, p. 633) has suggested that Layton's greatest achievement as owner (and editor):

> was to have his *Economist* read widely in the corridors of power abroad as well as at home. It was cautious and slightly on the dull side of solid; but it carried great weight. *Economists* went to the foreign offices and to the central banks abroad rather than to the bookstalls. They were highly influential copies.

The paper gained in importance because Layton was important, 'and because the interlocking circles in which he moved gave him access to information, the dissemination of which in turn increased his and his 's influence'. Layton's move to buy the paper when it was placed on the market was largely designed to maintain its liberal political stance on economic policy issues, a task facilitated by his long editorship during the 1920s and 1930s.

Layton returned to government service during the Second World War, taking charge of the Ministry of Supply and Production at the personal request of

Winston Churchill. He was made Baron Layton of Dane Hill in 1947. As a long associate of Liberal politics in Britain and a lifelong holder of Liberal views, it was not surprising that he served as deputy leader of the Liberal Party in the House of Lords from 1952 to 1955. Layton therefore was a highly influential person over much of his adult life, first in his role of 'press baron' in the 1920s and 1930s, and then, more briefly, as a leading figure in the House of Lords. He died in January 1966, aged eighty-one, still vice-chairman of the board of *The Economist* (Milgate and Levy 1987b, III, pp. 149–150; Edwards 1993, pp. 606–610; Hubback, 1985; Witzel 2004, pp. 666–669).

Something more can be said about Layton's economic education at Cambridge. His extant lecture notes reveal that the lectures he attended in Michaelmas term 1905 were devoted to international trade and government activity. They commenced with a brief history of the subject and contained autobiographical fragments of how Marshall himself had come to economics. The lectures also raised methodological issues, including the view that flexible definitions were the most useful and that definitions should always be treated as a 'matter of convenience'. Then followed issues of capital theory, of economic progress with special reference to British coal and steel production; taxation and rent; the association between religious ideas and the durability of primitive socialist societies; and the effects of permanent peace on the rate of interest. Marshall's Lent term lectures for 1906 dealt with the quantity theory of money, the heading used by Layton in his notes. They also covered aspects of business fluctuations and explanations of speculation in both the money and stock markets. Layton later recalled that he literally 'soaked himself' in Marshallian economics through attending Marshall's lectures when a Cambridge economics student.

More generally, he indicated about Marshall's lectures, that:

> I do not think I shall be exaggerating if I said he never once repeated himself. It was commonly said among the undergraduates that he took his text out of that morning's *Times* and talked about anything that had struck him in the day's news. It would be nearer the mark to say he gave us the benefit of his current study on the book he was writing on industry and commerce.
>
> (cited in Hubback 1985, p. 18)

In short, by attending Marshall's lectures, Layton appears to have been given an extensive overview of Marshall's economics, reinforced when such lecture attendance was invariably supplemented for the better students by extensive reading from Marshall's *Principles of Economics* and by the writing of regular essays for him on set topics (see Groenewegen 1995a, pp. 319–320). That, and his own teaching experience at Cambridge from 1908, undoubtedly made it possible for Layton to write the two economics books he had published before the end of 1914.

II

Layton's preface to the first edition of his *Introduction to the Study of Prices* ends with a very handsome acknowledgement to the importance of Marshall as Layton's economics teacher. 'My indebtedness to the teaching and inspiration of Dr. Alfred Marshall will be evident to all who are acquainted with recent economic thought in England' (Layton 1912, 1922, p. vi). In this context, it may be recalled that Layton had attended Marshall's lectures on the quantity theory in 1906. However, in this book, Layton's indebtedness is more strikingly revealed by his references to Marshall's evidence to the Gold and Silver Commission of 1887 (Layton 1912, 1922, pp. 36, 82), to Marshall's 1887 article in the *Contemporary Review* on 'Fluctuations in Prices and the Precious Metals' (Layton 1912, 1922, p. 51). He also specifically acknowledged Marshall's argument on the general definition of 'national income' (Layton 1912, 1922, p. 5n. 1), as well as for the

> pregnant suggestion … that under an ideal system of currency prices should fall at such a rate that receivers of fixed incomes (such as annuitants, civil servants, etc.) should secure a fair proportion of man's increasing control over his material environment, *i.e.* the purchasing power of a given income should increase with every improvement in the arts of production, transport, etc.
>
> (Layton 1912, 1922, p. 106n. 1)

Finally, at the end of Appendix C, 'TheViscious Circle of Prices', Layton referred his readers 'to Marshall's *Principles of Economics*, Book V Chapter VI, for a detailed discussion of this question, and a statement of the theoretical conditions under which any single group can increase its proportionate share of the national dividend' (Layton 1912, 1922, p. 165). The impact of these references for the Marshallian qualities of Layton's *Study* is pursued later in this section, after an overview of Layton's argument in the book as a whole.

The 1912 edition of Layton's book on the price level consisted of nine chapters, seven appendices as well as a number of statistical charts showing the movement of wholesale prices since 1800, those of the price index number, of Sauerbeck's index number distinguishing food and materials, and of movements in money wages, real wages, retail prices and unemployment. Chapter I dealt with a statement of the problem, that is, the analysis of the general causes of fluctuations in the value of money, and their consequences for, and effects on, the various classes of society. Chapter II discussed the complex meaning to be attached to the notion of the general price level, while its consequences of changes in the general price level were discussed by its impact on various types of income recipients (Layton 1912, 1922, p. 15) and, following Marshall, its effects on the general productivity of industry. The last referred explicitly to Marshall's detailed evidence before the Gold and Silver Commission, in particularly to his lengthy answers for Q9816 to Q9831 (Marshall 1887a, 1926, pp. 90–100). In fact, the whole of Marshall's evidence to this Commission was viewed by Layton as relevant to the problem at hand, as noted by him at the end of Chapter IV (Layton 1912, 1922, p. 36). Chapter III discussed the wholesale index number's course over the whole of the nineteenth century; Chapter IV provided a 'digression of monetary theory in relation to prices' in which Layton expounded the merits of the quantity theory of money, to which he was introduced by Marshall's lectures in 1906. Chapters V, VI, VII and VIII then looked at the broad tendencies in price movements over discrete periods as respectively falling from 1820 to 1849, rising from 1849 to 1873, falling from 1874 to 1895, and rising from 1896 to 1910. Chapter X, added for the 1922 edition, discussed movements in prices and currency from 1913 to 1919, in order to indicate the changes in the behaviour of prices during the First World War and the first year of post-war reconstruction. Chapter IX, the final chapter of the 1912 edition, presented conclusions based on the evidence from the nineteenth and early twentieth century, as presented in the four previous chapters.

From this brief overview, it is easy to describe the contents of the book as reflecting a clear Marshallian principle in their construction: the presentation of the historical facts required theoretical explanation, and the theory needed to conform to the facts. In short, the essentially nineteenth century economic history of fluctuations in the price level and currency movements presented in the greater part of the book, both reflected, and depended on, the theory of price level fluctuations, as well as the theoretical principles underlying the nature and scope of the various price index numbers. Layton in this respect was therefore a true student of Marshall because he showed fact and theory to be highly interdependent in explanations of currency fluctuations and associated price level changes.

One further general observation can be made about a Marshallian aspect in Layton's study of prices. His approach to the quantity theory of money in Chapter IV is multi-faceted in the manner in which Marshall tended to approach that theory, a matter, moreover, which Marshall would have stressed in his lectures on the subject attended by Layton in 1906. A chart in that chapter (Layton 1912, 1922, p. 31) indicates no fewer than six factors relevant to estimating changes in the effective quantity of money, and another six factors relevant to estimating the volume of transactions to be defrayed by the effective quantity of money. As shown earlier (Chapter 2 above, pp. 15–16) in the context of Marshall's criticism of Nicholson's submission to the Gold and Silver Commission, this was very similar to Marshall's approach to the quantity theory.

On more closely examining Layton's citations of Marshall, it is easy to suggest that these were rather varied and far-reaching. Marshall's definition of national income as 'the net aggregate of commodities and capital, material and immaterial, including services produced annually by the labour of a country acting upon its natural resources (Layton 1912, 1922, p. 5n. 1; Marshall 1916, p. 523 which approximates this definition) is a case in point.

Layton (1912, 1922, p. 51 and n. 1) cited Marshall's essay 'On Remedies for Fluctuations of General Prices' on one of the effects of war on the price level,

'The war has taken men away from the workshop, has killed some, unfitted others for their work; they diverted industries to supply the material of war fare and had destroyed vast qualities of commodities of all kinds' (Marshall 1887b, 1925, pp. 194, 196). This was an interesting supply-side cause of rising prices during periods of war, effected by a diminished output of use for meeting monetary demands of consumers and producers. It also was one of the leading factors discussed in the explanation of rising prices (1849–1874), which included the Crimean War (1854–1856) discussed by Layton in Chapter IV.

Although there are no further references to Marshall's 1887 essay on remedies for fluctuating prices, the general thrust of that paper is nevertheless reflected in the contents of Layton's analysis. Layton's book reviews virtually all the issues raised by Marshall in his discussion of remedies for a fluctuating price level: that is, the 'evils of a fluctuating standard of money' with respect to income distribution; the failure of the precious metals to act 'as a good standard of value'; the possibility of replacing gold and silver as the customary standard of value; the use of 'a fixed-ratio mintage' for such a standard and whether this should be considered as a 'stable' form of bi-metallism; and finally Marshall's own solution to the problem by way of bi-metallic convertibility of a unit of purchasing power in terms of a basket of commodities which on average reflects the various tastes in consumption of all classes of society. Layton's concluding chapter addresses all of these matters, together with the stable currency proposals advanced over the years by Jevons, and by Irving Fisher in his *The Purchasing Power of Money* (Layton 1912, 1922, pp. 106–111).

Marshall's position on the 'divergence of interest between various sections of the community' is quoted by Layton from Marshall's evidence to the Gold and Silver Commission presented in 1887.

> I think that it wants very much stronger statistical evidence than one yet has to prove that the fall of prices diminishes perceptibly or in the long run the total productiveness of industry. Supposing that it does not diminish considerably the total productiveness of industry, then its effect is, I think, on the whole good, because it certainly tends to cause a better distribution of wealth than we would otherwise have.... And really I could not say that there was any serious attempt to prove anything else than a depression of prices, a depression of interest, and a depression of profits – there is that undoubtedly.

On the interjection of the Chairman of the Commission, 'Then do I understand you to think that the depression in those three respects [i.e. prices, interest and profits] is consistent with a condition of prosperity?', Marshall replied, 'Certainly; the employer gets less and the employee gets more' (Marshall 1887a, 1926, Qs 9816–9825, pp. 90–100, as cited in Layton 1912, 1922, pp. 11–12).

The redistribution of income from various parts of employers' income to that of labourers in the form of wages as part of the 'vicious circle of prices' was also raised in Appendix C of Layton's book, in the context of which he mentioned

Marshall's *Principles of Economics*, Book V Chapter VI, on the application of the theory of joint production to aspects of the theory of income distribution. This chapter showed that there were cases where a small section of labourers involved in the production of a commodity (a particular type of labour crucial to the production process) could snatch a special advantage in terms of higher wages from this strategically important role they played in that manufacture. Marshall's discussion in the *Principles* of this rather complicated matter is referred to the reader by Layton (1912, 1922, p. 165) as 'a detailed discussion of this question, and [for] a statement of the theoretical conditions under which any single group can increase its proportionate share of the national dividend'.

Layton's first book, therefore, clearly indicates its author's Marshallian credentials. Apart from the general acknowledgement provided in the preface of the benefits Layton had received from Marshall's economics teachings, Layton cited some of Marshall's major published work on monetary theory produced in 1887 in both his evidence to the Gold and Silver Commission, and in his article on remedies for fluctuations of general prices. In addition, Layton cited, and on at least one occasion referred his readers, to technical topics raised in Marshall's *Principles*. These were the definition of national income and the theoretical foundations on the distributional tactic open to specific groups in society interested in, and capable of, snatching benefits for themselves through redistribution as part of the theory of 'joint production'. Moreover, the nature of the argument in Marshall's 1887 article on remedies for price fluctuations was broadly reflected in Layton's treatment of this topic in his first book.

III

Layton's *The Relations of Capital and Labour*, the second of his two books, was written during 1913 and 1914 in the context of what he described as a period of considerable industrial unrest. Although the statistical data on industrial disputes for the years 1910 to 1913 were subject to considerable revision, both these data and the data on the working days lost for the United Kingdom clearly indicate a sharp increase in labour unrest during the three years following 1910. Table 9.1 gives the details:

As G.D.H. Cole (1913, 1917. pp. 403–410) argued, during the three years from 1910, 'the strike has shown its power', and the labour movement in general

Table 9.1 United Kingdom industrial disputes 1910–1913

Year	*Disputes*	*Working days lost ('000)*
1910	521	9,867
1911	872	10,155
1912	834	40,890
1913	1,459	11,631

Source: Mitchell and Deane 1962, pp. 71–72.

has been capable of achieving far better results for the working class in improving living standards and conditions of work than parliamentary cooperation between the Liberal Party and the still very small parliamentary Labour Party. This was despite the fact that not all strikes were successful. Nevertheless, '[b]oth the national Transport Strike of 1911 and the national Railway strike brought the workers in these industries large advances, and the recent [miner] strikes [1913] in the Black Country were also, in the main, very successful' (Cole 1913, 1917, p. 403). He concluded, 'the strike is not played out, and ... [if] real wages can be made to keep pace with the rise in prices, ... Labour [has to be] ceaselessly active in the economic sphere.' The issues of labour unrest which inspired Layton to write on the relations of capital and labour in 1913 was clearly a topic of major concern in the three years before the start of the First World War.

Layton had in fact two aims in writing his introductory book on *Relations of Capital and Labour*. The first was to provide factual and theoretical background to the period of major labour unrest during 1911, 1912 and 1913; the second was to expand this background by focusing on the fundamental considerations affecting relations between labour and capital, including the determinants of the national distribution of wealth, and of the prices to be paid to labour (the employees) and capital (the employers) to secure their willing service for the community in productive activity. Aspects of income distribution featured therefore in his two books under consideration.

The division of the contents of the book clearly indicates its dual purpose. Excluding the introductory chapter, the first thirteen of its sixteen chapters are devoted to the distributional issues or to detailed discussion of the factors influencing the determination of wage rates and profits. Only the final three chapters, comprising more than one fifth of the contents, addressed the topic of industrial disputes and the various means of their settlement. Of the thirteen chapters on wage and profit determination, only the first three are devoted to 'theory', the other ten deal with various applied issues which can influence the wage bargain. Thus Chapter 5 deals with grades of labour, Chapter 6 with local aspects in wage determination, Chapter 7 with changes in the price level, Chapter 8 with trade unions, Chapter 9 with the influence of efficiency, Chapter 10 with competitive forces, Chapter 11 with fairness, Chapter 12 with the influence of state regulation, Chapter 13 with the use of sliding-scales and profit-sharing arrangements, while Chapter 14 explains the process of collective bargaining. The wide range of influences on wage determination in practice provides the main thrust of the book.

By way of introduction, Chapter 1 surveys the various contemporary factors which have made the question of the relations of capital and labour such an important issue. According to Layton, these include the increasing recognition in society of the importance of social obligation and responsibility on the part of business (Layton 1914, p. 6); the rising influence of socialist ideas including syndicalism, the last as represented in the United States by the International Workers of the World movement (Layton 1914, pp. 7–8, 14–15); the growing perception of the inherent injustice of the 'extremes of wealth and poverty' existing side by side in 'progressive societies'. These are associated by Layton with the replacement of 'the hold of orthodox religion' for the mass of the working classes by secular, ethical beliefs in the necessity of social and economic justice (Layton 1914, pp. 7–8). Combined with a growth in community feeling of public responsibility for the improvement in the operation of the industrial system, these include the case of fair wages which ensure a reasonable standard of life for every worker (Layton 1914, pp. 17–18). The pages of Chapter 1 clearly announce an intention on Layton's part to treat the matter of contemporary capital and labour relations in the broadest possible manner and not simply in terms of the principles developed on this subject by the economic theorist.

This is not to say that Layton ignores the principles of economic theory. They come to the fore in Chapter 2 devoted to the theory of wages in terms of the productivity of labour, greatly enhanced over time by technical progress and the accumulation of capital as instruments of production. This makes the product of labour and capital essentially a joint product which can only completely belong to the labourers if all saving and accumulations for these means of production is done by them, so that they themselves own the capital with which they work. This argument leads Layton to what he called the essential principle of distribution:

> If there is genuine competition on both sides, the joint product of labour and capital will be divided according to the relative importance in production of capital and labour, and the need which each has for the co-operation of the other.
>
> (Layton 1914, p. 24)

For Layton this is essentially an issue of supply and demand. If many labourers are working with few tools or implements, the value of tools will be relatively great compared with that of labour. If additional capital becomes available, the workers in question will offer to buy it at a price 'determined by the addition to the total product which could be attributed to the new capital, in other words, what economists call the "marginal net product" of capital …' (Layton 1914, p. 24). However, if labour is scarce, the situation is reversed, and its marginal net product (or price) would be high relative to that of capital (Layton 1914, p. 25). Layton then deals with the operational question of whether a marginal net product is there to be found. While admitting that in practice this may not be the case '*in every trade*', Layton claims that the theory holds good 'if competition works out in detail in one industry', illustrating this by examples of plate layers in the railways and North Country farm labour. Hence, Layton stated that the conclusion remains valid that:

> the level of the whole wage system is set by the productivity of those labourers whom it is only just worth the employer's while to employ, and the rate of interest [as the price of capital] is determined by the productivity of the capital which it is only just worth his while to borrow.
>
> (Layton 1914, pp. 25–27)

Three aspects of this theory of distribution are then highlighted by Layton. First, the theory reflects little more than the general principle of supply and demand with its emphasis on the relative scarcity of capital and labour. Second, dynamic factors in the process cannot be ignored: for example, on the introduction of labour saving machinery, the initial fall in demand for labour is offset in the longer run by the growth in capital caused by the short-term rise in profits generated by the new machines. Third, emphasis on productivity in the theory implicitly rejects the classical subsistence theory of wages as irrelevant since it shows living standards for workers are a consequence and not a determinant of wages (Layton 1914, pp. 27–31).

Chapter 3 starts with the proposition 'that verification of this theory of wages by reference to the actual facts of industrial life [means] ... that many qualifications have to be made'. For example, the assumption of 'free and equal ... competition is far from being true' and monopoly aspects have to be frequently considered when discussing wages (Layton 1914, pp. 31–32). Nevertheless, Chapter 3 presents the actual statistical data on wages and interest rates for large parts of the nineteenth century and beyond in which patterns of wage growth and changes in interest rates are subdivided into three historical periods. The post mid-1890s situation, that is, the third and most recent of the three periods, is characterised by Layton as showing continuing improvements in industry, sharp rises in interest rates and profits, and slow increases in wages. The last are explained for Layton by the very rapid growth in the work force following the very high birth rate recorded for the 1870s, as compared with a much slower rate of saving (Layton 1914, pp. 37–40). Layton admits that the effective increase of domestic capital is impossible to measure statistically but argues that increased luxury spending by the well-to-do (on motor cars, for example), the sharp rise in foreign investment and increased unproductive spending on national security by government have substantially lowered the growth of capital, and thereby the demand for labour. Layton (1914, pp. 43–44) argued here specifically on Say's Law grounds that 'spending out of taxation does not increase the demand for labour by one penny piece, it only alters the character of the demand, but does not increase it'. In short, relative abundance of labour and relative scarcity of capital explain the relative slow wage growth from the mid-1890s demonstrated by the statistical data. Growth data in terms of either national income or national output were not yet consistently available on an official basis.

Profits and their determination are the subject of Chapter 4, since profits are what Layton (1914, p. 48) calls 'the third element in the problem'. Profits are defined as the price of direction and organisation of business by the *entrepreneur* both in initiating new undertakings and for having the responsibility for disposing of the product. Layton also describes profits as the residual from the proceeds of selling a firm's output after wages and interest have been paid. Profits, Layton added, need to be sufficient to cover the 'earnings of management' or what 'would have to be paid to a salaried manager' and to provide adequate compensation for risk. Any surplus above these is akin to a rent for special skills in organisation and management (Layton 1914, pp. 48–50), or what Marshall called quasi-rent. Given his assumption of competitive analysis the existence of monopoly profits is ignored in this context.

Layton made several other points on the nature of profits. Profits are paid out as dividends in the case of joint-stock companies. Under 'free competition' profits are reduced to 'normal' earnings of management and the necessary compensation for ordinary risk or, in short, 'to the level that is just adequate to induce *entrepreneurs* to remain in business' (Layton 1914, pp. 51–52). Few statistical data are available on profits but data regularly published on dividend payments are said to act as a reasonable proxy. Accounting profits require for their calculation that the value of capital is left intact where this includes the firm's 'goodwill', a rather difficult operation, though more or less reliable estimates are invariably made for business and taxation purposes. At the end of Chapter 4, Layton concludes 'that the grossest inequalities in the distribution of wealth are due neither to the rate of interest, nor to profits as ordinarily understood, but to speculation and alterations of capital values of various kinds', a view he may have heard expressed in Marshall's lectures. Values of land and other productive assets, as well as those of stocks and shares, are key examples as are the potential gains to be made from special knowledge (inside information) by those involved in the industry. These considerations in the end make the notion of profit a somewhat difficult one to handle. Because of them, after all, it fluctuates between 'fair and reasonable profits' and the 'excesses of the competitive system' (Layton 1914, p. 67).

Little needs to be said on Chapters 6 to 14 devoted to discussion of a wide range of relatively minor influences on wage (and occasionally profit) determination. As MacGregor (1914) indicated in his review, these chapters contain, among other things, an interesting discussion of the effects of scientific management and 'time and motion studies' on efficiency wages defined in the Marshallian manner 'with reference to the exertion and *efficiency* required of the worker' (Layton 1914, pp. 121–125; Marshall 1920, p. 549); on the relative merits of competition and socialism – 'the State becomes a very imperfect machine for interpreting the multiplicity of human wants' – (Layton 1914, pp. 129–130); on the definition of 'fair wages' in terms of 'the community's estimate of the value of the work done' (Layton 1914, pp. 152–154); and, in connection with state authorities determining 'minimum wages', the possible 'effects a somewhat rigid system will have on employment and on prices' (Layton 1914, pp. 168–169). The discussion, to quote MacGregor's review (1914, p. 450) is both 'concise' and 'scholarly', and presents a fine overview of the state of the art on this topic of 'Edwardian economics'.

The last three chapters of Layton's book address the key issue which prompted its writing: the incidence of labour unrest in 1910–1913 and its possible remedies. Chapter 15 examined the role of 'strikes and lock-outs … in our present economic system … by reviewing [Board of Trade] statistics of strikes in recent years' (Layton 1914, p. 203). Layton warned that this was a topic far removed 'from questions of economic theory' because passions and weak human nature tend to govern the ferocity of labour disputes (Layton 1914, p. 204). No less than nineteen persons were killed during the 1912 Rand strike in South

Africa (Layton 1914, pp. 204–208); the first general strikes in England were contemplated by Robert Owen's short-lived national unions in the 1830s; the 1889–1892 dockers' strike paved the way for much industrial unrest. Following a recommendation of the Labour Commission (of which Marshall had been a member), a Labour Department within the Board of Trade commenced the systematic collection of statistics on strikes and on labour disputes more generally (Layton 1914, pp. 209–211, the last page of which reproduces some of these data). These data revealed 1893, 1897, 1898, 1899, 1908, 1911, 1912 and 1913 as years in which working days lost from trade disputes exceeded ten million. Over 60 per cent of these disputes concerned wages, trade union rights just under 20 per cent, and work conditions including hours of labour accounting for the remaining 20 per cent. Of these disputes, 27 per cent were settled in favour of labour, 26 per cent in favour of the employers, with the remainder ending in various degrees of compromises, the latter increasingly likely outcomes of such disputes on the available statistical data (Layton 1914, pp. 214–215). Layton therefore asked the pertinent question of whether strike action could be argued to have benefited labour on the basis of the historical record. The generally small wage increases gained from what were termed successful outcomes for labour rarely matched the losses from reduced output and the general disorganisation of trade from transport or coal strikes. However, few wage rises would be recorded in the absence of strikes, Layton (1914, p. 217) suggested, supporting his argument by data collected by the Board of Trade. Considerations like this made the case for state intervention in labour disputes a strong one, and emphasised the need for developing a sound industrial policy to deal with the issue. They were therefore the topics Layton discussed in his final two chapters.

Chapter 16 examined the 'three ways in which a Government can influence industrial disputes'. First, the State may prohibit strike action altogether and compel the opposing parties to 'resort to arbitration'. Second, the State may require investigation by an independent tribunal before permitting strike action to take place. Third, the State may itself take on the role as independent arbitrator. All three alternatives were practised, Layton (1914, pp. 220–221) indicated; the first in New Zealand, the second in Canada, and the third in Great Britain. Appropriate policy for government, employers and workers is reviewed in Layton's last chapter. It suggested increased thrift as the best way to raise real wages (via the increasing demand for labour from the concomitant growth in capital). Among ways to achieve this beneficial outcome, Layton listed reduced luxury spending, the abolition of taxes on thrift such as death duties, as well as greater transparency in the reporting of profits by firms as a way of attracting new investment to the industry in question. Moreover, State regulation of conditions of work, wage policy to secure fair wages and, more debatable, satisfactory controls over the right to strike or to declare lock-outs ought to be established. Layton's book closes with an exhortation for more public education. This would avoid social indifference to the issue of capital-labour relations. More generally, it would ensure the public's right to know the facts through the dissemination of sound information on the subject by government agencies.

The Marshallian credentials of Layton's book are clearly visible. Its stress on the explanatory powers of supply and demand in the labour market is one example. Second, Layton's recognition of the need to be realistic in dealing with the capital-labour relationship reflects his Marshallian training as well as his close study of Marshall's work. The chapter on the theory of wages (Chapter 2) draws heavily on aspects of Marshall's views on the topic, particularly with respect to its starting point, which reflects on labour's renumeration in a primitive state of society when labourers owned their tools and implements and worked for themselves (Layton 1914, p. 18; cf. Marshall 1892, pp. 234–235, the work cited by Layton instead of the *Principles*). The basic contents of that chapter also reflects Marshall's position on the distribution of income between labour and capital in the terms of their net product as influenced by the rate of increase of population and that of the supply of capital (Layton 1914, pp. 26–27; cf. Marshall 1892, pp. 234–242). Chapter III devoted to wages and saving likewise resembled Marshall's position but the mode of reasoning and the illustrations are quite different, since Layton presented a detailed table of the progress of real wages from 1790 to 1910–1912 (Layton 1914, p. 33). However, the chapter also rejected the assumption of free and equal competition in this discussion as quite unrealistic (Layton 1914, p. 31) just as Marshall (1892, p. 256) had done with respect to perfect competition in the labour market. Layton's account, not surprisingly given his earlier work on the theory of prices (Layton 1912, 1922) also discussed the impact of prices on wages and even on the rate of interest. Layton's analysis of saving, it may be noted, also looked at saving in relation to taxation and government spending and the demand for labour where that demand is argued to be totally impervious to 'money spent out of taxation' (Layton 1914, p. 43). As indicated previously, Say's Law still guided this type of proposition in the opening decades of the twentieth century.

Layton's chapter on profits presents an entrepreneurial theory very much in the manner of Marshall. The entrepreneur who directs and organises modern business, and brings capital and labour together, obtains the 'earnings of management' and a risk premium from profits. The remaining profit goes as interest and dividends to debenture holders and shareholders (Layton 1914, pp. 48–51). Both authors treat profits explained in this manner as associated with joint-stock companies, run by modern managers who organise the operations of the business to the full extent. There are some differences in their treatment. Marshall, for example, stressed evolutionary principles with reference to 'survival of the fittest' when commenting on the rise and decline of business firms (Marshall 1892, pp. 287–288); Layton dwelt more fully on the role of profits and their distribution in company finance (Layton 1914, pp. 60–62), and on comparisons in this aspect between companies and unincorporated enterprise.

Layton's (1914) examination of grades of labour (Chapter 5) is very traditional, commencing with a summary of Smith's discussion of the subject and then developing this in a more modern context. This was also Marshall's approach to this topic, though he was less prone to comment on the unequal sharing of skills, and the many special limitations in their specific supplies.

Layton's treatment of this topic draws on some new as well as older research, and approvingly quotes Marshall on the relationship between normal earnings and the required supply of a particular skill. Local variations in wages (Layton 1914, Chapter 6), as apparent for example in wage differences between town and country, are likewise treated by Layton very much in the manner of Marshall.

However, Layton's Chapter 7 treats wages and prices, or the determination of real wages, far more fully than Marshall did. Layton's interest in this topic came partly from his previously published book on the theory of prices (Layton 1912, 1922, discussed in Section II above). This has no counterpart in Marshall's work. Marshall's chapter on 'progress', added to the *Principles* in its fifth edition of 1907 and the 1910 sixth edition, though parts of it came from the first and second editions (Guillebaud 1961, II p. 703), covers this material in relation to real wage progress as part of the progress of labour in less detail, largely because an extensive analysis of this topic had no real place in a volume of foundations.

Layton's treatment of trade unions and wages, which follows in his Chapter 8, is seen as continuing the discussion of the previous chapter. Marshall's chapter on trade unions, the final chapter of Book VI of the *Elements of Economics of Industry* was described in its preface as an almost essential adjunct to its Book VI on distribution, particularly its Chapter 12 on the influence of progress on value. Layton's discussion is much more widely focused. It addresses the interdependence of trade unionism and higher wages, the gradual evolution of trade unions, especially during the second half of the nineteenth century, the association between successful wage negotiations by trade unions and economic conditions, and the trade union weapon of strike action and its efficacy. Marshall (1892) in particular discussed the influence of trade unions on wages, including strikes and the threat of strikes, and also indicated how real the long-term effects on wages were of these strategies. Marshall emphasised that strong trade unions did much to enhance the standard of life, an especially positive impact of their existence on economic progress. This type of conclusion undoubtedly benefited from Marshall's friendship with some trade union leaders and his work on the Labour Commission. However, Marshall also claimed that the very high wages for American and Australian labour in the 1850s were not attributable to trade union action but associated with the gold discoveries. Much of Marshall's discussion was explicitly inspired by his participation in the work of the Labour Commission of the early 1890s (see Groenewegen 1995a, pp. 360–371). Layton's (1914) treatment of the topic is much more modern in many ways.

Layton's (1914) next two chapters on efficiency (Chapter 9) and competition (Chapter 10) likewise treat issues dealt with by Marshall, but often in a more modern setting. His illustrations in the first of these chapters based on Abbé's experiments in the Zeiss optical works in Germany came straight from Marshall, as did the references to Taylorism and scientific management in this context. Layton's treatment of the general and specific impacts of competition on wages is not directly reflected in Marshall's treatment of the subject but indirectly relies much on Marshall's work. The chapter explains the relationship between shifts in prices, wages and interest and economic organisation, arguing that competitive supply and demand forces regulate 'the economy far more efficiently than any system of collectivism or of state ownership'. This is Layton the 'economic liberal' at his best: contrasting state choice with individual choice; noting the superiority of private resource use guided by price signals over that of state direction and control, and the failures of 'communist experiments' in getting the 'fair' outcomes of which they boast. This is combined with praise for certain types of legal wage regulation, particularly when it equalises bargaining strengths between employers and employees and enhances efficiency in production. However, such practices may also drive capital investment out of regulated trades and thereby generate unemployment (Layton 1914, pp. 139–141).

This general discussion of the importance of competition and free markets introduces the final seven chapters on fair wages and the manner in which they can be achieved. Layton's discussion is here once again quite Marshallian. Marshall was a strong advocate of fair wages, and stressed the role for this notion in social policy. Much of that position was presented in Marshall's introduction to Price's *Industrial Peace* (Marshall 1887c), the key perspective of which forms the starting point for Layton's discussion (1914, pp. 146–147). Likewise, Layton's discussion of state regulation of workers with its strong condemnation of sweated labour is very Marshallian, as is its recommendation of establishing wage boards and the fixing of minimum wages. However, like Marshall, Layton fully appreciated the difficulties in setting minimum wages. Layton (1914) brought this discussion up to date in his Chapter 12. Likewise, Layton's perspectives on sliding scales of wages and the benefits of profit sharing follow in essence Marshall's views on these subjects, indirectly via the 1894 Report of the Labour Commission and more directly from Marshall's pronouncements in his *Elements* (Marshall 1892, pp. 301, 381n., 395n. and 172). They also draw on their development by Marshall's other pupils, in particular Fay and Ashley (Layton 1914, pp. 181–182, 184–186) including their reservations about its practical applications. Layton's discussion of collective bargaining (Chapter 14) draws more on the work of the Webbs (1897) on *Industrial Democracy* while that on strikes and lock-outs incorporates commentary on very recent disputes such as the 1912 Rand strike (Layton 1914, pp. 204–208), and the general perspective of recommendations on the subject by the Labour Commission (Layton 1914, pp. 209–212). These are illustrated by the relevant statistics. The subsequent chapters on 'state intervention in disputes' contrasts antipodean experiments in New Zealand, those in Canada and in the United Kingdom, including the impact thereon of recommendations from the Labour Commission (Layton 1914, p. 228). The final chapter on industrial policy pulls many of these considerations together, often in a critical manner which reminds readers that the state 'has not got a free hand in the matter of wages' including the enforcement of a fair wages policy and of minimum or standard work conditions (Layton 1914, pp. 243–244). However, Layton, in quite Marshallian fashion, strongly rejects the view attributed to Ramsay McDonald that the interests of employers and wage earners are necessarily antagonistic and irreconcilable (Layton 1914, p. 255) suggesting instead that their mutual interests in growth and development far outweigh any such differences. Cooperative industrial policy involving all sections of the community (employers, wage earners, the state and the general public) is the broad policy response offered. Layton's liberal response is well within the Marshallian tradition as expressed in Marshall's views on economic and social progress in the final chapters of both his *Principles* and his *Elements*, and the gloss thereon embodied in his 1907 'Social Possibilities of Economic Chivalry', with its concluding call for the widest possible social cooperation to achieve national social policy goals (Marshall 1907, 1925, pp. 342–346). Although seemingly contradicted by very recent experience in the growth of industrial disputes, the long-term social objective for economic liberals of industrial peace did not need to be jettisoned in the light of what was easily described as short period, selfish, trade union action.

The contents of Layton's (1914) book in short clearly demonstrate how much of Marshall's work Layton had imbibed as a student in Marshall's political economy courses at Cambridge and as a reader of Marshall's books. This is neither a startling nor a particularly novel conclusion. However, it validates the remark that Layton was a Marshallian *pur sang* in terms of both his liberal economic philosophy and in terms of his perspectives on the vexed question of capital-labour relations. The essentials of Layton's (1914) book in terms of theory are completely Marshallian; Layton's approach to the topic in presenting its findings in as realistic a manner as possible is likewise. Layton is therefore a major pupil of Marshall, one who scattered his teachings in a very wide manner through his journalism and his many and varied writings of which his book on *The Relations of Capital and Labour* is a particularly striking instance.

IV

There are only a few conclusions to be drawn from this analysis. Both of Layton's books examined in this chapter reflect a strong influence from Alfred Marshall and his published work, even if the direct reference or citation of Alfred Marshall's writings are relatively few (five in Layton 1912, 1922; four in Layton 1914). Much of the theory in these books is very compatible with Marshall's position expressed in his *Principles*, while in addition Layton used to advantage Marshall's contributions to the Royal Commission whether as giver of evidence (Royal Commission on Gold and Silver) or as member (Labour Commission), as well as a number of articles published by Marshall. Moreover, in the second of Layton's two books, Marshall's *Elements of the Economics of Industry* came to the fore as a reference, particularly because its final chapter contained Marshall's views on trade unions. Whether these considerations make these books Marshallian texts *pur sang* is something for which the contents of this chapter make a very positive case.

10 Charles Ryle Fay (1884–1961)

A devoted teacher of economic history and one of Marshall's favourite Cambridge pupils

Charles Ryle Fay (1884–1961), the Cambridge social and economic historian, became involved with Alfred Marshall as teacher of economics during his undergraduate years at Cambridge University (1902–1905). He was then a King's College student taking the History Tripos. During 1907–1908, Fay held the Shaw Research Scholarship at the London School of Economics, where he further worked on his 1908 Fellowship dissertation on cooperation, and befriended Edwin Cannan. He started teaching economic history for the new Economics and Politics Tripos from 1908 on the strength of his first class honours results for both parts of the History Tripos, and his election to a Fellowship at Christ College in 1908 on the basis of the dissertation on cooperation completed by that year under Marshall's guidance and supervision.

Chapter 10 assesses the Marshallian credentials of Fay's early economic writings as an economic historian. These are confined to his work on cooperation, a very Marshallian enterprise (Section II), and to his early work on social and economic history entitled *A Study of Life and Labour*, largely covering the nineteenth century. This was the topic on which Fay had initially lectured for Marshall and later for Pigou until the outbreak of war in 1914, and again from 1919 to 1921 (Section III). Section I of the chapter provides biographical details; Section IV presents some conclusions.

I

Charles Fay was born in Lancashire in 1884. His grandfather as a boy had worked on the construction of the first railway carriages for the Liverpool to Manchester Railway, and had later invented the chain brake used for the emergency stopping of trains (Milgate and Levy 1987a, p. 297). This was a good ancestry for the economic and social historian to be, who frequently wrote on the 'Industrial Revolution' as a tremendous source of progress and improved living standards. Becoming an academic historian required Fay to study at Cambridge during 1902–1905 for the History Tripos, the economic contents of which brought him into contact with Alfred Marshall.

As an undergraduate at King's College, Fay had met and befriended Maynard Keynes, an acquaintance that continued when both taught subjects for the

Economics Tripos before the First World War, and immediately thereafter from 1919 (Moggridge 1992, pp. 53–54, 172; Skidelsky 1983). Fay saw military service during the First World War, finishing up as Captain in the Machine Gun Corps. In 1919 he returned to Cambridge for two years to lecture in economic history, resigning in 1921 to take up the Chair of Economic History at Toronto. Fay's academic post in Canada, however, did not prevent frequent visits to England, including regular visits to Marshall up to 1924, the year of his death (Fay 1926, 1982). In 1931, a decade from taking up his Toronto position, Fay was back in his Cambridge Alma Mater as reader in economic history, a position he occupied until his retirement in 1949.

Over his lifetime, Fay published a substantial number of books. Ignoring a 1907 monograph on *King's College, Cambridge*, the first of these, *Cooperation at Home and Abroad*, his Fellowship dissertation, was published in 1908. It subsequently went through three further editions, the fourth in two volumes being published in 1936. These two volumes provided a reprint of the text of the second edition (only slightly different from that of the first edition) while the second volume provided the new material added for both the third and the fourth editions. The initial preparation of this first book by Fay on an economics topic was greatly assisted by Alfred Marshall, as indicated more fully in Section II of this chapter. In a letter to Foxwell dated 24 January 1908, Marshall described Fay's book on cooperation as 'a splendid piece of work' (in Whitaker 1996, III p. 197).

Other books on cooperation followed. A volume, *Co-partnership in Industry* appeared in 1913; *Agricultural Co-operation in the Canadian West*, the first fruits of his pen in print from his Canadian location, was published in 1925. Fay's study of *Two Empires*, appeared with Toronto University Press in 1928, in a simultaneous publication with Bowes & Bowes of Cambridge.

In 1920, Fay published *Life and Labour in the Nineteenth Century*, explicitly based on the lectures he had given at Cambridge during 1919, as well as those he had given before the war. Explaining the life and labour for Newfoundland was reserved by Fay for a later volume (Fay 1956). By 1928, Fay had considerably enlarged the scope of his economic and social history of the English nineteenth century of life and labour. It appeared under the title of *Great Britain from Adam Smith to the Present Day*. As a very readable economic and social history text, this book went through a further four editions in 1929, 1932, 1937 and 1950.

During the 1930s, Fay published *Youth and Power. The Diversions of an Economist* (Fay 1931), *The Corn Laws and Social England* (Fay 1932); *Imperial England and its Place in the Formation of Economic Doctrine 1600–1932* (Fay 1934) and in 1940, *English Economic History, mainly since 1700* (Fay 1940), another text frequently reprinted. More books appeared in the 1950s. These included *Huskisson and his Age* (Fay 1951a); *Palace of Industry 1851: A Study of the Great Exhibition and its Fruits* (Fay 1951b), and *Round About Industrial Britain 1830–1860* (Fay 1952), yet another economic and social history, this time dealing with a particularly significant episode in British nineteenth century industrial history. A brief volume, *The World of Adam Smith* (Fay 1960), based on a set of lectures Fay had given in Toronto in 1958, appeared the year before his death.

Fay also published more than twenty papers in academic journals, mainly in the *Economic Journal* but also in the *Canadian Journal of Economics, Economic History* (an occasional supplement to the *Economic Journal*) as well as single contributions to both the *Quarterly Journal of Economics* and the *American Economic Review*. The following should be especially noted. Apart from four book reviews and three obituaries, including one of his former London professor and friend, Edwin Cannan, in 1937, the articles dealt with issues of cooperative enterprise, various aspects of the corn trade in the nineteenth century, and some other issues in economic history. Fay also extensively published in other periodicals, often not of a strictly academic nature. Their contents were frequently reprinted in his various collections of articles and books of which Fay (1931) is a good example.

Fay's close contact with Marshall during the first two decades of the twentieth century can be indicated as follows. On his own account, Fay (1925b) had attended some of Marshall's lectures from his second year at Cambridge in 1902, and he was part of the small audience at Marshall's last lecture presented on 21 May 1908, immediately before his retirement that year. Fay's published reminiscences report various other, more social contacts with Marshall and comment as well as on the assistance Marshall gave Fay in his early work. In turn, Fay assisted Marshall by proof reading the last three editions of the *Principles of Economics* for which he was explicitly thanked in their prefaces. Moreover, Marshall (1919, p. 813n. 2) referred to Fay's *Copartnership* (1913) but *Money, Credit and Commerce* (Marshall 1923) failed to mention Fay's work on cooperation when that topic was mentioned in the context of index number.

Seven letters from Marshall to Fay are extant, three each from 1906 and 1908, and one from 1915. The 1906 correspondence deals with matters associated with the book on cooperation, then in preparation; two 1908 letters mention its publication and its review in *The Economist* which associated the work with Fay's research under Cannan at the London School of Economics. The third letter referred to Fay's teaching on life and labour as a historical short course. Marshall's last letter to Fay (23 February 1915, in Whitaker 1996, III p. 321) congratulated Fay on his promotion to captain, and commented on his projected study of *Life and Labour* (Fay 1920). However, a letter from Mavor to Marshall (dated 21 February 1923) reports on a conversation he had with Fay on the then recently published *Money, Credit and Commerce*, and on the great value of *Industry and Trade* for teaching. Mavor added that Fay was only one of three economics teachers directly influenced by Marshall (in Whitaker 1996, III p. 393).

II

Fay's first book was his Fellowship dissertation, *Cooperation at Home and Abroad* (Fay 1908, 1936). It had been prepared under Marshall's supervision from 1906 and was quite a substantial book, a little less than 400 pages. Fay (1960, 1982) recounts his first encounter with Marshall on this matter at Balliol Croft in October 1906. It was then, at the suggestion of Pigou, that he sought Marshall's advice on the topic for his Fellowship dissertation. Fay recounted this occasion:

> How well I remember my first, strange, experience at Balliol Croft. It was in 1906, when I was starting to dissert. Pigou had sent me to Marshall for an interview. He listened to me, approved the notion of what became 'Cooperation at Home and Abroad', and, spreading a row of books on his sofa, said 'Smell these, when you've had enough, blow down the tube and Mary will bring you some tea.' Being quite dazed, I'd soon had enough, so blew down the tube. 'Yes, Mr. Fay?' 'Mary, bring up the tea please.'
>
> A stately tread brought up the tray, and in walked NOT the house-keeper, but Mrs. Marshall!! I can still feel the thrill of horror that ran down my spine when I realised who Mary was.
>
> (Fay 1960, 1982, p. 87)

Earlier, for Pigou's *Memorials of Alfred Marshall* (Fay 1925b, pp. 74–77), Fay recalled this occasion in more detail, thereby indicating that the matter of Marshall's role in this dissertation topic choice was more drawn out than he remembered half a century later. Fay was sent by Pigou to Marshall for advice on his dissertation topic. He therefore duly went to Balliol Croft, where Marshall read him a long list of potential topics from a 'small black book', among which were included 'The Recent German Commercial Crisis', which sounded suitable as a potential topic to Fay. Marshall however ruled that it would not suit Fay at all, nor that a topic dealing with the Argentine economy which sounded attractive to Fay, would be really suitable. Fay's choice of a comparison between English and German labour met with Marshall's approval as a topic Fay could easily attempt. Marshall then selected about thirty books from his library shelves, most of them in German, for Fay to examine by himself. It was then that Marshall invited Fay 'to blow down the tube and Sarah will bring you some tea' (Sarah being the Marshalls' house maid), when Fay had completed his preliminary perusal of the literature Marshall had selected for him. Fay's account continued:

> In response to a blow, the tea came in on a low tea trolley and I ate and drank alone. I went away too late for Hall, staggering under an armload of books, and next day came back with a bag for the balance. I had had them nearly for three years. Gradually I arrived at my subject – Co-operation. I was under a bond with him to write down on a separate page in my notebook the proposed title, altering it each week till it fitted my ambition. At last it became 'Co-operation at Home and Abroad, an analysis and description'....
>
> (Fay 1925b, pp. 74–75)

Unfortunately, this recollection betrays nothing of the process by which the comparison of English and German labour was transformed into an internationally comparative study of cooperation dealing with Great Britain, as well as with Germany, France, Belgium and Italy, in a largely descriptive way. Furthermore, although some of the books carried away at Marshall's behest on that occasion in October 1906 may have been suitable for the later topic, it seems strange that Fay kept all of them for nearly three years when some of their immediate relevance for his final dissertation topic was rather small. However, Fay also recalled in 1925 that when the dissertation topic had been determined, Marshall 'supplied all the books which I was to take away in a cab' and which, from the several trips Fay had to make from Marshall's library to the cab, would have amounted to more than thirty. It may be noted as well that at least part of the earlier topic, that dealing with English labour, became a subject in its own right for Fay's next major project, as is discussed in Section III of this chapter.

The structure of Fay's finished dissertation on *Cooperation at Home and Abroad* is as follows. The published version was divided into four parts. These respectively dealt with cooperative enterprises in banking and other credit providers; agricultural societies involved in production and/or marketing; workers' societies in production in the form of small workshops or smallish manufacturing enterprises, some of which had distinct socialist origins in some countries; and finally cooperative stores at either the retail or the wholesale level. Considerable attention was devoted to distributional and pricing aspects. For example, Fay discussed at length whether profits were distributed as dividends to workers or customers or in the form of direct profit sharing as appropriate for cooperative enterprises involved in production. Pricing policies of cooperative enterprises were analysed in terms of whether conventional market prices were charged, or prices somewhat above market prices, or whether prices were cost based, enabling distribution of 'profits' directly to consumers through lower prices.

As previously mentioned, the study contained a substantial European dimension. The various parts generally tended to start with the evolution of British practice, sometimes split up between England and Scotland when differences were sufficiently large to make the separate analysis relevant. Ireland was also given separate treatment, while continental Europe was represented in all parts by Germany, Switzerland, France, Belgium and Italy, though with considerable differences in the degree of detail. Danish cooperative agricultural enterprises (especially in dairying) were discussed at considerable length in Part II. Virtually all of the data, including that of a statistical nature, derived from nineteenth century practice brought up to date, wherever possible, to a year of the first decade of the twentieth century.

Fay's work on cooperation is not a text whose argument is easily, and succinctly, summarised given its largely descriptive nature. The cooperative society is defined by him as

> an association for the purpose of joint trading, originally among the weak and conducted always in an unselfish spirit, on such terms that all who are

> prepared to assume the duties of membership share in its rewards in proportion to the degree in which they make use of their association.
>
> (Fay 1908, 1936, p. 5)

Fay justified this somewhat broad definition on the ground that a narrower one ran the risk of excluding organisations that either claim, or are actually organised, to be cooperative in their operations. The major types of cooperative enterprises which were covered in the book were classified in the four parts (already outlined) of which the first three dealt with cooperative associations of producers while only the fourth could be considered as a consumers' cooperative.

Fay deliberately excluded some specific forms of cooperative enterprise. These omissions included building societies and cooperative credit institutions for financing the purchase of new or existing houses; friendly societies designed to offer medical services to their members; and cooperative insurance firms or mutualities especially dedicated to life and accident insurance (Fay 1908, 1936, p. 9). Furthermore, given the growth of large-scale industry, especially in manufacturing, Fay argued that this development was significantly reducing the scope for cooperative endeavours in manufacturing since sufficient capital was difficult to raise by a cooperative form of organisation to make such large-scale production feasible under this form of organisation of ownership. Hence cooperatives in manufacturing production were set to decline in practical importance, though this did not apply to agriculture where the benefits of scale economies, when applicable, were heavily curtailed in practice.

A taste of Fay's work on cooperation can be given by quoting a rather typical argument from this detailed study. In the context of his discussion of cooperative dairying in Europe, Fay (1908, 1936, pp. 156–157) argued:

> The *sine qua non* for the establishment of a co-operative dairy is the existence of a sufficient number of cows in the district, or the assurance that an immediate deficiency in this respect can be quickly made up. The farmers must not live so far from the dairy that the milk supplies cannot be conveyed fresh each morning to the receiving centre. If they lived too far off, the economies of concentrated production will be out-weighed by the dearness and the irregularity of transport; for it is necessary that the milk should be sent fresh each morning. It does, however, happen that there are single little farms or small clusters of little farms scattered over the country, which possess a limited number of cows, say 300 or less. These farmers are too far from the existing nearest creamery and are at the same time not numerous or rich enough to build an efficient dairy of their own, costing perhaps £1,000. If they try to gather in neighbouring farmers, they may overlap with the existing creamery, thus creating waste and fraction. To obviate this difficulty auxiliary dairies can be established, to perform the preliminary process of separating the skim milk from the cream, which is then dispatched to the central creamery. By this device the milk is treated while still fresh, and the more valuable extract, which is only a quarter the

> bulk of the milk, can bear the comparatively reduced costs of long-distance transport, from which it incurs no damage. As an auxiliary cost at most £500 to build, it is within the scope of a poorer association. If its trade grows, it can be connected with an independent creamery. The arrangement of terms between the auxiliary and the central dairy can be settled without difficulty with the help of a chemical expert and a book-keeper. These auxiliaries exist in most countries.

In concluding his work on agricultural cooperation, Fay (1908, 1936, p. 214) stated concisely:

> We may therefore present as our broad conclusions: (1) that statistical evidence proves the vitality and slow expansion of other forms of cultivation than that which we call distinctively big, and in particular small cultivating ownership; (2) that the province of small-scale farming is permanently assured and capable of expansion; (3) that this expansion is directly stimulated by the trend of international agriculture.
>
> Combining these results with those of previous chapters, in which we have shewn the supreme importance of co-operation to the small farmer in particular, we may submit that co-operation is not only *a* but *the* cornerstone in the development of modern agriculture (Fay's emphasis in this quotation).

There are direct, and indirect, signs of Marshall's influence visible in this book. Take first the indirect signs. The topic of cooperative enterprise, and its association with profit sharing, was one dear to Marshall's heart. In 1889, Marshall had addressed the twenty-first Annual Cooperative Congress at Ipswich on the general subject of cooperation (Marshall 1889, 1925b, pp. 227–255) in which he pontificated on the basic principles of this thriving, even if recent, social movement. In his *Principles*, likewise, Marshall had extensively addressed the benefits of cooperation and profit sharing as part of contemporary economic and social progress. Cooperation was there favourably compared with competition (Marshall 1920, pp. 8–9), with some measure of business management (Marshall 1920, pp. 305–309), associated with profit sharing in its highest form (Marshall 1920, p. 627). Moreover, agricultural cooperation as practised in Denmark, Italy, Germany and Ireland, especially as applied to dairying, was very favourably compared with its progress in England (Marshall 1920, pp. 655–656). More sophisticated systems of profit sharing are treated as examples of progress in relation to the standard of life (Marshall 1920, p. 706). For Marshall, cooperative activity and profit sharing were clearly higher forms of business organisation made possible by social advance and progress. The topic of cooperation was therefore a quite Marshallian one and, given the fact that nothing is really known about how precisely cooperation as a comparative study emerged as Fay's dissertation topic, Marshall's undoubtedly considerable influence on this process is difficult to deny.

There are also direct acknowledgements of Marshall's influence on the final product. Marshall is thanked in the preface (Fay 1908, 1936, p. viii) as one of two teachers (the other is Cannan) with whom Fay had been in a great deal of contact during the three years of writing his dissertation. The opening paragraph of its text draws attention to Marshall's definition of economics in the *Principles* as 'a study of mankind in the ordinary business of life' making Fay's study an economic one because cooperation 'is one way of conducting certain parts of this business'. Elsewhere dairying (especially in Denmark) is noted as a strikingly successful form of cooperation in which large-scale production plays a significant part (Marshall 1920, p. 159). Marshall's views on the comparative skills of the large-scale farmer and the large manufacturer are approvingly quoted (Fay 1908, 1936, pp. 211–212) but the somewhat limited scope for this to eventuate implies 'little inducement for really able men to enter the business of farming' (Fay 1908, 1936, p. 652). In Part III, Fay (1908, 1936, p. 256n. 2, 257n. 1) cited Marshall twice on the meaning of cooperation as a form of business organisation, in parts of which the 'weakness of separating risk and control can be avoided'. However, on aggregate the direct references to Marshall are rather few, about one for every hundred pages. Nevertheless, Fay's text clearly falls well within the Marshall research programme.

III

Life and Labour in the Nineteenth Century, the book based on Fay's lectures published in 1920, was also the second major book Fay had completed while Marshall was still alive. It may be recalled from Section I that Marshall had paid Fay £100 per annum out of his own pocket to lecture on this topic for the Economics Tripos and had likewise encouraged him to do so when Fay took up the Shaw studentship at the London School of Economics for a period of two years. In a letter written from the Tyrol, Marshall suggested that even if in London, Fay could lecture on England in the nineteenth century during 1907–1908 or, on the supposition that MacGregor repeated the lectures he had given in 1905–1906 during 1907–1908, Fay could give them in 1908–1909 (Marshall to Fay, 7 August 1906, in Whitaker III, pp. 141–143). Fay did in fact both go to London (where he studied with, and befriended Edwin Cannan), and afterwards taught nineteenth century English economic history for Marshall from 1907–1908, and subsequently for Pigou until the outbreak of the First World War in 1914. In 1919, on his return to Cambridge from military service, Fay presented a similar course of lectures 'to students of economics, among whom were members of the Royal Navy and students from the army of the United States' (Fay 1920, p. iii), the contents of which went into the 1920 book.

The book as published claimed its contents were based 'on the substance of lectures delivered at Cambridge University in the year 1919', without mentioning their presentation before the start of the First World War. Its preface largely discussed its major sources, which on this account consisted of industry studies, 'Blue Books', leading secondary works on the nineteenth century, as well as items from the classics of economic literature housed in the Goldsmiths' Library at London University (and then physically situated in the Imperial Institute at South Kensington).

Fay divided his study of nineteenth century life and labour into two parts. There are nine chapters in Part I devoted to political, social and economic developments from 1815 to 1830. The thirteen chapters in Part II cover these issues from 1830 to the 'present day'. Businessmen, and workers for that matter, if induced to read the book, were advised to go straight to Chapter XIV as their starting point. This dealt with industrial and other development from the 1840s. The book concluded with an Appendix on the location of industry in the north of England, drawn from the 1913 Census of Production, and illustrated with a large, fold-out map on the subject. The detailed index is surprisingly without any entry for Marshall or any of his publications, and Marshall is in fact not mentioned at all in this second book by 'one of his favourite pupils'.

Fay's text blended social, political and economic history together with some history of economic and social thought. Its first chapter is devoted to the international background (1815–1830), and includes brief sections dealing with 'Castlereagh, Canning and Wellington', 'the Holy Alliance and the Triple Alliance', 'the Policy of England', 'the United States of America and the Monroe Doctrine', and concludes with a section, 'Today, and One Hundred Years Ago'. Among other things, this section comments on the similarities and important differences between the post-Napoleonic-wars adjustments from 1815 and the Versailles arrangements for the post-First World War era. Given its prominence in post-First World War international affairs, Fay (1920, p. 11) also draws attention to similar features (then and now) for Russia: its substantial contribution to the defeat of Napoleon (as to a lesser extent to that of Germany in the First World War), as well as to the strangeness of its society to Western minds in 1815, and especially following the 1917 Bolshevik Revolution. This last mentioned world event probably explains the book's pronounced emphasis on socialism.

The emergence of British socialism in fact covers virtually half of the other chapters in its Part I. Chapter V distinguishes two types of association: 'individualistic societies (as advocated by Jeremy Bentham, whose tremendous influence is briefly documented in Chapter IV), and the origins of British socialism in its communal variety as represented by Owen, and in its more individualistic guise represented by Cobbett (Chapters VI and VIII respectively). The remaining three chapters discuss other political and social aspects of these fifteen years: repression and reform of British institutions (Chapter III), the spirit of association (Chapter V) and the old Poor Law (dating back at least to Tudor times) and the new one (derived from the 1834 Poor Law Reform Bill associated with Nassau Senior). At the start of Chapter VIII, Fay (1920, p. 75) refers to these three forms of association as 'old Toryism (1800–1830)', 'individualism (1825–1870)' and 'collectivism (1865–1900)'.

Fay sympathetically associated Owenite socialism with cooperation, since Owen's social experiments at Lanark embodied the application of cooperative principles to retail trading as well as to production. The chapter on Owen (Fay

1920, Chapter VI) starts with a brief account of a personal pilgrimage Fay made in 1913 to the site of New Lanark. It then gives an overview of this experience (Section 2), a discussion of the nature of the New Lanark enterprise (Section 3), followed by the 'community experiments' from which, Fay indicated, 'the eminently solid Co-operative Movement was born' (Fay 1920, p. 59). The details of this in Owen's time are presented in Section 6, while his other contributions (equitable labour exchanges, trades unions and further community experiment) bring the chapter to a close.

Part II of Fay's book also begins with an introductory chapter surveying the political background to the period covered. This is presented in terms of the era of Palmerston from 1830 and that of Sailisbury and Grey from 1885.

> In the middle is an 'interminable period' dominated by Gladstone and Disraeli. Free trade and its consequences play an important role in this part (Cobdenism, Anti-Corn Law League), followed by a discussion of Chartism as a political reform movement, and a depiction of the industrial scene, 1842 …

as a type of snapshot analysis (Fay 1920, p. 171). The focus shifts from the railway navvy (its Section 1) to the countryside and its 'deadness' (Section 2), rural domestic industry (Section 3), 'factory districts' resembling Marshall's 'industrial districts', but their analysis is not nearly taken as far by the 'pupil', who in fact kept the whole of this discussion at a very descriptive level. The evidence is, however, drawn from 'Blue Books', Fay's basic source for his 'industrial' snapshots and a source which Marshall, of course, also greatly exploited and contributed to.

Mining is discussed in Chapter 15. It starts with a brief section on the importance of coal in English industrial history. It then briefly investigates the conditions of miners (Section 2), the employment of women and children in mines (Section 3), before illustrating various abuses in the prevailing wage system in kind. These included the 'butty system' as practised in South Staffordshire, the truck system of payment in kind, including the experiments therein by Robert Owen (truck at Lanark, payment in non-legal tender coin in the labour exchanges). Two chapters on the historical foundations of capitalism follow. They initially investigate the notion of 'Industrial Revolution' as developed by Toynbee, its manifestations in agriculture and in the cotton industry, and its selective absorption into political economy. Large-scale, localised industry is discussed with reference to the Midlands (Fay 1920, pp. 205–206), as are some of its foundations in terms of mechanisation, with illustrations drawn from lace making, stocking knitting and handloom weaving in the various branches of the textile industry. These also offer explanations of declining wages and prices, and conclude with a neat summary of nineteenth century and labour as viewed by Fay in terms of its general characteristics.

> Direct employment, net wages, steam power, large scale industry, these are the things which capitalism, studied objectively, implies. Under it, the

> standard of working class living steadily improved, and the owners of capital saved much more than they spent. But it does not follow that what worked in the 19th century will work in the 20th. For the conditions of competition on which the old system was based are being transformed by the Combine on the one hand and the Trade Union on the other. Furthermore, the whole fabric of economic life has been stirred by the upheaval of war. Capitalism is now challenged less on account of its antecedents than on account of the outlook and supposed motives of those who are held responsible for it. The 'Co-operative Commonwealth' is matched against Capitalism. It should be possible to do justice to these new aspirations without reading irrelevant notions into the history of the 19th century.
>
> (Fay 1920, p. 226)

The final five chapters of the book raise a miscellany of issues. Chapter 18 reviews Britain as 'a nation of shopkeepers' in terms of the necessary institutions (shops, fairs, markets, bread, clothing and their improvements, partly on cooperative lines). Chapter 19 investigates development of the cooperative movement from 1884, linking it with Christian Socialism, and providing a statistical analysis of cooperative stores based on his 1908 monograph (discussed in Section II above). The revival of British socialism is the subject of Chapter 20, viewed eclectically to cover Marx, Henry George, the Fabian Society, the Independent Labour Party and the Labour Party, concluding with a comparative section on English and European socialism. This section emphasises reformist versus revolutionary aims, different progress under democratic as against authoritarian forms of government, of which England and Germany are respectively taken as clear illustrations (Fay 1920, pp. 256–257). Positive conclusions are drawn in the final two chapters: the spirit of the century (Chapter 21) is portrayed as its general drive to social betterment via publicity and information gathering, a free press, popular education such as adult education for workers, publication of parliamentary papers, investigation and legislation including the Factory Acts, the Mines Acts, the Truck Acts, recognition of Trade Unions as legal entities and the greater recognition of employers' responsibilities for the welfare of their workers. The 'century' decade by decade is used to indicate crucial aspects of the heritage of the past in driving social movements of reform and change. Its final section reminds readers that life consists of work and play, and that 'today', at the start of the twentieth century, opportunities for the players and watchers of sport, have grown enormously, just as in so many other aspects of working class life (dress, food, working conditions) have greatly improved. The book thereby ends on an optimistic note of progress and its continuation.

This, indirectly, is another broad similarity between Fay's book and Marshall's *Principles of Economics*. It, after all, also ended very much on the high note of the increasing opportunities provided for progress through education, rising standards of living and especially the good prospects for further increases in the standard of life. More generally, some resemblance can be seen between the text of Fay's book and that of Marshall's Appendices A and B in the *Principles* when such a comparison is confined to their discussion of nineteenth century developments. Emphasis on the importance of free trade and of free enterprise to this progress is fully shared by Fay in his discussion of nineteenth century economic history. The importance of his book on cooperation for part of the argument at least of his first economic history text, can likewise be noted, given Marshall's original influence on this work, as indicated in the previous section.

IV

Fay's early years at Cambridge as student and as lecturer in economic history were marked by a solid acquaintance with, and great admiration for Marshall. Fay was already attending some of Marshall's lectures as an undergraduate while he was studying history; he was greatly indebted to Marshall for his informal supervision and other assistance while preparing his Fellowship dissertation on cooperation, if not for basically suggesting its actual topic to him. Moreover, Marshal paid £100 from his own pocket by way of salary for Fay's teaching of economic history during the early years of the Economics Tripos. However, Marshall's considerable influence on, and friendship with Fay, which endured in varying degrees until not long before Marshall's death in 1924, coincided with Fay's friendship with Cannan. Cannan's guidance had also been freely available to Fay during his studies at London as the holder of a Shaw Research Studentship from 1906 to 1908 while he was working on the Fellowship dissertation. For this reason, Cannan was thanked for his assistance in the preface of this book, together with Marshall, as was previously noted. Furthermore, Fay's later substantial devotion to the life and times of Adam Smith probably owed as much to Cannan as to Marshall, even if Fay's first prolonged contact with Cannan took place in the wake of Cannan's extensive preparation of his edition of the *Wealth of Nations*. This was first published in 1904, and was the version mainly used by Fay when preparing his later work on Smith and his times.

As shown in Section II of this chapter, Marshall's influence is considerably more visible in the work on cooperation. This is fully acknowledged in its preface. After all, the book contained five specific references to Marshall's *Principles*, even if this significant Marshall citation was omitted from both its index and its selective biography. As distinctly indicated in the second last paragraph of Section II, this was clearly one of various reasons why Fay's *Cooperation at Home and Abroad* is so easily described as a Marshallian text. Other reason related to the importance of the topic of cooperation and the associated one of profit sharing to Marshall's vision of what he called economic progress, and to the fact that what little theory was included in Fay's largely descriptive study, was very Marshallian. Examples are the emphasis on economies of scale, localised specialisation, and the benefits these can provide for ensuring the survival and prosperity of small farmers. Finally, as mentioned in the last two sentences of Section II, a strong Marshallian tone to the work is not surprising, given the assistance Marshall had given to its preparation at a time when he was still very active in economic study and mentally alert.

Fay's second major economics study discussed in this chapter, his *Life and Labour in the Nineteenth Century*, is less demonstrably Marshallian even if its origins were to be found in Fay's teaching of the subject which had commenced while Marshall was still professor of economics during the early years of the Economics Tripos. As noted in Section III, there are no direct references to Marshall's work in this book, and only the tone of certain of its parts suggest a distinct Marshallian flavour. For example, Fay's arguments in the book resemble some of the parts devoted to the nineteenth century in the historical Appendices A and B of the *Principles of Economics*; emphasis on economic and social progress at the end of the nineteenth century in both books provide another broad similarity. Furthermore, combining Owen, Marx and Henry George as socialists was a perspective which came easily to Marshall, and which appeared just as easily in Fay's treatment of the topic. In addition, Fay's distinct use of the notion of factory districts as areas of local specialisation is a sign of Marshallian influence even if Fay only treated these topics in a most descriptive fashion and nowhere analytically developed them in the manner of Marshall. Finally, the considerable emphasis given to cooperation in Fay's book provides yet a further indication of the impact on Fay of Marshall's opinion on the importance of this topic for the serious economics student.

How Marshallian an author does this make Fay? It may be noted here first that these Marshallian characteristics were largely confined to Fay's early books on cooperation and on British life and labour in the nineteenth century, written directly and indirectly under varying degrees of Marshall's personal supervision and guidance. The later books on economic history, generally speaking, seem less Marshallian, even if their discussion of industrial progress in Britain and Canada drew on Marshall's perspectives on industrial organisation and the importance of the size of the firm for economic development. Fay also never lost his faith in the effectiveness of the market, and in his liberal views of the nature of economic and social policy based thereon. Like Marshall, he staunchly supported both free trade and free enterprise, even if he generally envisaged Canadian and British industrial development in manufacture and agriculture as able to take place within a cooperative organisational framework. These were all general propositions, easily sustained for Fay from Marshall's economic work on such topics, which in any case remained standard economic theory of industrial organisation for much of Fay's active life as an economic historian and economist. Last, but by no means least, until his death Fay stood as a constant reminder of the importance of Marshall's enormous contributions to Cambridge economics and the influence it had, and continued to exert, on economic studies. In short, Fay may be said to have assiduously assisted, even if in his own specific way, the spreading of Marshall's economic organon through his writings and his teaching in England and Canada.

11 Gerald Shove (1888–1947)

An enduring Marshallian loyalist

In Austin Robinson's (1977) authoritative portrait of the Cambridge Economics Faculty in 1930–1931, Shove is included as part of the pre-1914 generation, who studied economics for the second part of the Tripos, gaining a first class result on the strength of some brilliant answers in his examination papers (Kahn 1987, p. 327). With Marshall's retirement in 1908, this meant that he had not been personally taught by the Cambridge economist whose work he so greatly admired for the rest of his life. Earlier, Shove had secured what was called 'a disastrous Second Class result' in the Classical Tripos.

More interestingly, Robinson (1977, p. 28) commenced his paragraph devoted to Shove with the express wish 'that someone would write a good account of Gerald Shove and his work', a wish never fulfilled during Robinson's lifetime (he died in 1993), nor, as far as I am aware, thereafter. Robinson's 1977 paragraph on Shove continues:

> In the later 1930s and in the early post-1945 period he was one of the most interesting and effective of Cambridge lecturers. But this was, in a sense, a re-incarnation. I was his pupil in 1921–2 and attended his inordinately dull lectures on trade union organisation. He had been a brilliant student in the 1910–14 period, whose conscience had made him a pacifist when war came.
>
> On the fringe of the Bloomsbury group, he had endured all the miseries of being a pacifist in a world that was war-mad. With my own generation of prematurely adult war veterans with a contempt for pacifists he found it difficult to establish an easy and relaxed intimacy. He and Fredegond, his poet wife, were infinitely kind. But I got at that stage very little from his teaching – he was then so painfully shy. It was in 1929–30 that he had a sabbatical year and came back a wholly different person. But even after that it is not, I think, wholly unfair to him to say that his gifts were critical rather than creative. In some way he resembled Dennis Robertson in always wanting to insist that the world is not as simple as the simpler economic models of it – that nothing is wholly black or white, but everything grey. His central interests were at that time in the rethinking of Marshallian value theory – the other of our two revolutions. With Keynes, as with all of us, Shove was an invaluable critic. But, as I say, his qualities as a critic were always greater as

> a creator of models of what he would have regarded as oversimplifications. In relation to the *General Theory* work, there is no question that in the later stages Keynes was discussing with him the arguments with Pigou and getting from him valuable comments on that. But I do not think he played any major part in the first stages. There is certainly no written record of comments on drafts. He took no part that I can remember in the work of the 'Circus'.
>
> (Robinson 1977, p. 28)

Shove's other famous Cambridge economics student, Richard Kahn, also left a brief account of Shove and his work, published in *The New Palgrave* (Kahn 1987, IV pp. 327–328), and partly based on his King's College obituary published in 1947 (Rosselli 2005, p. 366n. 2). This account mentions the uneven academic record and its brilliance in economics, the slow academic promotion thereafter – 1923: university lecturer, 1926: Fellow of King's College (but not his, very late, promotion to Reader in 1945) – as well as his early good connections in the Faculty. These included Keynes from 1908, to whom Whitaker (1996, III p. 273n. 6) adds friendships with Robertson, Henderson and Dalton, made initially through debating at the Union. During the war (1914–1918) Shove gained notoriety as a pacifist in the company of quite a few other members of the Bloomsbury circle, and from the 1920s as a deep critical thinker on economic issues, especially those arising during the debates on the Marshallian theory of value in the 1920s and 1930s. By the 1930s, his name appeared occasionally in the prefaces of books (e.g. Joan Robinson, 1933, as discussed later in this chapter).

Kahn (1987, IV p. 328) adds that Shove was 'a fastidious self-critic' who wrote an enormous amount of economics even though he only rarely published. Sadly, the unpublished writings were lost to later generations since Shove's testatory request that his unpublished papers be destroyed, was fastidiously carried out. His published work comprises several journal articles, a few 'notes' or short papers, the more famous pieces devoted to Marshall's economics and to the cost controversies of the 1920s and 1930s. He also published some book reviews (one, of Joan Robinson's *Essay on Marxian Economics* almost at article length) including a rarely mentioned review of Marshall's *Industry and Trade* published in the *Athenaeum* (31 October 1919, reprinted in Groenewegen 1998, II pp. 158–160).

This chapter examines Shove's published output in the following manner. After a section devoted to an overview of Shove's life and writings (Section I), the subsequent three sections in turn examine Shove's economic work. Section II reviews Shove's work published in articles, particularly that devoted to the debate on Marshall's theory of value during the later 1920s, early 1930s; Section III discusses his book reviews of Joan Robinson's *Theory of Imperfect Competition* (1933), of her *Essay on Marxian Economics* (1942) and of Hicks's *Theory of Wages* (Shove 1933b); while Section IV surveys his more general assessment of the place of Marshall's *Principles* in the development of economic theory (published in the 1942 *Economic Journal*) together with his review of Marshall's

Industry and Trade in the *Athenaeum* (Shove 1919, 1998). These extant sources of Shove's economics will be supplemented on occasions by what can be drawn from surviving notes taken from his 1928–1929 Lectures by John Saltmarsh, but not from Shove's paper presented to the 1925 meeting of the British Association for the Advancement of Science, now apparently lost. A final section draws some conclusions, with special reference to demonstrating that the second part of the paper's title, 'an enduring Marshallian loyalist', is fully justified. Perhaps this is not the monograph of Shove's life and work that Austin Robinson desired, but at least a reasonable foundation for such a piece.

I

Gerald Shove was born at 354 Queen Court, Ospringe, on 21 November 1888, the child of Herbert Samuel Shove and Bertha Shove, née Miller. He was educated at Uppingham School and in December 1906 won a scholarship to King's College, Cambridge. He entered Cambridge in 1907 to study classics. His result of a second class in the first part of the Classical Tripos meant he lost his King's College Scholarship (Kahn 1987, p. 327). He then (in 1908, the year of Marshall's retirement from the Cambridge chair) enrolled in the second part of the Economics and Political Sciences Tripos, in which he obtained a first class result. Kahn (1987, p. 327) writes in this context that this examination outcome came from 'only a few answers' in the various papers '[b]ut they were of such outstanding merit that he was placed in the First Class of Part II of the Economics Tripos'. This result may have been assisted by Shove's considerable, and early, friendship with Maynard Keynes and close acquaintance with other King's College economists such as Pigou and Dalton. Shove in fact was part of the splendid cohort of pre-1914 graduates in economics at Cambridge, which included Lavington (1910), Hubert Henderson and Dennis Robertson (1911), Claude Guillebaud (1913) and Philip Sargant-Florence (1914).

Shove's early, and close friendship with Keynes needs some elaboration. It started in July 1908, as Keynes reported to Duncan Grant (27 July 1908): 'Shove I've now seen twice. He's much the best of them – quite a cut above the others in my opinion. Indeed he is quite charming, though not very clever, I dare say, and quite nice to look at' (cited in Skidelsky 1983, p. 195). In 1909, their friendship was sufficiently close for Keynes to assist in getting Shove elected to the Apostles (Moggridge 1992, p. 185). By 1911, Skidelsky (1983, p. 265) claims that Shove was Keynes's closest friend, despite his tendency to black moods, offset for Keynes by Shove's 'vehement, biting edge and blasphemous, daredevil side' as attractive qualities. They apparently accompanied each other in observing university sportsmen at athletic events, and Shove was recorded to have been quite overcome at one stage 'by the beauty of Noel Baker, a King's undergraduate'. In 1911, Shove accompanied Keynes on a trip to Ireland (Moggridge 1992, p. 191), and in 1912 joined Keynes and Duncan Grant on an 'eating and gambling holiday at Monte Carlo' (Skidelsky 1983, p. 271). By then, Shove was already a close associate in the Bloomsbury circle, an association undoubtedly further assisted by early friendship with Lytton Strachey (also started in 1908), a friendship particularly robust during 1911 and 1912 (Holroyd, 1971, 1979, pp. 377, 428, 463). On occasions, Shove occupied Virginia Woolf's rooms in her absence (Skidelsky 1983, p. 271) and Keynes let the upper rooms of his flat in Gordon Square to Shove in April 1915.

Somewhat contradicting Shove's later reputation as a very shy person, anecdotes preserved from his life among the Bloomsbury group give another impression. The biographer of Lytton Strachey (Holroyd 1971, 1979, pp. 521, 538) records hilarious lunches at Simpson's with Shove among the frequent participants, and Shove's presence, very drunk and dressed in a top hat, at a Bloomsbury evening party. Skidelsky (1983, p. 300) mentions a night at the Café Royal in 1915 at which Shove ended up 'enthroned in the centre of the room, crowned with roses'. The party associated with Shove's election to the Apostles in the summer of 1909 was also a very drunken affair with Shove so inebriated that he was unable to walk (Skidelsky 1983, pp. 234–235). Perhaps this type of drunken activity encouraged Shove's marriage later in 1915 to Newnham student Fredegond Maitland, a niece of Virginia Woolf, given his need, as he apparently once put it himself, 'to be looked after' (Skidelsky 1983, p. 328). Their marriage lasted a lifetime, and was celebrated some years after his death by his wife's memoir on their life together, *Fredegond and Gerald Shove*, published by Cambridge University Press in 1952.

These years of partying as a young Cambridge graduate also failed to enhance Shove's initial academic prospects. When Shove submitted a fellowship dissertation on the local government rating system for King's College in 1914, Pigou and Cannan as examiners wrote very 'dismissive reports' on his efforts. Keynes was extremely annoyed with this formal outcome. He therefore circulated a note of dissent to the Fellowship electors which was so hostile to Pigou's and Cannan's judgement that Clapham, another Fellow of King's, considered it nothing short of 'insulting'. Keynes's defence of his friend failed to convince the electors in 1914 and it was not until 1926 that he finally succeeded in getting Shove the fellowship (Skidelsky 1983, pp. 213–214). Perhaps Keynes also secured book reviews for his friend and protégé over these years, of which the little noticed review of Marshall's *Industry and Trade* for the 1919 *Athenaeum* is an isolated example.

Shove did not gain his university lectureship until 1923, but he had been involved with teaching well before then. After the war, for example, he took over Keynes's college teaching for some time as a useful source of additional income. As Austin Robinson (1977) recalled, his 1921–1922 lectures included 'inordinately dull teaching on trade union organisation'. Work on this topic may have been inspired by Shove's flirtations with Fabian socialism, in which he engaged as early as 1908. A letter to Keynes (15 September 1910) compared the faith in socialism of some of those attending Fabian meetings (particularly James Strachey) to the Christian faith in which Shove at this stage (see Skidelsky 1983, pp. 234–235, and pp. 240–241 on Fabian socialism) was no longer a true believer even if he continued to describe himself as such in public. His pacifist stance and conscientious objection to military service during the First World War can be recalled at this stage. He then 'ran' a pacifist monthly called *Face the Facts* and became one of Lady Ottoline Morell's 'honorary gardeners' at Garsington (Collard 1990, p. 178).

By the end of the 1920s, Shove's lectures were devoted to the Marshallian theory of value, with special reference to the nature of competition, the laws of returns, the representative firm, attempts by firms to influence the market by price reduction strategies and by incurring advertising expenses, the importance of time (both short and long period) to Marshallian value analysis, the notion of quasi-rent, and the equilibrium output conditions for the firm in terms of equating marginal cost and marginal revenue (Shove, Lectures 1928–1929, from John Saltmarsh's lecture notes preserved at King's College, Cambridge). Most of these topics featured in the cost controversy debates in which many Cambridge economists were then very much engaged, and to which Shove himself contributed with distinction. In 1928, he published his article on 'Varying Costs and Marginal Net Products' in the *Economic Journal* (Shove 1928); Shove's 'Increasing Returns and the Representative Firm' (Shove 1930, 1996) appeared two years later in the *Economic Journal* as his contribution to the symposium on this topic organised by its editor, in which Piero Sraffa and Dennis Robertson also participated. In 1933, he published a further, lengthy note on 'The Imperfection of the Market', a topic on which he had been lecturing for some years. No further journal publications at article length were then recorded until his assessment of the status of Marshall's *Principles of Economics* on the centenary of Marshall's birth (Shove 1942, 1982), prepared for publication in the *Economic Journal* at the invitation of Keynes as editor.

Although Robinson (1977) indicated that Shove was not a participant in the 'circus', that important economics discussion group of the early 1930s which debated the implications of Keynes' *Treatise of Money* for understanding and finding solutions to problems associated with the great depression, Shove was part of a Keynes study group (together with Dennis Robertson and Roy Harrod) which debated the implications of Pigou's *Theory of Unemployment* in 1934 (Moggridge 1992, p. 566). Some years later, and with reference to Pigou's article, 'Real and Money Wage Rates in Relation to Unemployment', Shove told Kahn 'that without exception this is the worst article he has ever read' (Kahn 1984, p. 196). However, Shove was not thanked by Keynes in the preface of the *General Theory*.

Shove was also an active member of the Cambridge Political Economy Club for a considerable period, and by 1923 had become one of its senior members in terms of regular attendance, even if he was also 'shy and withdrawn' during its debates on current topics (Skidelsky 1992, pp. 5, 287). In fact, Shove, together with other members of the older generations of Cambridge economics – Dennis Robertson, Ralph Hawtrey, Hubert Henderson – were part of the academic community with whom Keynes could have good conversations during the 1930s. Skidelsky (1992, pp. 424, 512) also records that Shove attended a lecture by Keynes in October 1934, which Shove described as 'the best lecture he had ever heard in his life'. By then, Shove was passing on from his concentrated work on the defence of Marshall even if the topics on the theory of the firm on which he taught at the end of the 1920s continued to be the mainstay of his Cambridge university lectures, together with at least some classes on trade union organisation and the theory of distribution. From 1929 to 1945, Shove was Secretary of the Faculty Board (Carabelli 2005, p. 208).

For 1930, Plumptre (1975, p. 250) provided an interesting comparison of Keynes's student supervisions with those of Shove. Plumptre frequently experienced Shove as a replacement tutor for Keynes, given Keynes's busy life outside College:

> There was a great difference between Keynes's supervision of undergraduates in economics while I was in King's and other supervision which was given at the same time, and there is something to be learned from the contrast. Mr Gerald Shove was bearing the brunt of it. He is, in many ways, the best teacher I ever had; he always took pains to discuss our written work in detail and to make us talk about it. He would choose subjects that were not too far beyond us; often they would involve examination of some limited but important points in the theory of value. He talked easily and, almost more important, he was easy to talk to. Not so Keynes! His overwhelming brilliance made interruption undesirable and argument almost out of the question....

Given their friendship and shared interest in economics, it is not surprising that Shove was on the list of those to whom Keynes sent a complimentary copy of his *General Theory* on its publication. Skidelsky (2000, p. 18) also reports that in 1938 Shove was asked to deliver Keynes's paper on buffer stocks to a meeting of Section F (Economics) of the British Association on 19 August of that year. This avoided talk of the prospects of a second world war since the paper largely discussed government social and strategic raw materials policy, not as a security measure but as an aid to price stability in peace time by guarding against cost price fluctuations from drastically changing primary resources supplies (cf. Harrod 1951, pp. 484–485). Shove, in addition, continued to read and comment on his older friend's work. For example, commenting in April 1943 on the Keynes Plan for Post-War Reconstruction with special reference to international trade, he noted, '[It] is masterly. It combines the clarity of Mill, the ingenuity of Ricardo & the wisdom of Marshall' (in Moggridge 1992, p. 670). Not long after this, Shove's last book review, that of Joan Robinson's *Essay on Marxian Economics* appeared in the *Economic Journal* (Shove 1944). Shove died three years later, in 1947. Richard Kahn, his former student at King's and later colleague, wrote Shove's Fellow's obituary for King's College. Surprisingly, no obituary of Shove appeared in the *Economic Journal.*

Shove's defence of Marshall's wisdom in addressing economic questions during the 1930s and after is the major concern of this chapter. Shove, the Marshallian loyalist, after all, is the title of this chapter. This is addressed in the subsequent sections dealing respectively with his defence of Marshall in his journal articles, in his book reviews, and in the other extant Shove material of relevance to this study.

II

Shove's first article published in the *Economic Journal* presented criticism of Pigou's *Economics of Welfare* for its use of imprecise language with respect to analysing the impact of a change of output on prices, on rent of the producer, and on consumers' benefit, criticism to which Marshall's *Principles of Economics* on the same topic was, according to Shove, immune. Identifying a change of output with a change in scale, which can be either one of increasing, or of diminishing returns, such changes are associated with either a diminution or an increase in price. Whether this price change affects the welfare of the consumer (or the 'purchaser', the term Shove tended to use in this context) or the landlord (rent recipient) or investor, is the point at issue for Shove (1928, p. 260), particularly since Pigou's analysis in his *Economics of Welfare* needed qualification.

Shove argued that one 'effect which a change in the scale of production has upon rents' depends on its impact on marginal cost, on prices and on the average cost of production given that such changes in cost 'are often shared by *all* producers and affect *every* unit of output' (Shove 1928, pp. 259–260; his italics in the quotation). When this was taken into consideration, a qualification to the analysis as presented by Pigou was necessary. Shove (1928, pp. 260–262) demonstrated that:

> whether the loss (or gain) to the consumer from an expansion of output exactly matches 'the corresponding and equivalent gain' going to the 'landlord', does *not* depend on whether the commodity is produced under conditions of diminishing, increasing or constant returns.

This result required the same assumption as that made by Pigou, an assumption Shove (1928, p. 262) suggested, which 'is not likely to be often fulfilled in practice', since changes in the scale of production always affect the facilities for producing a substantial part, if not the whole of that output. Marshall had argued this point persuasively in the context of agriculture, from which it followed, Shove implied, that 'the odds are against economies of this kind being exactly offset by analogous diseconomies'.

Shove then examined the case where the landlord's gain differed from the 'burden thrown upon the consumers'. Here again, inclusion of what happens to average cost may alter the results reached by Pigou. This brought Shove (1928, p. 265) to his major conclusion:

> What then becomes of the doctrine that it is in the social interest to give a bounty to industries showing increasing returns and to tax those showing diminishing returns. Stated in this unqualified form it collapses. Nor can it

> be defended without further qualification in the form in which it is now presented by Professor Pigou, viz. that there is a 'presumption in favour of State bounties to industries in which the law of increasing returns operates strongly, and in which conditions are such that effects upon rents may be ignored.' The effects of rents must be allowed for in both types of industry, not in one only.
>
> (Shove 1928, pp. 265)

Shove (1928, pp. 265–266) then emphasised that 'in the form in which it was first enunciated by Marshall the doctrine remains unshaken'. Marshall, unlike Pigou, had allowed for the fact that in general:

> the ratio of marginal to final trade costs [the addition to aggregate costs (other than rent) occasioned by a unit expansion of output], varies from industry to industry and, though it is usually greater than one, in some cases it may be less.

Only in perfect competition will resources tend to be distributed between different industries to equate marginal cost and the value of a unit of product (price) in each industry. Since perfect competition was not likely to occur in practice, there is no certainty whatsoever about these results.

Shove's (1928) paper directed attention to three matters which remained of enduring interest to him. First were the consequences of the laws of returns; second, the realism from introducing degrees of imperfect competition to the argument, thereby rejecting the assumption of perfect competition (which Marshall had argued could lead only to 'play results'); third, the fact that Marshall in his *Principles* tended to present these issues in a far more realistic manner than Pigou.

Shove's second, and most famous contribution to the *Economic Journal*, was his article on 'The Representative Firm and Increasing Returns', a part of the symposium on these issues contained in its March 1930 issue, in which Dennis Robertson and Pierro Sraffa also participated. It was a revised version of a paper Shove had originally submitted to the *Journal* on 'The External and Internal Economies of Large-scale Production', altered to meet the requirements of the symposium at the request of Keynes, who as editor had organised to have these contentious issues debated. Shove's (1930, 1996) paper defended, and sought to clarify, Marshall's notion of the 'representative firm' as a device for dealing with the economics of an industry, made up from a number of quite heterogeneous individual firms. In addition, it sought to explain the distinction between 'internal' and 'external' economies in large-scale production to a greater extent than usual (the original subject of the paper), particularly since Marshall himself had left these terms somewhat vague. This second major aim of the paper as actually published reflected the author's more limited intentions as to subject matter when submitting its original version. These two issues form the major topics raised in the paper's two sections, though further comments on the representative firm intrude into Shove's clarification of the concepts of external and internal economies.

Shove's defence of the representative firm stressed the wide variety of its uses in analysis, its satisfactory nature as a tool of analysis to explain what it was intended to clarify, even if it was not indispensable for analysing 'competitive equilibrium'. The representative firm, Shove (1930, 1996, pp. 51–52) claimed, was particularly useful for analysing industries in which some entrepreneurs earn rents from special aptitudes; some entrepreneurs enjoy larger than normal earnings; profits vary over the life-cycle of individual firms in the industry so that industry earnings depend on the age composition of the firms of which it is composed; while finally, equilibrium for the industry does not imply equilibrium of the individual firms of which it consists. Taken together, these points indicated that earning capacity of resources invested in an industry partly reflected the manner of its distribution among individual firms, such as the scale of operation of these business units. Equilibrium distribution of these resources then depended not on the absolutely most advantageous, but on the advantageous relative to the initial distribution of resources (Shove 1930, 1996, pp. 52–53), making for multiple equilibria of the industry. Changes within firms within the industry with respect to earnings prospects are in a continuous state of flux, creating further difficulties for specifying the requirements of equilibrium. In this context, Shove (1930, 1996, p. 53) also drew attention to the fact that in some circumstances, change can only be fruitfully made at the industry level and not at the level of individual firms (his unelaborated examples were cotton-spinning and coal). Moreover, heterogeneity is the stuff of which the real world and its problems consist (Shove 1930, 1996, p. 54). This allowed Shove to criticise Robertson's attempt to construct aggregate supply curves of the various factors of production, an impossible task when quantity rather than value of factors is to be used. Here again, heterogeneity between firms in the industry is the key, as Marshall (1916, p. 355) had suggested when stressing differences in expenditure on individual factors for firms in the same industry. Here, Shove admitted, the representative firm could, unfortunately, do little to help.

The second part of Shove's paper examined the distinction between internal and external economies, an issue of considerable importance in the context of analysing the nature of competition in industries and firms where such economies were significant. Shove (1930, 1996, p. 55) commenced by arguing that 'Marshall (intentionally, no doubt) left his definition of these terms a little vague' but for him they dealt essentially with the following aspects of industrial behaviour. Internal economies for a firm related to 'the advantages which a firm derives from the organisation of *the resources which it employs directly*', external economies from:

> the advantages … from the organisation of *those outside resources, not in its own direct employment, whose services or product it uses*, in common with other firms in the industry (for example, transport facilities, communications, trade journals, produce exchanges, subsidiary industries, the traditions and 'atmosphere' of the locality, and so on).
>
> (Shove 1930, 1996, p. 55; Shove's italics in the quotation)

An increase in the scale of industry may, but need not, give rise to both internal and external economies. Shove considered implications of the distinction for the size of the firm and the industry, and indicated that equilibrium when such economies exist, tends to be 'monopolistically competitive' rather than simply pertaining to monopoly as Sraffa (1926) had suggested (Shove 1930, 1996, pp. 60–61). Although the representative firm can play a part in this analysis, it need not do so (Shove 1930, 1996, pp. 62–63).

Shove then briefly linked the speed at which an individual firm can grow to an increase in the volume of trade of the industry (Shove 1930, 1996, p. 63), the problems addressed by Allyn Young (1928) in his article on 'Increasing Returns and Economic Progress', with its analysis of organisational changes created by increased division of labour (specialisation) among firms in the industry. An example of such changes in the textile industry was the separation of spinning firms, weaving firms and dyeing firms into new forms of industrial organisation from the textile industry broadly conceived (Shove 1930, 1996, pp. 64–65). This type of consideration made the notion of internal and external economies very difficult to handle, even if it remained important when the economies of large-scale industry existed 'as positive and of considerable magnitude' (Shove 1930, 1996, p. 65). As Marshall himself had noted, these difficulties become even greater when long-lived joint-stock companies started to dominate the industry (Shove 1930, 1996, p. 64).

Shove's third *Economic Journal* article (Shove 1933a) was appropriately devoted to some aspects of imperfections in the market. It was essentially a comment on Joan Robinson's article, 'Imperfect Competition and Falling Supply Price', which had investigated the proposition that when falling average costs were established, it necessarily followed that supply price was falling. Shove denied ever having held such a proposition. He had adopted the weaker argument 'that "falling average costs to the firm" will *often*, but *not always or necessarily* lead to "falling supply price for the commodity"' (Shove 1933a, p. 113, his italics in the quotation). Shove then proceeded to note some further points of difference on the issue between them, including of what he perceived to be Joan Robinson's method of establishing this proposition.

One point related to Joan Robinson's reliance on a theorem developed by Richard Kahn on the equilibrium position under such conditions, requiring 'the individual demand curve for the firm to be tangential to its average cost curve' (Shove 1933a, p. 114). In this context, Shove queried the precise nature of this average cost curve, in particular its degree of independence of the demand curve, looking in detail at the various examples provided by Joan Robinson in this connection. The details of this discussion need not be examined, but their impact was to enable Shove's questioning of the generality of Kahn's theory of equilibrium in terms of average costs. In addition, Shove queried Joan Robinson's treatment of normal profit and equilibrium, particularly when entry was free. Generally speaking, the questions Shove raised were all designed to point out:

> what I conceive to be the fundamental dilemma presented in all these attempts to treat these matters precisely. So long as we are content with rough and ready indication of the forces at work, we can keep fairly near the facts: but any attempt to make our treatment exact is apt to lead either to a degree of abstraction which renders the apparatus inapplicable to the actual phenomena we set out to explain or to a degree of complication which makes it cumbrous to use.
>
> (Shove 1933a, p. 121)

On this realistic, Marshallian basis, Shove constructed an alternative line of approach, designed to throw 'some [additional] light on the complicated' matter before them. This classified total costs in terms of minimum and special costs, and proposed some further, modified equilibrium conditions. These suggested:

> expenditure of this kind [on 'advertising, facilities, transport'] is expanded up to the point at which the final increment of it causes an equal addition to the selling value of the output (or if there are several such points, then the one of them which yields the greatest excess of total selling value over total costs).

In addition, 'the price of the firm's final increment of output must be equal to the saving in cost (including advertising and market costs if any) which it would make if it refrained from producing it while keeping prices unchanged'. Third, equilibrium for Shove required that selling price should not be less than unit average cost nor more than the price which will attract new entrants (Shove 1933a, p. 122). This argument could be tackled by sophisticated analytical apparatus (of the type employed by Kahn and Robinson) while it also reminded that cost depended on demand as well as size of the firm, and that realistic economic theory needed to develop a set of tools which could accommodate this broader cost theory 'closely connected to the actual character of the market' (Shove 1933a, p. 124).

The three contributions at article length examined in Section II have some basic matters in common. All three opposed the overly abstract, precise inferences from economic theory – whether *à la* Pigou as in 1928, *à la* Robertson and Sraffa as in the 1930 symposium, or those of Kahn and Joan Robinson as in Shove's 1933 reflections on imperfect competition. Marshall's superior, vaguer method is explicitly preferred in the first two of Shove's articles; indirectly in the third in the quote given on the previous page. Marshall, however, himself deserved occasional criticism, as in the context of his 'loose' definitions of internal and external economies in his *Principles of Economics*. As the true student of Marshall he claimed to be, Shove greatly preferred descriptive generalisations from 'the facts' to the clear, mistakenly precise, statements of theory. This type of defence of Marshall's 'practice' also emerged in Shove's few book reviews for the *Economic Journal*, as indicated in the next section.

III

Shove published three book reviews in the *Economic Journal*, two in 1933 and one in 1944. The last review appeared three years before his death as his final publication. The reviews he published tended to be relatively long. Twelve pages were devoted to his highly critical comments on Hicks's *Theory of Wages* (Shove 1933b); about four pages to his review of Joan Robinson's *The Economics of Imperfect Competition* (Shove 1933c), and no less than fourteen pages to reviewing Joan Robinson's *Essay on Marxian Economics* (Shove 1944). As mentioned previously, a fourth Shove review is extant, that of Marshall's *Industry and Trade*, published in the *Athenaeum* in 1919, but its discussion is postponed to the next section.

Shove's lengthy review of Hicks's *Theory of Wages* is very critical. Its opening sentence proclaimed that Hicks had not accomplished the task he had set himself in restating the theory of wages 'in a form reasonably abreast of modern economic knowledge' (Shove 1933b, p. 460). Nor did Hicks, Shove (1933b, p. 461) went on to say, provide a study of the relationship between earnings and the number of available workers, a connection he claimed was not part of the theory of wages but of the theory of population. Other parts of wage theory, 'the reaction of wage rates to the supply of capital' were also not fully worked out by Hicks. 'In short,' Shove (1933b, p. 462) argued, 'it is impossible to extract from Mr. Hicks' pages any precise and comprehensive formulation of the forces determining either the level of wages generally or the relation between the rates ruling in different industries, occupations and places …'. The title and preface of the book promised more 'comprehensive' and 'ambitious' treatment, than the book in fact delivered.

Some of the review space was devoted by Shove to rescue Marshall's treatment of wages in the *Principles* from Hicks's direct and indirect criticism. Thus Marshall's marginal productivity explanation (demand side) of wages, did not rule out the possibility of unemployment (Shove 1933b, p. 463), while its confinement by Marshall to competitive conditions in a perfect market was also insufficiently appreciated by Hicks. Nor did Hicks satisfactorily handle the relationship between marginal productivity theory and the profit maximisation condition of equating marginal production expenses with marginal revenue.

Hicks's book has other problems for Shove. For example, it failed to treat the central notion of 'exploitation' in wage theory with the importance it deserved (Shove 1933b, p. 466). Monopolistic power over wages for Hicks was too 'narrowly limited' by the potential competition which Hicks saw as an ever present quality of any market (Shove 1933a, p. 467), contrary to the view that 'any degree of market imperfection … (to say nothing of open or tacit understanding [between employers] such as Smith envisaged) opens the door to exploitation of one type or the other to some degree' (Shove 1933b, p. 468).

Hicks's book did have some merits in Shove's view. It introduced the potentially valuable concept of 'elasticity of substitution' of a factor of production, thereby usefully modifying Marshall's 'four rules' in the *Principles* for 'determining the elasticity of a derived demand'. However, Hicks's approach in the book was essentially that of 'pure theory'. Its application to problems of the real world caused Shove (1933b, p. 468) to have 'some misgivings', particularly when 'rigid assumptions' deprived the theoretical conclusions Hicks had reached of any degree of generality. Shove (1933b, pp. 469–471) was also rather critical of Hicks's lengthy discussion claiming excessive wages (those 'higher than would have been paid in a competitive market') whether induced by trade union activity or not, to increase unemployment. Part of this can be attributed to the impetus given by such high wage rates to substituting more capital for labour in the production process (a proposition of which Shove 1933b, pp. 470–471, was rather dubious), particularly because its capital-theoretic foundations were lacking in Hicks's book. Nor did Hicks adequately deal with monetary reactions to changes in wages policy (Shove 1933b, p. 472) including those via the rate of interest. He thereby further raised the 'obscurity and lack of precision' in the argument of these chapters, arising from what Shove believed to be the far too narrow focus on wages Hicks gave in his book. Shove, therefore, provided a solid indictment of inadequacy in treatment on a book proclaimed by its author to be a general theory of wages.

Given the fact that Shove had published a long 'note' on imperfections in the market' in the March issue of the 1933 *Economic Journal* which specifically commented on an earlier article by Joan Robinson on this topic, Shove's review of her book, *The Economics of Imperfect Competition*, was relatively short at a mere five pages. The review opens with Shove's statement that 'for a product of youth' (Joan Robinson was thirty, as compared with Shove's age, at the time, of thirty-six), the book was 'disappointingly conservative'. Its treatment of the subject of imperfect competition was very much on 'established lines' with the 'originality [of the book] … [very much] in the detail' (Shove 1933c, p. 657). Shove also indicated that the book's analytical foundations rested on two propositions: the Marshallian equilibrium analysis for the individual firm based on equating marginal cost and marginal revenue; second, the equality of price and average cost. These propositions could be generalised to all firms in an industry, not just to a 'representative firm' or to the 'marginal firm' (Shove 1933c, pp. 657–658).

Shove praised Joan Robinson for the book's clear definitions of terms, and forthright statement of necessary assumptions (Shove 1933c, p. 660), though he also diagnosed 'a tendency' in the author 'to evade difficulties' as in, for example, her treatment of 'normal profit' (Shove 1933c, pp. 659–660). Likewise, other terminology (the meaning of commodity, the nature of entrepreneurship) was left vague. Overall, the great virtue of the book was its 'restoration' of 'marginal revenue' to its rightful place as a counterpart to marginal cost (Shove 1933c, p. 660). However, Shove (1933c, p. 661) argued that 'the author is too prone to attribute fallacies to other writers on insufficient grounds. Mr. John Hicks (p. 97), Prof. Taussig (p. 155) and Marshall (pp. 49, 155, 168) are, for example, treated in this way'.

Shove's grounds for this opinion with respect to Joan Robinson's treatment of Marshall were as follows. Joan Robinson's (1933, p. 49) claim that Marshall related cost and price decreases with increases in demand was far too general a statement for Marshall on this point. Second, there was Joan Robinson's (1933, p. 155 and note) attribution of a view to Marshall's *Industry and Trade* which, as she admitted in the accompanying footnote, was never formally set out by Marshall in the text cited. Third, a contradiction in Marshall's *Principles* (Joan Robinson 1933, p. 168) is just not there to be found. It contrasted Marshall's loose discussion of competition with the costs saving in a monopoly (Marshall 1920, p. 484) from advertising, marketing and like costs. Such cost saving would arise as well if the monopolist's cost function was compared on this type of expenses with the cost function of firms in imperfect competition. In short, Joan Robinson's specific criticisms of Marshall's work all rest on too strict a reading of his text, even when Marshall clearly intended it to be read in a more general way. Shove would have been particularly annoyed with Joan Robinson's criticisms of Marshall because they implied a rigour for Marshall's analysis which he deliberately refrained from in most cases, a quality of Marshall's work which Shove particularly admired in Marshall's method, as indicated on various occasions in the previous section.

Shove's third *Economic Journal* review appeared eleven years later. It commented on Joan Robinson's *Essay on Marxian Economics*, two years after its publication in 1942. It was a long review, fourteen pages, much of it devoted to criticising Joan Robinson's 'misrepresentations' of Marshall, whose views she had taken, as she had done to a lesser extent with Pigou's, as representative of 'orthodox' economics in contrast with the economics of Marx. A good example of such comparisons is her remark about the use of coloured terminology in that orthodox economics for comparison with Marx's practice: for example, his use of the notion of 'rate of exploitation', Marshall's use of the term, 'waiting', and Pigou's use of 'exploitation' to designate the difference between real wages under perfect competition and monopoly (Joan Robinson 1942, 1949, pp. 19, 21).

The opening pages of Shove's review addressed some aspects of Robinson's treatment of Marx. Shove identified this as both sympathetic and critical. An illustration of the former for Shove was her (wrong, according to Shove) attribution of a theory of effective demand to Marx; her critical attitude came out for him in the discussion of value theory though here she herself was wrong, according to him, when explaining the use of cost prices in a socialist economy (Shove 1944, pp. 49–50).

In the context of her treatment of Marshall in the review, Shove raised the following points. First, Marshall's own predictions of socially just societies (made in both the *Principles* and in some of the material reproduced in Pigou's 1925 edition of *Memorials of Alfred Marshall*) were never mentioned by Joan Robinson in her comparisons of Marshall with Marx. Second, Joan Robinson's (1942, 1949, p. 73) identification of 'orthodox' (read Marshallian) theory with perfect competition was described by Shove (1944, pp. 51–52) as completely erroneous since Marshall held perfect competition to be untenable from both the abstract theory and the 'realistic' point of view. This was clearly stated in his *Principles*, and probably suggested by his strong dislike of the 1879 *Economics of Industry*, the immature work which had assumed perfect competition for much of its analysis.

Shove (1944, pp. 53–59) spent almost half of the space for the review in criticising Joan Robinson's interpretation of 'waiting' (especially that contained in Chapter VII, 'The Orthodox Theory of Profit'). In this connection, Shove (1944, p. 55) carefully paraphrased Marshall's views on waiting and capital theory, in the following three points:

1 'Waiting' means neither saving nor owning capital, but the postponement of gratifications;
2 in order that capital equipment should be produced or replaced a decision must be taken that gratifications shall be deferred by using resources for this purpose rather than in acquiring more immediately consumable commodities;
3 the return obtained from capital is an inducement to take this decision – necessary, not in all circumstances and in all cases, but in the circumstances of modern industry so far as the marginal saver (or marginal increment of waiting) is concerned.

In addition, Shove (1944, p. 55) bitterly complained that Joan Robinson had totally ignored Marshall's concept of quasi-rent as part of his explanation of the return to fixed capital, and that she had failed to grasp his analysis of the rate of interest, its association with the marginal product of capital and variations in the size of the capital stock. A fall in the rate of interest, associated with a fall in the marginal product of capital and a reduced capital stock, over the longer run encouraged resources to be moved into additions to the capital stock (Shove 1944, p. 57). Joan Robinson's erroneous views on these various aspects of Marshall's theory, undoubtedly induced Shove's (1944, p. 61) concluding remark: 'It is to be hoped that Mrs Robinson will on some future occasion give us a more detailed and more fully documented examination of Marshallian and post-Marshallian theories.'

Shove's reviews of Joan Robinson's books reflect in part views he had expressed in their correspondence, letters preserved unlike so much of his other non-published writings. Thus Shove's letter of 10 August 1933 (Rosselli 2005, p. 363) precisely reflected the main praise he gave of her 1933 book in the *Economic Journal*, though the overall tone of Shove's review was not enthusiastic. In connection with the review of her *Essay on Marxian Economics*, Joan Robinson initiated a correspondence to explain her position on aspects of the review. She particularly protested about Shove's excessive praise of Marshall in the review, especially in the context of the rate of interest, saving and investment (Rosselli 2005, pp. 364–365). Joan Robinson's conclusion in the context of the 1930 Symposium that 'Gerald's stuff is really hopeless' would have been reinforced by her experiences with him a decade later in a review context.

IV

Both Shove's (1919) review of *Industry and Trade* and his 1942 birth centenary appraisal of Marshall's *Principles of Economics* reflect on the major contributions to modern economics made by Marshall, the economist. This is done very succinctly in the opening paragraph of the 1919 review in a comparison with J.S. Mill's approach to political economy and with that assumed to be his readers' response to the subject. It can therefore be quoted in full:

> Alfred Marshall's 'Principles of Economics' marked an era in the development of the science. Partly through the reverence which was accorded to John Stuart Mill by the mildly educated classes (who but half understood his work), but more particularly through the writings of second- and third-rate popularisers, Victorian England came to regard political economy almost as a minor branch of the Utilitarian philosophy and to elevate – or degrade – it to the rank of polite learning suitable for the instruction of young ladies at the high schools. The complicated character of modern business changed all that, and economics is now established as a specialised and highly technical science. Many causes and many men contributed to this result, but the tendencies which were making towards the new phase were gathered up, weighed and developed in Dr. Marshall's book – published nearly 30 years ago. More than any other writer, Dr. Marshall can claim to be the founder of modern economics.
>
> (Shove 1919, 1998, p. 158)

The review continued with a brief summary of the three 'books' or parts which made up *Industry and Trade.* Shove saw that contents essentially as a survey of the rise of monopolistic competition, emerging from the development on the technical side of industry, from the growth of large-scale enterprise and the spread of joint-stock companies, of scientific management, and of the shading together of competition and monopoly in the practical development of 'modern business' (Shove 1919, 1998, pp. 158–159). 'Trusts and cartels' were analysed in terms of German and American experience, and in more detail in the context of British developments. The author's erudition on display in the work was 'immense', and was 'probably more penetrating than any living economist can command' (Shove 1919, 1998, p. 160). The writing was also 'never for display', but simply designed to reveal the truth about these matters in so far as that can be done. However, *Industry and Trade* was not the 'monumental book' Marshall produced in the *Principles,* even if it provided 'a well-balanced picture of the main forces and tendencies which were at work in the organisation of business on the eve of the war' (Shove 1919, 1998, p. 160). Shove's review thereby explicitly mentioned one weakness of *Industry and Trade,* that is, the rapidity with which its contents were becoming 'history'. Shove also raised the 'unsatisfactory feature' of the book's 'moral tone … altogether out of place … in a scientific treatise' (Shove 1919, 1998, p. 159), and mentioned its replacement of 'economic man' as the centre of attention for the *Principles* by the new captains of industry as modern heroes glamorised by the American movie industry, a far-fetched picture substantially removed from that of the 'real life' the book attempted to portray (Shove 1919, 1998, p. 160).

Shove's 1942 appraisal of the place of Marshall's *Principles* in the development of economic theory begins with a strong denial of the appropriateness in viewing the book's contents as a 'synthesis' of Ricardian (or J.S. Mill's) doctrines and the utility theory of Jevons and the Austrians. For Shove, Marshall's work is of pure Ricardian stock, directly evolved from the British classical tradition: Smith, Ricardo and Mill (Shove 1942, 1982, p. 133). The validity of this position is demonstrated by Shove through pointing out the gaps in their analysis which the Marshallian apparatus cleverly filled. These relate to the necessity of both supply and demand conditions for a general theory of value; of combining scale factors and factor payments to solve for cost of production; third, the need to combine supply and demand factors in satisfactorily explaining long-period value theory; and, fourth, in the context of short period labour costs, the demand side explanation of capital requires a clear analysis of the growth of capital as associated with the rate of profit or returns to capital (Shove 1942, 1982, pp. 134–136). Marshall, Shove argued, clearly filled these gaps as demonstrated succinctly in the mathematical appendix, particularly in the equations announced to be leading up the major note XXI of that Appendix.

The last note was the backbone of the theory, and a proposition which Marshall attempted, during his long lifetime, to make as realistic as possible (Shove 1942, 1982, p. 137). As a real Marshall connoisseur, Shove indicated this position was more clearly presented in the organisation of the material for the first edition, than in subsequent editions, particularly the definitive eighth edition. He also insisted that Marshall's views had developed before, and independently, of Jevons and the Austrian economists (Shove 1942, 1979, pp. 137–138). After all, as Marshall himself had recollected in material now published in Pigou's 1925 *Memorials of Alfred Marshall*, he had gained the substance of the new economics from von Thünen, and its mathematical form from Cournot's work, both of whose views he had studied by the end of the 1860s after his decision to leave mathematics and the natural sciences, and to study economics in earnest.

In other respects, Marshall was much more a follower of Adam Smith. His historical, statistical and other factual studies; his use of government reports, necessary means by which to fulfil his desire of combining realism with theory, attested to this affiliation (Shove 1942, 1982, p. 142). Shove also doubted that there was serious influence from the historical school, though Hegel's *Philosophy of History* may have been instructive to the young Marshall in his search for realism in economic argument. In a similar way, Marshall's strong belief in 'freedom of enterprise' was matched by a desire to remove its potentially undesirable social consequences by both individual and state action, thereby removing the stigma of 'dismal science' when describing the character of political economy. Hence scientific endeavour was able to combine with the science of character (Mill's 'ethology') to create political economy afresh as a science of society. Moreover, for Marshall, biological evolution became a hallmark in economic progress and understanding, turning economics into a science relative to time and place. Much of this transformation Marshall achieved in the pages of his *Principles*.

In England, Marshall's *Principles* gradually gained the status which Mill's *Principles* had enjoyed from the middle of the nineteenth century. By the middle of the twentieth century, Marshall's book had become a third watershed in the development of economics following those of Smith's *Wealth of Nations* and Ricardo's *Principles*. Marshall's book by then had also strongly influenced the development of United States economics, while in European economics, it, together with the work of Walras, had likewise become the dominant influence (Shove 1942, 1982, pp. 147–149).

Shove admitted that in some respects Marshall's major work had begun to date, even though less so than the work of most of his contemporaries. 'The decay of what may be called "atomic" competition', and its virtual replacement by monopolistic competition had become a major change between Marshall's world of analysis and that of economists in the 1940s. Marshall had gradually realised this himself as subtle changes in the wording of later editions of the *Principles* indicate (Shove 1942, 1982, pp. 152–153). Recent developments in imperfect competition theory in fact reflect much of Alfred Marshall's thought on the subject, such as the important equilibrium condition of equating marginal cost and marginal revenue for the firm, and, for the industry, equating the receipts and costs of the marginal firm.

However, in many other aspects Marshall's approach to economics in his *Principles* had been less successful. For example, his valiant attempts to combine realism with economic theory had not been followed by later generations of economists. Value and distribution theory had become far more abstract than was the situation in his day. Likewise, Marshall's strong hopes for an economic biology had not been realised, and theoretical physics provides more of a beacon to the contemporary economic theorist. Economics had also become much more mathematical than Marshall would have wished.

Irreversible processes, the type of dynamic developments Marshall had wished to catch with his mecca of economic biology, remained as important for analysis as in his day, even if they were not treated in this manner by contemporary economic theory. Part of this lack of progress, Shove (1942, 1982, pp. 156–157) explained by the fact that post-Marshall economics in the 1930s had become immersed in solving the problem of unemployment and the theory of output as a whole, which needed to be developed in a monetary economy. Marshall, following J.S. Mill, Shove (1942, 1982, pp. 157–158) admitted, had perceived the weakness in Say's Law by indicating 'the power to buy' did not necessarily imply the wish to buy, so that general demand failure, as Malthus had appreciated in his debate on the issue with Ricardo was a distinct possibility in certain circumstances. Reintegrating money with value and distribution theory had become an urgent necessity if this task was to be adequately attempted.

Shove (1942, 1982, pp. 158–159) recognised clearly that some Marshallian tools (his examples include 'mutual determination', 'balancing of cost and advantage', 'short- and long-period elements in costs' and 'the notion of elasticity') had still a useful role to play in economic analysis, as was shown by Keynes's recent work. Shove's concluding paragraphs suggested that some Marshallian concepts (his notion of 'real cost' is the example) were useful for discussing incentives in a socialist economy like the USSR, while other tools (Marshall's 'ingenious notion' of 'compromise benefit' as modestly applied in his *Industry and Trade*) may still play a part in future analysis of 'the economics of group-action, of collective control, massive competition and mass bargaining' (Shove 1942, 1982, p. 159). Shove's concluding sentences (1942, 1982, p. 159) are worth quoting as a final word on what Marshall still has to offer:

> What we can say with confidence is that Marshall's *Principles* contributed to the corpus of scientific ideas elements which were not only 'architectonic' and 'in some sense his own', but are still 'an existing yeast working in the Cosmos' and far from dying. On the evidence so far available, its author abundantly deserves the title 'classical' even on his own somewhat exacting standard.

That Marshall's *Principles* is now a classical text remains as true at the start of the twenty-first century as it was when Shove wrote these words in 1942.

Both of Shove's specific pieces on Marshall's major books discussed in this section are critical, even if their general tone is that of praise for the Cambridge economist. In 1919, Shove indicated that realistic analysis of the type presented in Marshall's *Industry and Trade*, tended to date quickly. In 1942, Shove admitted that intellectual obsolescence equally applied to Marshall's *Principles*, even if its relevance had been more enduring. Realism and practical relevance, as shown in early sections, were virtues in economic argument greatly admired by Shove. Shove's willingness to criticise Marshall on this score, which was in fact an inevitable quality of economic theory, says a great deal for his objectivity in assessing Marshall's work. These assessments therefore married substantial praise of Marshall's major books with pertinent and significant criticism. What other conclusions can be more generally derived from this overview of Shove's published work, are discussed in Section V of this chapter.

V

As Austin Robinson indicated in his remarks quoted at the start of this chapter, Shove's 'sabbatical year' in 1929–1930 had made him a different person. The early 1930s were undoubtedly the period when he published most of his work, that is, two of his *Economic Journal* articles and two of his four book reviews. Other work appeared sporadically in 1919 and 1928, and there was another, brief burst of activity in the early 1940s. Much of Shove's work had to be pushed out of him, and here Keynes as editor and friend was probably the key factor in getting him to write for publication.

Some common streams run through Shove's limited published output. First, it all falls within the theory of value, broadly conceived as including the theory of the competitive firm, the theory of market imperfections, and the theory of distribution. Second, they are all critical, not only in the book reviews of John Hicks and Joan Robinson. The 1928 article criticised Pigou's treatment of Marshall's welfare economics; the 1930 contribution complained about Robertson's and Sraffa's misunderstandings of the role of the representative firm. The 1919 review and the 1942 article even criticised Marshall, as do, to a lesser extent, Shove's other papers and reviews. However, the criticisms bestowed on Marshall are always relative. Marshall failed to make himself sufficiently clear on some points; he left definitional statements a little too vague, he was occasionally too imprecise. Against this, there are Marshall's great advantages, especially those exhibited within the pages of the *Principles.*

First of all, these include Marshall's quest for realism, which often included a concomitant warning of the dangers of too much precision, too much generalisation, too much exact and precise theory, when insufficiently backed by supporting facts. Marshall's abiding quest for these facts was visible in his immense study of history, in his fact-finding tours and *wander-jahre* in factories, in his reading of government blue books, and in his international comparisons shedding light on different national systems of economic development. Marshall's stress on the tremendous value of economic biology was also part of his never-ending search for realism, unsuccessful though he had been in applying that 'mecca of the economist'.

Despite these criticisms, Shove in his published work and his lectures continued to support the Marshallian research programme, as he saw it revealed through his study of the *Principles.* Theoretical exposition in the *Principles* for Shove was generally placed in a setting where its potential practical uses were always kept in view, and where warnings of the dangers in misapplication were generally explicitly provided. This Marshallian practice for Shove contrasted particularly strongly with the expository practice of Pigou, Marshall's successor, with its elaborations of theory untested, and unleavened, by the facts. Lack of realism was Shove's general criticism of his professor and former teacher at Cambridge.

What other qualities are visible in Shove's published work? Great originality and theoretical innovation were not attributes for which that work was later noted. This can be illustrated from references to him in works devoted to the development of 'modern economics'. Hutchison (1953, p. 69) mentioned Shove's praise for Marshall's 'restless quest after realism' and later noted Shove's 1928 contribution to careful elaboration of the meaning to be given to Marshall's concepts of internal and external economies. Shackle (1967, pp. 43, 44, 45) mentions Shove as having appreciated the dilemma for competitive industry from the existence of increasing returns, his attempt to rehabilitate the representative firm in that context, and his appeal to the evolutionary aspects of Marshall's theory. Seligman (1963, p. 484) only mentions Shove as one of many Cambridge economists critical of attempts to apply Marshall's subsidy scheme for increasing returns industries, since associated losses of rent could wipe out the benefits from increased consumer surplus when these industries expanded their output. The commentators therefore capture both Shove's great admiration and his occasional positive criticism and correction of Marshall's theoretical construction in the *Principles*. As Chapter 11 has elaborated at much greater length, this is what made Shove a true, and an enduring Marshallian loyalist during his decades as Cambridge economics teacher.

12 Conclusions

Ten 'Minor Marshallians' – spreading Marshall's organon of economics to later generations

The Cambridge School of Economics was created gradually over the decades following Marshall's installation in the Cambridge Economics Chair in 1885. His inaugural lecture, as indicated later in this chapter, announced his intention to form a Cambridge School of Economics for spreading the benefits of good economics to the whole of Great Britain and eventually to the world at large. By 1888 Foxwell could say that 'half the Economics chairs of the United Kingdom are occupied by his students'. J.S. Nicholson was by then Professor of Economics at Edinburgh University for eight years, but none of the other nine minor Marshallians treated in this book were teachers of economics by 1888. However, at the start of the twentieth century, Flux was professor at Manchester, Sanger was teaching economics at University College, London, Chapman succeeded Flux as professor of economics at Manchester by 1901, Clapham was professor at Leeds from 1902, while the remaining five commenced economics teaching after the establishment of the Cambridge Economics Tripos in 1903. With the exception of Lavington and Shove, all these minor Marshallians had been taught by Marshall, most before the creation of the Tripos, Layton and Fay being the exceptions. As Collard (1990, p. 170) put it, 'The Production of Cambridge Economics by means of Cambridge economists' clearly had its beginning in these years.

The preceding ten chapters traced the impact of Marshall's teaching, whether in lectures or through his published work, on the ten minor Marshallians, individually examined for their Marshallian credentials. This was done by assessing that impact by a detailed study of a sample of their published work. A variety of patterns were disclosed, some critical of Marshall, some less so, irrespective of whether Marshall's impact had come directly via his teaching, or indirectly via his published work. Some broad generalisations can be made about the nature of Marshall's contributions most admired by his ten 'students' who are included in this study.

The most important feature of the Marshall legacy left to these ten economists and economic historians was Marshall's stress on the necessity for good economics to blend fact with theory. This view of the nature of good economics was accepted by every one of the ten minor Marshallians under consideration, both explicitly and as revealed by their own practice. Their strong support for

Marshall's plea for a realistic economics had critical implications for the appreciation of his own work for some of the ten. For example, Nicholson severely criticised the lack of realism in consumers' surplus, which for him made it difficult to use for practical application in tax or welfare policy. On the other hand, Chapman, MacGregor and Lavington viewed consumer surplus as one of Marshall's major theoretical innovations. It was also the tool, Marshall predicted during his final lecture in 1908, whose use would outlast all those present in his audience. This was one Marshall prediction from that lecture which time has definitely shown to have been correct.

Moreover, MacGregor claimed realism in economics combined with the process of industrial and other types of economic and social development implied that sooner or later most of Marshall's (and his own) theoretical concepts would have to be jettisoned as out of date. This view was also strongly upheld by Shove, initially in his review of *Industry and Trade*, but more trenchantly in his centenary assessment of Marshall's work where he argued this quality of eventual obsolescence applied with equal force to Marshall's contributions in the *Principles*. Clapham argued in his famous article on 'Empty Economic Boxes' that concepts like increasing and diminishing returns were difficult to discover within the operations of actual industrial enterprises, despite the general theoretical merits these analytical tools of classification were thought to have. However, the laws of returns as dealt with by Marshall, and in particular their refinement in the associated notions of internal and external economies of scale were strongly praised as very useful tools in industry economics by Chapman and by Shove. In this context, Marshall's advocacy of his policy proposal for penalising diminishing returns industries by a tax and using its revenue to finance bounties for increasing returns industries was strongly criticised by Clapham as an empty policy box, while it was praised as an interesting, even if difficult to apply, policy suggestion by Chapman, by MacGregor, by Fay and by Shove.

Quasi-rent, another Marshall innovation in theory, although criticised and rejected by Nicholson, was praised as a useful, and hence important, new concept by Flux, Chapman, Layton and Shove. Marshall's notion of the representative firm was treated as much more problematic by some of the minor Marshallians. Flux completely rejected its usefulness as an economics tool of analysis. However, MacGregor claimed it to be one of the three major analytical contributions made by Marshall of enormous use in the emerging field of industry economics, while Shove vigorously defended its value as a tool of analysis against misrepresentations by Robertson and criticism from Sraffa and Joan Robinson.

In the context of competition, Chapman, MacGregor, Layton and Shove, all strongly indicated that for Marshall competition often entailed monopolistic elements, and that it was therefore quite compatible with scale economies. It never implied pure or perfect competition. This, Marshall had totally rejected as unrealistic and as an abstract form of market situation impossible to exist in practice. Further in the context of realism, it may also be noted that the treatment of mathematics and diagrams by those of the ten minor Marshallians who used these tools of analysis (Flux and MacGregor) followed Marshall's practice of putting the mathematics in an appendix and the diagrams in the footnotes. As part of the burgeoning interest in industry economics by some of the minor Marshallians (especially by MacGregor, Lavington and Shove), both MacGregor and Lavington accepted Marshall's device of the particular expenses curve as an interesting and original analytical device. MacGregor's centenary appraisal of Marshall and his work also signalled his treatment of price analysis (supply and demand) and the importance of time (market period, short and long periods) and his concomitant use of varying elasticities as important analytical innovations.

In what would now be called macro-analysis, Lavington, in his book on the trade cycle, elaborated on much of Marshall's work on that topic as presented in the 1879 *Economics of Industry* while he also drew on Robertson's research for his 1915 *Study of Industrial Fluctuations*. In addition, Lavington and Shove also positively evaluated Marshall's savings-investment analysis as an important part of his economic system. Alfred Marshall's broad treatment of the quantity theory of money in his evidence to the Gold and Silver Commission, was both praised and followed by Layton's work on the theory of prices, and also fully accepted by Lavington even if initially it had been quite wrongly criticised by Nicholson in his submission to the Gold and Silver Commission. With respect to the treatment and development of these branches of Marshall's economics, his followers made good use of his official papers represented by such submissions, especially those on monetary questions including the Gold and Silver Commission, and that on the Depression of Trade. More generally, Marshall's firm belief in economic progress and the rise in both living standards and standard of life which accompanied such progress, was particularly strongly supported by Fay. In this context it may also be noted that Fay discussed socialism, and the cooperative movement as its preferred form, very much in the manner of Marshall.

Much of this brilliance of Marshall's economic innovations spilled over into general admiration, sometimes critical, of Marshall's major publication, *The Principles of Economics.* This was invariably described as a major theoretical tour de force by all ten minor Marshallians including Nicholson, even if in his review of the first edition, he had criticised its history as 'old-fashioned' if not 'wrong', and its organisation and structure as deficient and repetitive. MacGregor by contrast praised the unity of the supply and demand system of analysis underlying the *Principles*: things are demanded by consumers, they are therefore produced, the commodities produced are exchanged at competitive prices, and the incomes derived from that production distributed to the various productive classes. Although, as already indicated in this chapter, many of these admirers of the *Principles* recognised its inevitable progress to eventual intellectual obsolescence, because its originally highly realistic background would necessarily disappear from the inevitable change and development in business practice taking place over time. This was seen as an even greater risk for the finished 'companion volume' of the *Principles, Industry and Trade,* and for the final volume from the 'master', *Money, Credit and Commerce.* The last, it may be noted, appeared only to have been used for teaching by MacGregor at Oxford, during the 1930s. *Industry and Trade* fared a great deal better in this respect.

Spreading the Marshall 'Organon'

In his inaugural lecture, 'The Present Position of Economics', Marshall (1885, 1925), among many other things, carefully discussed the meaning of his notion of the 'organon' of modern (that is, contemporary) economics. The 'part of economic doctrine, which alone can claim universality, has no dogmas. It is not a body of concrete truth, but an engine for the discovery of concrete truth …' (Marshall 1885, 1925, p. 259). Marshall provided an analogy from the theory of mechanics, and the way it was used to solve practical problems of immense benefit to the art of bridge building. In spite of this acknowledged practicality in applying the theory of mechanics, there was 'no universal organon of mechanical reasoning'.

The 'organon' of political economy, Marshall (1885, 1925, pp. 159–162) further explained, would 'ultimately' contain an element of 'perfectly pure or abstract theory', but it would also embrace measurable aspects of motivation, in practice measured by money. Marshall discussed this more fully in what follows:

> This organon deals with the play of measurable forces for and against one another, balancing one another and being substituted for one another, though the persons concerned may be in classes or in countries that have little direct intercourse. And it sets out that most complex play of human motives that changes the purchasing power of money, and thus alters the measure of all motives.
>
> Lastly, taking account of the fact that the same sum of money measures a greater pleasure for the poor man than for the rich, it helps in determining the relations between the money gain that a nation gets from any given social or industrial change and the totals increase in happiness arising from it. This task most properly belongs to the economic organon, though it has been much neglected by economists till recently. If more attention had been paid to it, we would have avoided many of those unintelligent applications of the doctrine of *laisser-faire*, which assume that whatever increases wealth must necessarily increase well-being. By a natural reaction many of the social reformers of to-day, in their desire to improve the distribution, are reckless as to the effects of their schemes on the production of wealth. They argue that, if the distribution of wealth were somewhat improved, its inequalities being somewhat diminished, the present or even a rather smaller national income would suffice for all the reasonable needs of man. But statistics prove that this is not the case.
>
> (Marshall 1885, 1925, p. 162, his italics in the quotation)

The economic organon, as Marshall made abundantly clear in his inaugural lecture, rested on a combination of pure and abstract theory with a careful study of the facts. 'Measurable motives' as an essential component of the organon implicitly emphasised this crucial combination of 'induction' and 'deduction', and that combination alone made safe and reasonable inferences about economic topics possible. In the quote from his inaugural lecture just given, Marshall illustrated this aspect of the organon by his references to mistaken policy proposals of income redistribution from the rich to the poor, with their potential for unintended consequences on wealth creation and future possibilities for living standards and standard of life, and the 'unintelligent', (because unscientific?) applications from laissez-faire doctrine. Economics for Marshall was therefore a very complex body of thought and analysis, combining theory with observation, measurement with application, science with policy prescription. All of these issues were further developed in his 'mission statement' as the new professor of economics at Cambridge, presented in his inaugural lecture. They were subsequently embodied in Marshall's *Principles of Economics* which expressed the meaning he gave to economic science as the 'study of mankind in the ordinary business of life [examining] ... that part of individual and social action which is most closely connected with the attainment and with the use of the material requisites of well-being' (Marshall 1920, p. 1; somewhat differently worded in Marshall 1890, p. 1, a matter not noted in the Guillebaud variorum edition). Marshall's *magnum opus* gradually became a major tool in the spreading of his 'organon' over the greater part of the world.

Marshall's professorial responsibilities in the way he defined them are crystallised in the final paragraph of his inaugural lecture, which became his effective creed as professor of economics at Cambridge over the next twenty-three years.

> It will be my most cherished ambition, my highest endeavour, to do what with my poor ability and my limited strength I may, to increase the numbers of those, whom Cambridge, the great mother of strong men, sends out into the world with cool heads and warm hearts, willing to give some at least of their best powers to grappling with the social suffering around them; resolved not to rest content till they have done what in them lies to discover how far it is possible to open up to all the material means of a refined and noble life.
>
> (Marshall 1885, 1925, p. 174)

The ten previous chapters discussed ten of the men whom Marshall, directly or indirectly, caught for economics while professor at Cambridge (for the whole of their lives in the case of nine of them, Sanger the only exception). In various ways, they helped the world to better understand the manner by which social suffering could be reduced and greater material opportunities could be provided to society at large.

Can it be said that the careers of these ten 'minor' Marshallians support a Marshall 'success story' as professor of economics at Cambridge who directly, or indirectly, guided their economic endeavours to do good? In many respects, the preceding chapters have shown this to be the case, though in a somewhat limited way. The careers of the ten minor Marshallians assisted the spread of the economic organon to later generations at Cambridge, and to economics students at Oxford, London, Manchester, Leeds, Sheffield and other parts of Great Britain. They also revealed its spread to Canada even if not its diffusion to the United States. This was achieved later, largely through the *Principles* and, through Marshall's many personal contacts with American economists, to the United States. However, the internationalisation of economics from Cambridge was also illustrated with the spread of sources on which the ten drew for their work. These frequently included German works on economics and, to a lesser extent, works by French and Italian authors. Spreading the organon is therefore a strong, unifying feature of this study of the academic activities of the ten minor Marshallians it contains.

The individual research conducted by these minor Marshallians also tended to fit neatly into the wider economic research programme Marshall wanted to initiate. This was particularly the case with respect to the initial research undertaken by MacGregor, by Fay and by Clapham. MacGregor, on his own account guided herein by Marshall, set out to study aspects of industry economics, especially issues associated with the development and operation of trusts and cartels, and their impact on competition. Fay, it will be recalled from Chapter 10, owed his first research topic of cooperative organisations for his Fellowship dissertation directly to Marshall. He was also encouraged by Marshall to work on life and labour in the nineteenth century, the subject of some of his lectures at Cambridge and an interesting piece of research in social and economic history. Clapham was strongly encouraged by Marshall to specialise in economic history. Irrespective of Marshall's wishes, this was the road taken by Clapham. He first analysed the economic history of the woollen and worsted industries in England, he then produced a comparative study of economic development (1815–1914) in France and Germany and, though Marshall did not live to see it, completed a monumental three-volume British Economic History. Chapman's work, although not discussed in any detail in Chapter 5, partly covered aspects of British industrial history with his studies of the Lancashire cotton industry and, more generally, on the cotton industry and trade. He also produced a small Marshallian text on political economy, and brought the three volumes of Brassey's *Work and Wages* up to date, a task Marshall would have greatly appreciated.

Both Layton and Lavington produced work on monetary and financial economics, as indeed did Joseph Nicholson, Marshall's oldest 'pupil' discussed in this book. Layton did so in his discussion of the theory of prices in which he made great use of Marshall's broad views on the validity of the quantity theory; Lavington in his analysis of the British capital market, a topic on which Marshall had been virtually silent until the appearance in 1923 of his *Money, Credit and Commerce*; and Nicholson in his *Treatise of Money and Monetary Essays*, respectively evaluated in Chapters 9, 8 and 2. Marshall, however, was not impressed by Nicholson's work, publicly criticising Nicholson's submission to the Gold and Silver Commission, and privately informing Foxwell of the poor and slovenly nature of Nicholson's work, especially that on theory. In the context of this paragraph, it can be added that Lavington also published on the trade cycle, and in the final years of his life produced two articles in the field of industry economics. Layton published his second book on the relations of capital and labour, a topic addressed more narrowly in Nicholson's prize-winning Cobden Club Essay on Labour and Machinery. As mentioned in the previous paragraph, Chapman's substantial updating of Brassey's *Work and Wages* also falls within this research programme. In addition, Sanger and Chapman wrote on taxation theory, and contributed to public finance.

Matters of pure theory were especially addressed by Flux and Sanger. Not surprisingly, they were also the more adept mathematical economists among the ten. They both, like Marshall, were Cambridge wranglers (high in the first class honours list of the Mathematical Tripos. Flux was (bracketed) first wrangler in 1887; six years later, Sanger was second wrangler in 1893. Flux's mathematical style was illustrated in Chapter 3 by his review of Wicksteed's 'Co-ordination of the Laws of Distribution', and by the Marshallian manner in which he treated the mathematics in his *Principles of Economics* by neatly placing it an appendix. Sanger's mathematical economics was discussed in Chapter 4 in terms of his 1894 paper on demand theory written with Johnson, and his survey of 'recent contributions to mathematical economics' published in the 1893 *Economic Journal*. Neither of them stayed in academic economics: Flux on his return from Canada moved to the Board of Trade, Sanger left economics altogether for legal practice as a barrister.

This leaves the 'Benjamin' of the ten minor Marshalians, Gerald Shove. As put in the title of the preceding chapter, he was a very loyal preserver and defender of the Marshall economic organon, even if he had also explicitly pointed to the inevitable obsolescence of both Marshall's *Principles* and his *Industry and Trade*. Chapter 11 also showed how Shove staunchly defended Marshall's 'theory of value' during the cost controversies, including the concept of the representative firm which he tried to save from Robertson's and Sraffa's misrepresentations. In addition, Shove reviewed Hicks's *Theory of Wages* and Joan Robinson's *Economics of Imperfect Competition* and *Essay on Marxian Economics*. Much of Shove's criticism in these reviews constituted a defence of Marshall. Marshall's theory of wages was depicted as superior to that presented by Hicks. Shove condemned Robinson for failing to appreciate the important work Marshall had done on imperfect competition, for her misunderstanding of Marshall's complex views on the nature of competition, and with respect to her work on Marxian economics, her failure to grasp the real foundations of Marshall's savings-investment analysis. Finally, Shove's centenary reappraisal of Marshall's work indicated both its successes and failures. The last explicitly included the lack of success of Marshall's plea for combining fact with theory, in fact, for realism in economic theory; Shove also pointed to Marshall's inability to put into practice his notion of the value of economic biology in economic argument. For Shove, important features of Marshall's 'economic organon' were therefore clearly crumbling by the early 1940s, and much of contemporary economics was rejecting its Marshallian heritage.

A significant number of Marshall's better students chose to spread his economic organon to future generations of economics students at Cambridge and elsewhere. It is almost self-evident that the three 'major' Marshallians – Pigou, Keynes and Robertson – did so both as teachers at Cambridge and in their many books. They were joined in this task by a generation or two of 'minor' Marshallians, of whom ten were individually investigated to shed light on the nature and extent of their Marshallian views. Their activities likewise indicate how very successfully Marshall's aims at Cambridge were achieved through the economists he trained during his years as professor at Cambridge. Both 'Marshall and his book', to paraphrase one 'minor' Marshallian (MacGregor 1942, 1982, p. 114), were extensively drawn upon over the many years they were used by them as students, and as teachers. All of them, in varying degrees, did so loyally, critically and effectively, as the preceding chapters have demonstrated.

Bibliography

[V.W.B.] (1943) 'Sir William Flux (1867–1942)', *Canadian Journal of Economics and Political Science* 9(1), February, pp. 74–76.

Baumol, W.J. and Goldfield, S.M. (eds) (1968) *Precursors of Mathematical Economics: An Anthology*, London: London School of Economics, Series of Reprints of Scarce Works on Political Economy, No. 19.

Blaug, M. (1962, 1996) *Economic Theory in Retrospect*, London: Heinemann, first edition; Cambridge: Cambridge University Press, fifth edition.

Bridel, Pascal (1987) *Cambridge Monetary Thought. The Development of Saving-Investment Analysis from Marshall to Keynes*, London: Macmillan.

Cannan, Edwin (1895) 'Inequality in Local Rates and its Economic Justification', *Economic Journal* 5(1), March, pp. 22–34.

Cannan, Edwin (1922) 'Review of Lavington, *The Trade Cycle*', *Economic Journal* 32(3), September, pp. 355–359.

Carabelli, Anna (2005) 'A Life-long Friendship. The Correspondence between Keynes and Shove', in Maria Cristina Marcuzzo and Annalisa Rosselli (eds) *Economists in Cambridge. A Study through their Correspondence 1907–1946*, London: Routledge, chapter 7, pp. 196–215.

Chapman, S.J. (1899) *Local Government and State Aid*, London: Swan, Sonnenschein & Company.

Chapman, S.J. (1904) *Work and Wages in Continuation of Lord Brassey's Work and Wages*, Volume 1, *Foreign Competition*, London: Longmans, Green and Company.

Chapman, S.J. (1908) *Work and Wages in Continuation of Lord Brassey's Work and Wages*, Volume 2, *Wages and Employment*, London: Longmans, Green and Company.

Chapman, S.J. (1909) 'Hours of Labour', *Economic Journal* 19(3), September, pp. 354–373.

Chapman, S.J. (1912) *Political Economy*, London: William and Norgate, Home University Library.

Chapman, S.J. (1913, 1959) 'The Utility of Income and Progressive Taxation', *Economic Journal* 23(1), March, pp. 25–35, reprinted in R.A. Musgrave and C.S. Shoup (eds) American Economic Association, *Readings in the Economics of Taxation*, London: George Allen and Unwin, chapter 1, pp. 3–12.

Chapman, S.J. (1914) *Work and Wages in Continuation of Lord Brassey's Work and Wages*, Volume 3, *Social Betterment*, London: Longmans, Green and Company.

Chapman, S.J. (1942) 'Obituary: Sir Alfred Flux', *Economic Journal* 52(208), December, pp. 400–403.

Chapman, S.J. and Knoop, D. (1904) 'Anticipations in the Cotton Market', *Economic Journal* 14(4), December, pp. 541–554.

Chapman S.J. and Knoop, D. (1906) 'Dealing in Futures on the Cotton Market', *Journal of the Royal Statistical Society* 69(2), June, pp. 321–364.

Clapham, J.H. (1921, 1951) *The Economic Development of France and Germany 1815–1914*, fourth edition, Cambridge: Cambridge University Press.

Clapham, J.H. (1922a, 1953) 'Of Empty Economic Boxes', *Economic Journal* 32, pp. 305–314, reprinted in K.E. Boulding and G.J. Stigler (eds) American Economic Association, *Readings in Price Theory*, London: Allen and Unwin, pp. 119–130.

Clapham, J.H. (1922b) 'The Empty Economic Boxes: A Rejoinder', *Economic Journal* 32(125), December, pp. 560–563.

Clapham, J.H. (1926) *An Economic History of Modern Britain. The Early Railway Age 1820–1850*, first edition, Cambridge: Cambridge University Press.

Clapham, J.H. (1931, 1948) 'Economic History', in E.R.A. Seligman (ed.) *Encyclopaedia of the Social Sciences*, New York: Macmillan, Volume 5, pp. 327–330.

Clapham, J.H. (1936) 'Marshall and Dutch Shipbuilding', *Economic Journal, Economic History Supplement* III(2), February, pp. 212–213.

Clay, H. (1959) 'Flux: Sir Alfred William', in *The Dictionary of National Biography 1941–50*, Oxford: Oxford University Press, pp. 262–263.

Cole, G.D.H. (1913, 1917) *The World of Labour. A Discussion of the Present and Future of Trade Unionism*, third edition, London: G. Bell and Sons.

Collard, David (1981) 'A.C. Pigou 1877–1959', in D.P. O'Brien and J.R. Presley (eds) *Pioneers of Modern Economics in Britain*, London: Macmillan, chapter 4, pp. 105–139.

Collard, David (1990) 'Cambridge After Marshall', in J.K. Whitaker (ed.) *Centenary Essays on Alfred Marshall*, Cambridge: Cambridge University Press, chapter 7, pp. 164–192.

Cournot, A.A. (1838, 1963) *The Mathematical Principles of the Theory of Wealth*, Homewood, IL: Irwin Paperback Classics.

Cournot, A.A. (1877, 1982) *Revue sommaire des doctrines oeconomiques*, Paris: J. Vrin.

Deane, Phyllis (1987) 'Clapham, John Harold (1873–1946)', in John Eatwell, Peter Newman and Murray Milgate (eds) *The New Palgrave. A Dictionary of Economics*, London: Macmillan, Volume 1, pp. 427–428.

Deane, Phyllis (2001) *The Life and Times of John Neville Keynes*, Cheltenham: Edward Elgar.

Ebenstein, Alan (2004) 'Clapham, John Harold (1873–1946), in Donald Rutherford (ed.) *The Biographical Dictionary of British Economists*, Bristol: Thoemmes Continuum, Volume 1, pp. 222–223.

Edgeworth, F.Y. (1897) 'The Pure Theory of Taxation, Parts I–III', *Economic Journal* 7(1, 2, 4), March, June, December, pp. 46–70, 226–238, 550–571.

Edwards, Ruth Dudley (1993) *The Pursuit of Reason. The Economist 1843–1993*, London: Hamish Hamilton.

Eshag, Eprime (1963) *From Marshall to Keynes*, Oxford: Blackwell.

Fay, C.R. (1908, 1936) *Cooperation at Home and Abroad*, London: P.S. King, two volumes.

Fay, C.R. (1913) *Copartnership in Industry*, Cambridge: Cambridge University Press.

Fay, C.R. (1920) *Life and Labour in the Nineteenth Century*, Cambridge: Cambridge University Press.

Fay, C.R. (1925a) *Agricultural Co-operation in the Canadian West*, London: P.S. King.

Fay, C.R. (1925b) 'Reminiscences', in A.C. Pigou (ed.) *Memorials of Alfred Marshall*, London: Macmillan for the Royal Economic Society, pp. 74–77.

Fay, C.R. (1926, 1982) 'Reminiscences of a Deputy Librarian', in J.C. Wood (ed.) *Alfred Marshall. Critical Assessments*, London: Croom Helm, Volume 1, pp. 87–90.

Fay, C.R. (1927) 'Obituary of F. Lavington', *Economic Journal* 37(3), September, pp. 504–505.

Fay, C.R. (1928a) *Two Empires*, Toronto: Toronto University Press.

Fay, C.R. (1928b) *Great Britain from Adam Smith to the Present Day*, London: Longmans, Green and Company [second edition 1929, third edition 1932, fourth edition 1937, fifth edition 1950].

Fay, C.R. (1931) *Youth and Power. The Diversions of an Economist*, London: Longmans, Green and Company.

Fay, C.R. (1934) *Imperial Economy and its Place in the Formation of Economic Doctrine 1600–1932*, Oxford: Clarendon Press.

Fay, C.R. (1951a) *Huskisson and his Age*, London: Longmans.

Fay, C.R. (1951b) *Palace of Industry 1851: A Study of the Great Exhibition and its Fruits*, Cambridge: Cambridge University Press.

Fay, C.R. (1952) *Round About Industrial Britain 1830–1860*, Toronto: Toronto University Press.

Fay, C.R. (1956) *Life and Labour in Newfoundland*, Cambridge: W. Heffer and Sons.

Fay, C.R. (1960) *The World of Adam Smith*, Cambridge: W. Heffer and Sons.

Fishburn, Geoffrey (2008) '*The Economic Review* 1894–1914', paper presented at the 21st Conference of the History of Economic Thought Society of Australia, Parramatta: University of Western Sydney, 9–11 July.

Fletcher, Gordon (2000) *Understanding Dennis Robertson. The Man and his Work*, Cheltenham: Edward Elgar.

Flux, A.W. (1894, 1968), 'Review of P.H. Wicksteed's "Essay on the Co-ordination of the Laws of Distribution" ', *Economic Journal* 4(2), June, pp. 308–313; reprinted in William J. Baumol and Stephen M. Goldfield (eds) *Precursors of Mathematical Economics: An Anthology*, London: London School of Economics Series of Reprints of Scarce Works in Economics, No. 19, pp. 326–331.

Flux, A.W. (1904a, 1923) *Economic Principles*, London: Methuen and Company, first and second editions.

Flux, A.W. (1904b) 'The Variation of Productive Forces: further comment', *Quarterly Journal of Economics* 18(2), February, pp. 280–286.

Flux, A.W. (1906, 1965) editor with an introduction, in W.S. Jevons, *The Coal Question* (1865), New York: Augustus M. Kelley.

Friedman, Milton (1990) 'Bi-metallism Revisited', *Journal of Economic Perspectives* 4(4), Fall, pp. 85–104.

Graaf, J. de V. (1987) 'Pigou, Arthur Cecil (1877–1959)', *The New Palgrave. A Dictionary of Economics*, London: Macmillan, Volume 3, pp. 876–879.

Groenewegen, Peter (1995a) *A Soaring Eagle. Alfred Marshall 1842–1924*, Cheltenham: Edward Elgar.

Groenewegen, Peter (1995b) 'Keynes and Marshall: Methodology, Society, Politics', in Allen F. Cottrell and Michael S. Lawlor (eds) *New Perspectives on Keynes*, Durham, NC: Duke University Press, pp. 129–155.

Groenewegen, Peter (ed.) (1996) *Official Papers of Alfred Marshall. A Supplement*, Cambridge: Cambridge University Press for the Royal Economic Society.

Groenewegen, Peter (ed.) (1998) *Alfred Marshall. Critical Responses*, London: Routledge, 2 volumes.

Guillebaud, C.W. (ed.) (1961) Alfred Marshall, *Principles of Economics*, ninth variorum edition, London: Macmillan for the Royal Economic Society, 2 volumes.

[H.L.] (1942) 'Sir Alfred William Flux C.B.', *Journal of the Royal Statistical Society* 105(2), pp. 144–147.

Haberler, G. von (1937, 1952) *Prosperity and Depression*, New York: United Nations, third edition.

Harrod, R.F. (1966) *The Life of John Maynard Keynes*, London: Macmillan.

Holroyd, Michael (1971, 1979) *Lytton Strachey. A Biography*, Harmondsworth: Penguin Books.

Hubback, David (1985) *No Ordinary Press Baron. A Life of Walter Layton*, London: Weidenfeld and Nicolson.

Hutchison, T.W. (1953) *A Review of Economic Doctrines 1870–1929*, Oxford: Clarendon Press.

Johnson, W.E. and Sanger, C.P. (1894) 'On Certain Questions Connected with Demand', *Cambridge Economic Club*, Easter Term, 1894, pp. 1–8, in William J. Baumol and Stephen M. Goldfield (eds) *Precursors in Mathematical Economics: An Anthology*, London: London School of Economics Series of Reprints of Scarce Works in Economics (1968) No. 19, chapter 5, pp. 42–48.

Kadish, Alon (1994) *Historians, Economists and Economic Historians*, New York: Routledge.

Kahn, Richard F. (1984) *The Making of Keynes's General Theory*, Raffaele Mattaioli Foundation, Cambridge: Cambridge University Press.

Kahn, Richard F. (1987), 'Shove, Gerald Frank (1888–1947)', in John Eatwell, Peter Newman and Murray Milgate (eds) *The New Palgrave. A Dictionary of Economics*, London: Macmillan, Volume 4, pp. 327–328.

Keynes, J.M. (1930) 'C.P. Sanger', *Economic Journal* 40(1), March, in J.M. Keynes, *Essays in Biography*, in *The Collected Writings of John Maynard Keynes*, London: Macmillan, for the Royal Economic Society, 1972, Volume X, pp. 324–325.

Keynes, J.M. (1971) *Activities 1906–1914* in *The Collected Writings of John Maynard Keynes*, London: Macmillan, for the Royal Economic Society, Volume XV.

Keynes, J.M. (1972) *Essays in Biography*, in *The Collected Witings of John Maynard Keynes*, London: Macmillan, for the Royal Economic Society.

King's College (1949) *John Harold Chapman 1873–1946, Fellow, Tutor and Vice-Provost. A Memoir*, Cambridge: printed for King's College.

Knight, F.H. (1921) *Risk, Uncertainty and Profits*, Boston and New York: Houghton, Mifflin & Co.

Lavington, F. (1911) 'The Social Importance of Banking', *Economic Journal* 21(1), March, pp. 53–60.

Lavington, F. (1912) 'Uncertainty in its Relation to the Rate of Interest', *Economic Journal* 22(3), September, pp. 398–409.

Lavington, F. (1913) 'The Social Interest in Speculation', *Economic Journal* 23(1), March, pp. 36–52.

Lavington, F. (1921, 1929) *The English Capital Market*, London: Methuen & Company.

Lavington, F. (1922) *The Trade Cycle*, London: P.S. King.

Lavington, F. (1923) 'The Indian Fiscal Commission 1921–22', *Economic Journal* 33(1), March, pp. 51–59.

Lavington, F. (1924) 'Short and Long Rates of Interest', *Economica* 4(7), November, pp. 291–303.

Lavington, F. (1925) 'An Approach to the Theory of Business Risks, Part I', *Economic Journal* 35(2), June, pp. 186–199.

Lavington F. (1926a) 'An Approach to the Theory of Business Risks, Part II', *Economic Journal* 36(2), June, pp. 192–302.

Lavington, F. (1926b) 'Monopoly and Business Stability', *Economica* 6(2), June, pp. 135–147.

Lavington, F. (1927) 'Technical Influences on Vertical Integration', *Economica* 7(1), March, pp. 27–36.

Layton, Walter T. (1912, 1922) *An Introduction to the Theory of Prices*, London: Macmillan.

Layton, Walter T. (1914) *The Relations of Capital and Labour*, London and Glasgow: Collins.

Lee, F.S. (2004) 'D.H. MacGregor', in Donald Rutherford (ed.) *The Biographical Dictionary of British Economists*, Bristol: Thoemmes Continuum, Volume 2, pp. 705–708.

Lemberger, J. (1921) 'Review of Lavington, *The English Capital Market*', *Economic Journal* 31(4), December, pp. 516–519.

MacGregor, D.H. (1906, 1966) *Industrial Combination*, London: Routledge, Thoemmes Press.

MacGregor, D.H. (1914) 'Review of Walter Layton, *The Relations of Capital and Labour*', *Economic Journal* 24(95), September, pp. 449–450.

MacGregor, D.H. (1934) *Enterprise, Purpose and Profit*, Oxford: Clarendon Press.

MacGregor, D.H. (1942, 1982) 'Marshall and his Book', *Economica*, N.S. 9 November, pp. 313–324, in J. Cunningham-Wood (ed.) *Alfred Marshall. Critical Assessments*, London: Croom Helm, Volume 2, pp. 114–126.

Marshall, Alfred (1879, 1930) *The Pure Theory of International Trade*, London: The London School of Economics and Political Sciences, Reprints of Scarce Tracts No. 1.

Marshall, Alfred (1885, 1925) 'The Present Position of Economics', in A.C. Pigou (ed.) *Memorials of Alfred Marshall*, London: Macmillan, for the Royal Economic Society, pp. 152–174.

Marshall, Alfred (1886, 1926) 'Royal Commission on the Depression of Trade. Answers to Questions', in J.M. Keynes (ed.) *Official Papers of Alfred Marshall*, London: Macmillan, for the Royal Economic Society, pp. 1–16.

Marshall, Alfred (1887a, 1926) 'Evidence to the Gold and Silver Commission', in J.M. Keynes (ed.) *Official Papers of Alfred Marshall*, London: Macmillan, for the Royal Economic Society, pp. 17–195.

Marshall (1887b, 1925) 'Remedies for Fluctuations in General Prices', in A.C. Pigou (ed.) *Memorials of Alfred Marshall*, London: Macmillan, for the Royal Economic Society, pp. 188–211.

Marshall, Alfred (1887c) 'Introduction to L.L. Price, *Industrial Peace*', London: Macmillan.

Marshall, Alfred (1888, 1996) 'Note on Professor Nicholson's Paper for the Gold and Silver Commission', in Peter Groenewegen (ed.) *Official Papers of Alfred Marshall. A Supplement*, Cambridge: Cambridge University Press, for the Royal Economic Society, pp. 70–77.

Marshall, Alfred (1889, 1925) 'Co-operation', in A.C. Pigou (ed.) *Memorials of Alfred Marshall*, London: Macmillan, for the Royal Economic Society, pp. 227–255.

Marshall, Alfred (1890a) 'Some Aspects of Competition', in A.C. Pigou (ed.) *Memorials of Alfred Marshall*, London: Macmillan, for the Royal Economic Society, pp. 256–291.

Marshall, Alfred (1890b) *Principles of Economics*, London: Macmillan, first edition.

Marshall, Alfred (1891) *Principles of Economics*, London: Macmillan, second edition.

Marshall, Alfred (1892) *Elements of the Economics of Industry*, London: Macmillan.

Marshall, Alfred (1895) *Principles of Economics*, London: Macmillan, third edition.

Marshall, Alfred (1897, 1925) 'The Old Generation of Economists and the New', in A.C. Pigou (ed.) *Memorials of Alfred Marshall*, London: Macmillan, for the Royal Economic Society, pp. 295–311.

Marshall, Alfred (1897, 1926) 'Memorandum and Evidence on the Classification and Incidence of Local Taxes', in J.M. Keynes (ed.) *Official Papers of Alfred Marshall*, London: Macmillan, for the Royal Economic Society, pp. 329–364.

Marshall, Alfred (1898) *Principles of Economics*, London: Macmillan, fourth edition.

Marshall, Alfred (1902) *A Plea for a Curriculum in Economics and Associated Branches of Political Science*, Cambridge: Cambridge University Press.

Marshall, Alfred (1906) *Principles of Economics*, London: Macmillan, fifth edition.

Marshall, Alfred (1907, 1925) 'Social Possibilities of Economic Chivalry', in A.C. Pigou (ed.) *Memorials of Alfred Marshall*, London: Macmillan, for the Royal Economic Society, pp. 323–346.

Marshall, Alfred (1910) *Principles of Economics*, London: Macmillan, sixth edition.

Marshall, Alfred (1916) *Principles of Economics*, London: Macmillan, seventh edition.

Marshall, Alfred (1919) *Industry and Trade*, London: Macmillan.

Marshall, Alfred (1920), *Principles of Economics*, London: Macmillan, eighth edition.

Marshall, Alfred (1923) *Money, Credit and Commerce*, London: Macmillan.

Marshall, Alfred and Marshall, Mary Paley (1879) *The Economics of Industry*, London: Macmillan.

Marshall Library of Economics (1927) *Catalogue*, Cambridge: Faculty of Economics and University Press.

Milgate, Murray and Levy, Alistair (1987a) 'Fay, Charles Ryle (1884–1941)', *The New Palgrave. A Dictionary of Economics*, London: Macmillan, Volume 2, pp. 297–298.

Milgate, Murray and Levy, Alistair (1987b) 'Layton, Walter Thomas (1884–1966)', *The New Palgrave. A Dictionary of Economics*, London: Macmillan, Volume 3, pp. 149–150.

Mitchell, B.R. and Deane, Phyllis (1962) *Abstract of British Historical Statistics*, Cambridge: Cambridge University Press.

Moggridge, D.E. (1992) *Maynard Keynes. An Economist's Biography*, London: Routledge.

Murphy, Antoin (1997) *John Law. Economic Theorist and Policy Maker*, Oxford: Clarendon Press.

Nicholson, J.S. (1888, 1895a) *Treatise of Money and Essays on Monetary Problems*, London: A. & C. Black.

Nicholson, J.S. (1888, 1895b) 'Causes of Movements in General Prices', in J.S. Nicholson, *Treatise of Money and Essays on Monetary Problems*, London: A. & C. Black, pp. 342–379.

Nicholson, J.S. (1891) 'The Living Capital of the United Kingdom', *Economic Journal* 1(1), March, pp. 95–107.

Nicholson, J.S. (1892) *The Effects of Machinery on Wages*, London: Swann Sonnenschein & Co., second edition.

Nicholson, J.S. (1893, 1962) 'The Reaction in Favour of the Classical Economy', in R.L. Smyth (ed.) *Essays in Economic Method*, London: Duckworth, pp. 112–125.

Nicholson, J.S. (1893, 1897, 1901) *Principles of Political Economy*, London: A. & C. Black, Volumes I, II and III.

Nicholson, J.S. (1894) 'The Measurement of Utility by Money', *Economic Journal* 4(2), pp. 342–347.

Nicholson, J.S. (1895) *A Treatise of Money and Essays on Monetary Problems*, London: Charles Black, third edition.

Nicholson, J.S. (1903a) 'The Use and Abuse of Authority in Economics', *Economic Journal* 13(4), December, pp. 554–566.

Nicholson, J.S. (1903b) *Elements of Political Economy*, London: Macmillan.

O'Donnell, R.M. (1989) *Keynes: Philosophy, Economics and Politics*, London: Macmillan.

Patinkin, Don (1965) *Money, Interest and Prices*, New York: Harper & Row, second edition.

Patinkin, Don (1976) *Keynes's Monetary Thought*, Durham, NC: Duke University Press.

Pigou, A.C. (1917/18) 'The Exchange Value of Legal Tender Money', *Quarterly Journal of Economics* 32(1), November, pp. 38–65.

Pigou, A.C. (1920, 1921) *Economics of Welfare*, London: Macmillan.

Pigou, A.C. (ed.) (1925) *Memorials of Alfred Marshall*, London: Macmillan, for the Royal Economic Society.

Pigou, A.C. (1927) *Industrial Fluctuations*, London: Macmillan.

Plumptre, A.F.W. (1975) 'Maynard Keynes as a Teacher', in Milo Keynes (ed.) *Essays on John Maynard Keynes*, Cambridge: Cambridge University Press.

Presley, John R. (1978) *Robertsonian Economics*, London: Macmillan.

Presley, John R. (ed.) (1992) *Essays in Robertsonian Economics*, London: Macmillan.

Robertson, D.H. (1915) *A Study of Industrial Fluctuations*, London: P.S.King & Son.

Robinson, A.E.G. (1977) 'Keynes and his Cambridge Colleagues', in Don Patinkin and J. Clark Leith (eds) *Keynes, Cambridge and the General Theory*, London: Macmillan, pp. 25–38.

Robinson, Joan (1933) *The Theory of Imperfect Competition*, London: Macmillan.

Robinson, Joan (1934, 1960) 'Euler's Theorem and the Problem of Distribution', *Economic Journal* 44(3), September, in Joan Robinson, *Collected Economic Papers*, Oxford: Blackwell, Volume 1, pp. 1–19.

Robinson, Joan (1942, 1949) *An Essay on Marxian Economics*, London: Macmillan.

Rosselli, Analisa (2005) 'The Defenders of the Marshallian Tradition: Shove and the Correspondence with Kahn, J. Robinson and Sraffa', in Maria Cristina Marcuzzo and Annalisa Rosselli (eds) *Economists at Cambridge. A Study through their Correspondence*, London: Routledge, pp. 350–370.

Rutherford, Donald (2004) 'Joseph Shield Nicholson (1850–1927), in Donald Rutherford, ed., *The Biographical Dictionary of British Economists*, Bristol: Thoemmes Continuum, Volume 2, pp. 854–858.

Sanger, C.P. (1895a) 'Recent Contributions to Mathematical Economics', *Economic Journal* 5(1), March, pp. 113–128.

Sanger, C.P. (1895b) 'The Fair Number of Apprentices in a Trade', *Economic Journal* 5(4) December, pp. 616–636.

Sanger, C.P. (1896a) 'The Hungarian Zone System', *Economic Journal* 6(2), June, pp. 294–295.

Sanger, C.P. (1896b) 'Hungarian Zone Tariff', *Economic Journal* 6(4), December, pp. 630–632.

Sanger, C.P. (1897) 'Review of E. Montel, *Le Leggi dell'interesse*', *Economic Journal* 7(2), June, pp. 255–256.

Sanger, C.P. (1899a) 'Is the English System of Taxation Fair?', *Economic Journal* 9(1), March, pp. 10–17.

Sanger, C.P. (1899b) 'Review of F.W. Lawrence, *Local Variations in Wages*', *Economic Journal* 9(3), September, pp. 421–424.

Sanger, C.P. (1901a) 'Report of the Local Taxation Commission: Review Article', *Economic Journal* 11(3), September, pp. 321–333.

Sanger, C.P. (1901b) 'Review of A.L. Bowley, *Elements of Statistics*', *Economic Journal* 11(2), June, pp. 193–197.

Sanger, C.P. (1902a) 'Review of Frederico Flora, *Le finanze degli stati composti*', *Economic Journal* 12(1), March, pp. 70–72.

Sanger, C.P. (1902b) 'Review of Eteocle Lorini, *La Repubblica Argentina e i suoi maggiori Problemi di Economia e di Finanza*', *Economic Journal* 12(4), December, pp. 528–530.

Sanger, C.P. (1902c) 'Review of Adolphe Landry, *L'utilité sociale de propriété*', *Economic Journal* 12(1), March, pp. 69–70.

Sanger, C.P. (1902d) 'Review of Pierre du Maroussem, *Les enquêtes, practique e théorie*', *Economic Journal* 12(1), March, pp. 67–69.

Sanger, C.P. (1903) 'The Legal View of Profits', *Economic Journal* 13(2), June, pp. 177–185.

Sanger, C.P. (1904a) 'Review of J.B. Clark, *The Problem of Monopoly*', *Economic Journal* 14(4), December, pp. 603–604.

Sanger, C.P. (1904b) 'Review of G. de Leener, *Les Syndicats Industrielles de Belgique*', *Economic Journal* 14(3), September, pp. 47–48.

Sanger, C.P. (1908) 'Review of Irving Fisher, *Appreciation and Interest*', *Economic Journal* 18(1), March, pp. 66–9.

Sanger, C.P. (1913), 'Review of Walter Leaf, *Troy: A Study of Homeric Geography*', *Economic Journal* 23(2), June, pp. 239–241.

Sanger, C.P. (1915a) 'Review of H.N. Brailsford, *The War of Steel and Gold*', *Economic Journal* 25(2), June, pp. 241–243.

Sanger, C.P. (1915b) 'Review of Richard Ely, *Property and Contract in their Relation to the Distribution of Wealth*', *Economic Journal* 25(3), September, pp. 224–226.

Sanger, C.P. (1924, 1998) 'Obituary of Alfred Marshall', *Nation and Atheneum*, 19 July 1924, in Peter Groenewegen (ed.) *Alfred Marshall. Critical Responses*, London: Routledge, Volume 1, pp. 31–33.

Sanger, C.P. (1926a) *The Structure of Wuthering Heights*, London: Leonard and Virginia Woolf, at the Hogarth Press.

Sanger, C.P. (1926b) 'Review of *Memorials of Alfred Marshall*', *Economic Journal* 36(1), March, pp. 83–84.

Sanger, C.P and Norton, H.T.J. (1915) *England's Guarantee to Belgium and Luxembourg*, London: Allen & Unwin.

Schumpeter, J.A. (1954) *History of Economic Analysis*, London: Allen and Unwin.

Scott, W.R. (1927) 'Obituary of J.S. Nicholson', *Economic Journal* 37(3), September, pp. 495–502.

Seligman, Ben B. (1963) *Main Currents in Modern Economics*, New York: The Free Press of Glencoe.

Shackle, G.L.S. (1967) *The Years of High Theory. Invention and Tradition in Economic Thought 1926–1939*, Cambridge: Cambridge University Press.

Shove, F. (1952) *Fredegonde and Gerald Shove*, Cambridge: Cambridge University Press.

Shove, G.F. (1919, 1998) 'Review of *Industry and Trade*', *Athenaeum*, 31 October, in Peter Groenewegen (ed.) *Alfred Marshall. Critical Responses*, London: Routledge, Volume 2, pp. 158–160.

Shove, G.F. (1928) 'Varying Costs and Marginal Net Products', *Economic Journal*, 38(2), June, pp. 258–266.

Shove, G.F. (1928–1929) Lecture Notes, taken by John Saltmarsh, Kahn Papers, King's College, Cambridge [notes kindly supplied by Annalisa Rosselli].

Shove, G.F. (1930, 1996) 'The Representative Firm and Increasing Returns', *Economic Journal* 40(1), March, pp. 94–116, in J.C. Wood (ed.) *Alfred Marshall. Critical Responses*, London: Routledge, Volume 5, pp. 50–69.

Shove, G.F. (1933a), 'The Imperfection of the Market', *Economic Journal* 43(1), March pp. 213–224.

Shove, G.F. (1933b) 'Review of J.R. Hicks, *The Theory of Wages*', *Economic Journal* 43(3), September, pp. 460–472.

Shove, G.F. (1933c) 'Review of Joan Robinson, *The Economics of Imperfect Competition*', *Economic Journal* 43(4), December, pp. 657–661.

Shove, G.F. (1942, 1982) 'The Place of Marshall's *Principles* in the Development of Economic Theory', *Economic Journal* 52(4), December, pp. 249–329, in J.C. Wood (ed.) *Alfred Marshall. Critical Assessments*, London: Croom Helm, Volume 2, pp. 132–165.

Shove, G.F. (1944) 'Mrs Robinson on Marxian Economics', *Economic Journal* 54(1), April, pp. 47–61.

Skidelsky, Robert (1983) *John Maynard Keynes. Hopes Betrayed 1883–1920*, London: Macmillan.

Skidelsky, Robert (1992) *John Maynard Keynes. The Economist as Saviour 1920–1937*, London: Macmillan.

Skidelsky, Robert (2000) *John Maynard Keynes. Fighting for Britain 1937–46*, London: Macmillan.

Sraffa, Piero (1926) 'The Laws of Returns under Competitive Conditions', *Economic Journal* 36(3), September, pp. 535–550.

Stigler, G.J. (1940) *Production and Distribution Theories. The Formative Period*, New York: Macmillan.

Trevelyan, G.M. (1946) 'Obituary of Sir John Clapham', *Economic Journal* 56(3), September, reprinted in King's College (1949), pp. 19–28.

Webb, Sidney and Webb, Beatrice (1897) *Industrial Democracy*, London: Longmans, Green and Company.

Whitaker, J.K. (ed.) (1965) *Early Economic Writings of Alfred Marshall*, London: Macmillan, for the Royal Economic Society, two volumes.

Whitaker, J.K. (1987a) 'Flux, Alfred William (1867–1942)', in John Eatwell, Murray Milgate and Peter Newman (eds) *The New Palgrave. A Dictionary of Economics*, London: Macmillan, Volume 2, pp. 395–396.

Whitaker, J.K. (1987b) 'Charles Percy Sanger (1871–1930)', in John Eatwell, Murray Milgate and Peter Newman (eds) *The New Palgrave. A Dictionary of Economics*, London: Macmillan, Volume 4, pp. 241–242.

Whitaker, J.K. (ed.) (1990) *Centenary Essays on Alfred Marshall*, Cambridge: Cambridge University Press, for the Royal Economic Society.

Whitaker, J.K. (ed.) (1996) *The Correspondence of Alfred Marshall. Economist*, Cambridge: Cambridge University Press, for the Royal Economic Society, three volumes.

Whitaker, J.K. (2004) 'Alfred William Flux (1867–1942)', in Donald Rutherford (ed.) *The Biographical Dictionary of British Economists*, Bristol: Thoemmes Continuum, Volume 1, pp. 393–394.

Winch, Donald (1969, 1972) *Economics and Policy. A Historical Survey*, London: Collins/Fontana.

Witzel, Morgan (2004) 'Layton, Walter (1884–1966)', in Donald Rutherford (ed.) *The Biographical Dictionary of British Economists*, London: Thoemmes Continuum, Volume 2, pp. 666–669.

Wright, H. (1927) 'Obituary of F. Lavington', *Economic Journal* 37(3), September, pp. 503–504.

Young, Allyn (1928) 'Increasing Returns and Economic Progress', *Economic Journal* 38(4), December, pp, 527–542.

Young, Warren and Lee, Fredric S. (1993) *Oxford Economics and Economists*, London and Basingstoke: Macmillan.

Index